STRANGENESS AND BEAUTY

'It is the addition of strangeness to beauty, that constitutes the romantic character in art . . .'

Walter Pater

STRANGENESS AND BEAUTY

AN ANTHOLOGY OF AESTHETIC CRITICISM
1840–1910

Volume 2 · Pater to Arthur Symons

EDITED BY

ERIC WARNER
Lecturer and Fellow in English,
Fitzwilliam College, Cambridge

AND

GRAHAM HOUGH
Emeritus Professor of English,
University of Cambridge

CAMBRIDGE UNIVERSITY PRESS

CAMBRIDGE
LONDON NEW YORK NEW ROCHELLE
MELBOURNE SYDNEY

Published by the Press Syndicate of the University of Cambridge
The Pitt Building, Trumpington Street, Cambridge CB2 1RP
32 East 57th Street, New York, NY 10022, USA
296 Beaconsfield Parade, Middle Park, Melbourne 3206, Australia

First published 1983

Printed in Great Britain by The Pitman Press, Bath

Library of Congress catalogue card number: 82–9708

British Library Cataloguing in Publication Data

Strangeness and beauty: an anthology of
aesthetic criticism 1840–1910.
Vol. 2: Pater to Arthur Symons
1. Aesthetics—Criticism and interpretation
I. Warner, Eric II. Hough, Graham
700′.1 BH39

ISBN 0 521 23895 1 vol. 1 hard covers
ISBN 0 521 28290 x vol. 1 paperback
ISBN 0 521 23896 x vol. 2 hard covers
ISBN 0 521 28291 8 vol. 2 paperback

Contents

Illustrations

Acknowledgements

During the course of this project the authors have enjoyed the care, concern and co-operation of many people. Among those who deserve special thanks are Wayne Markert, who gave us the benefit of his superior knowledge of Arthur Symons, and John Taylor, who elucidated many of the more difficult Classical references. R. V. Holdsworth, Kathleen Wheeler, and Duncan Raynor also offered useful comments, as did Paul Snowdon and Bernard Richards at an early stage. We must also express our gratitude to Margaret Weedon, Eileen Crampton, and the staff of the English Faculty Library at Oxford for their substantial help in preparing the manuscript. Caroline Murray took great pains with the subediting of this manuscript and to her as well thanks are due. Finally, our greatest debt is to our editor, Terence Moore, whose interest in and enthusiasm for this work have been evident at every stage, and without whom it would scarcely have been completed.

Note on the text

Unless otherwise stated, all extracts published here were taken from the collections cited in the first entry in the Guide to further reading supplied for each author. Extracts from essays which first appeared as magazine articles are identified in the Notes.

Chronology

1819 Ruskin born. Queen Victoria born. Peterloo Massacre.

1821 Keats dies. Baudelaire born.

1822 Shelley dies. Victor Hugo publishes first volume of poems. Translation of Byron into French begun by Pichot (completed 1825).

1827 William Blake dies. Hugo publishes Preface to *Cromwell*, French Romantic manifesto declaring right to liberty in subject and treatment.

1828 Dante Gabriel Rossetti born.

1831 A. H. Hallam publishes review of Tennyson's poems, championing Shelley and Keats as 'poets of sensation'.

1834 Coleridge dies. Whistler born. William Morris born.

1835 Gautier publishes *Mademoiselle de Maupin* with strong romantic preface.

1837 Swinburne born.

1839 Walter Pater born. Mary Shelley's edition of husband's poems.

1843 Ruskin publishes first volume of *Modern Painters*. Wordsworth succeeds Southey as poet laureate.

1845 Baudelaire publishes first volume of art criticism, the *Salon of 1845*.

1846 Baudelaire publishes the *Salon of 1846*, expanding ideas and tone of previous year's work.

1848 Pre-Raphaelite Brotherhood formed. Poe publishes 'The Poetic Principle'. Monckton Miles's first collected edition of John Keats.

1849 Poe dies. Ruskin publishes *The Seven Lamps of Architecture*.

1850 Wordsworth dies.

1851 Turner dies. Ruskin writes two letters to *The Times* defending the Pre-Raphaelites.

1852 George Moore born. Gautier publishes *Émaux et Camées.*

1853 Ruskin completes *The Stones of Venice.*

1854 Oscar Wilde born. Arthur Rimbaud born.

1857 Baudelaire publishes *Les Fleurs du Mal*; prosecuted for offence to public morals and edition withdrawn.

1858 Morris publishes *'The Defence of Guenevere' and Other Poems.*

1859 Charles Darwin publishes *The Origin of Species.*

1861 Rossetti publishes first book of poems, mainly translations from Dante. Baudelaire issues second edition of *Les Fleurs du Mal.*

1862 Ruskin publishes *Unto This Last.*

1864 Pater elected Fellow of Brasenose College.

1865 William Butler Yeats born. Arthur Symons born.

1866 Swinburne publishes *Poems and Ballads, First Series.*

1867 Baudelaire dies.

1870 Ruskin elected Slade Professor at Oxford. Rossetti's second volume of poems published.

1872 Gautier dies.

1873 Pater publishes *The Renaissance.*

1878 Whistler brings libel suit against Ruskin.

1882 Rossetti dies. James Joyce born.

1885 Victor Hugo dies. Pater publishes *Marius the Epicurean.* Whistler delivers the 'Ten O'Clock Lecture'.

1888 Pater publishes third edition of *The Renaissance*, restoring a toned-down version of the 'Conclusion'. George Moore publishes *The Confessions of a Young Man.*

1889 Yeats publishes *The Wanderings of Oisin and Other Poems.*

1890 Whistler publishes *The Gentle Art of Making Enemies.* Morris starts the Kelmscott Press.

1891 Rimbaud dies. Wilde publishes *The Picture of Dorian Gray*. Morris publishes *News from Nowhere*.

1893 Symons publishes *The Decadent Movement in Literature*. Yeats publishes his edition of *The Poems of William Blake*.

1894 Pater dies. The first number of *The Yellow Book* appears.

1895 'The Importance of Being Earnest' is produced; Wilde is convicted of homosexual practices and sentenced to two years' imprisonment.

1896 Morris dies. Symons becomes editor of *The Savoy*.

1899 Symons publishes *The Symbolist Movement in Literature*.

1900 Ruskin dies.

Introduction

The presiding genius in this second part of our anthology is Pater, as that of the first was Ruskin. Twenty years younger, Pater must be considered in most important respects as Ruskin's disciple, and the continuator of his aesthetic gospel. They are at one in their exaltation of the sensuous imagination, their reliance on the refined and educated senses as the principal avenue to an ultimately spiritual fulfilment. And much of Pater's response to the visual arts is a direct consequence of the teaching provided by Ruskin. But with Pater the sensibilities of the nineteenth century take a decidedly new turn. Ruskin saw the education of the senses as a means of subtilizing and enriching the moral and religious life; and by this he meant moral and religious life conceived in fundamentally orthodox terms. In his early days he was a devout evangelical Christian; and even after his 'unconversion' and the development of remarkably independent views of man and society he always saw the life of the imagination and the pursuit of the arts as making a major contribution to traditional moral and civic virtue. But for Pater beauty was always allied with a certain strangeness; it takes on a wayward air, and it begins to seem possible that a devotion to the arts might lead away from the straight and narrow path altogether. Aucassin, the hero of one of the old French romances of which Pater writes in *The Renaissance*, decides that he has no business in heaven among the worn-out old priests, but will go to hell with the fair knights and the fair clerks and the warriors who die in battle and the courteous ladies who have two or three lovers besides their wedded lords. Pater decorously refrains from associating himself with these rebellious sentiments, but the tone of his writing is such as to admit their possibility. Religion is a supreme aesthetic experience, but it has no particular connection with restrictive morality, and none at all with the bourgeois virtues.

Many of those who came under Pater's influence were not inhibited by his decorum and restraint. Hence, in the seventies and eighties, a new note comes into the criticism of literature and the arts – the assertion, sometimes tacit, sometimes open and vociferous, of a position outside the social order and its accepted values. It marks the final dissolution of the Victorian alliance between High Art and the Establishment. Pater's fastidious withdrawal from the contagion of the world was abetted by others with mockery and disdain. George Moore, Wilde and Whistler are all dandies, scoffers and professional immoralists. This was not new in a European setting; Gautier's preface to *Mademoiselle de Maupin*, to which these attitudes owe much, came out in 1835. But it was new to England; and the gaiety and frivolity of tone of much of this writing does not imply triviality; it was part of a real campaign. Pater's conclusion to *The Renaissance* does not look subversive, but it is; Wilde's epigrams and Moore's Parisian reminiscences do not look more than squibs, but they pack a considerable charge; and all herald a lasting change in the climate in which the arts have their being.

The slogan we always think of in this connection is 'art for art's sake'; but this well-worn phrase includes more than one meaning. In the first place it means that art has its own ends, implicit in its own nature, independent of the moral and social order. All the writers we are considering would agree on this, and it could lead to an art that was aloof, self-centred, pure, and ultimately powerless. But in Pater, in some ways the most thorough-going of the late nineteenth-century aesthetes, there is the additional claim that the values of art should be the directing values of life itself: the true aim of all our busyness – law, politics, commerce and the rest – should be to provide for and to disseminate exquisite sensations. Art is not only to be uncontaminated by life, it is to be its ruler and guide.

These shifts of mood and attitude are all contributory to the wide-ranging movement of thought and feeling that we call Symbolism, the heir and successor to the Romanticism of the earlier part of the century. It has been the purpose of this anthology to trace the English branch of this movement to its roots, and in an extended sense, but a quite legitimate one, we can call the whole change and stirring in the arts that began with Ruskin and developed through the Pre-Raphaelites a Symbolist movement. Specifically, however, Symbolism is the name for a poetical movement that arose in France after the death of Baudelaire in 1867, and from that time on a powerful wave of French influence begins to affect English letters. Baudelaire's critical attitudes helped to shape those of Pater; George Moore educated himself in Paris, and in his own offhand way transmitted ideas derived from Gautier, Baudelaire and their successors. Arthur Symons, a younger man, developed along the same lines, and he achieved a more scholarly knowledge of Franch literature than either of them. His immensely influential book *The Symbolist Movement in Literature* appeared in 1899. It included essays on Mallarmé, Rimbaud, Verlaine, Villiers de l'Isle Adam and Laforgue, poets still little known in England at the relatively late date when Symons wrote. But what is perhaps his greatest service to poetry had come earlier; it was to transmit the Symbolist ideas to Yeats, his contemporary and the friend of his youth. And in Yeats's hands they were re-formed, combined with elements of his own instinctive genius, and given an assured status in the English language. Symons's influence does not end here; it forms one of the principal links between nineteenth-century poetics and the poetics of Modernism. His introduction of the French Symbolists to England gave a powerful impulse to the innovations of Eliot and Pound. As the final link in the chain connecting nineteenth-century aesthetic ideas with those of the early moderns, it is fitting that Symons brings these volumes to a close.

WALTER PATER (1839–94)

On the surface, Walter Horatio Pater's life of fifty-five years is remarkable for its lack of incident, a situation which Pater himself did much to further. The death of his father while he was an infant, and of his mother when he was fourteen, established patterns of isolation and self-communion which he retained throughout his life. His thirty years as a don at Brasenose College, Oxford, increased this sense of retreat; he developed an elaborate, mandarin courtesy which kept even familiars at arm's length, and his life fell into a rhythm of reading, writing and meditation in an inner world to which his closest friends had little real penetration. His letters are scrupulous in excluding passionate or intimate expression of any kind, and the sense of ordered restraint also marked his appearance, in the large brush moustache and trim military bearing that left the gathering 'aesthetic' acolytes in the later part of the century gaping with wonder. In short, Pater's mystique was the opposite of that of his disciple, Oscar Wilde: he endeavoured to make himself invisible. Much of the fascination that attended, and still attends, Pater is due to the fact that he scarcely seemed to have existed in the active world at all.

The more perceptive of his contemporaries, including Wilde and Henry James, saw through this facade and regarded Pater as a prime example of the man and his mask – which also helps explain his fascination for Yeats. They realized that it was above all in the work where the man was to be found, and that work is intriguing both for the degree to which it suggests more than it says, and the degree to which it conveys a sense of repression or restraint. Pater's early writings, culminating in *The Renaissance* (1873), were more forthright, but he lived at a time when Oxford dons were not encouraged to dally with unorthodox opinions. The frankest expression of his beliefs, in the 'Conclusion' to *The Renaissance*, instantly made Pater a cult figure among the young, and so alarmed the heartily orthodox establishment that he lost all chance of advancement in his chosen profession. He was denied a University Proctorship in 1874, and then, in a far more bitter blow, the Slade Professorship of Art in 1885. To some extent it is fair to say that Pater spent the rest of his life trying to live down the success of *The Renaissance*, and he developed a highly indirect, elusive form of expression which veiled both his lack of Christian belief and his homoeroticism. Late in life he was reconciled with the University by virtue of his Classical writings and increasingly religiose deportment at Brasenose Chapel, even though a late essay such as 'Prosper Merimée' indicates that his fundamental beliefs had not changed.

If Pater the man is concentrated to an unusual degree in the work, we may ask how we are to approach the body of his writings. To begin with, Pater's intellectual foundations, his ruling ideas, were essentially romantic in nature. His childhood in the London suburb of Enfield was the happiest period in his life, commemorated in the highly autobiographical piece 'The Child in the House' (1878). This Edenic period vanished with the death of his mother, shortly after he was sent to the King's School, Canterbury, leaving him with a permanent sense of 'homesickness', 'the wistful yearning towards home' which surfaces throughout his work. Such a sense not only made him particularly sensitive to Wordsworth's meditations on childhood, but also established in him early the tendency to day-dream and self-communion which he was to cultivate all his life. As Pater's best critics have always realized, his work represents, in his own words, 'a prolonged quarrel with himself', a persistent and unending attempt to discover the secrets of his own nature, the workings of his own mind. Thus, like the romantic poets before him, all Pater's best work tends to transform itself into some form of imaginative autobiography.

Recoiling from the exuberant athleticism of public school, Pater's passion from the first was for reading and the satisfaction of intellectual curiosity. Before he left school he had devoured many of the great works of French and English romanticism of the turn of the century, and to this store was added the potent impress of the German romantic tradition, notably Hegel, when he came under Benjamin Jowett's influence as an Oxford undergraduate. His incessant allusions mark Pater as one of the most widely read in an age of widely read critics, and out of this confluence of ideas came a cluster of related romantic concepts which appear throughout his writing. Perhaps the most striking of these is Pater's own version of a natural supernaturalism, a transcendent ideal based wholly within the human and phenomenal worlds. This naturalized ideal, evident throughout Pater's writings, leads to the denial of all other-worldly claims for religion. Thus Pater is drawn to the physical beauties of the world and is full of admiration for ancient Greek culture, with its frank handling of the sensuous aspects of life. As he puts it in 'The Child in the House': 'certainly, he came more and more to be unable to care for, or think of soul but as in an actual body, or of any world but that wherein . . . men and women look so or so, and press actual hands'. The idea is also expressed conversely, intensifying and idealizing human beings to quasi-divine status, the most striking example being Pater's earliest recorded essay, 'Diaphaneitè' (q.v.), which suggests the divine transpicuousness of the fully imaginative soul.

More important for Pater's criticism are the related ideas of the subjective bases of knowledge and the importance of the imagination in human life. Such romantic concepts come to full flower when considering artistic genius, and it is in Pater's subsequent work, the essays which make up *The Renaissance*, that such ideas are refined. Treating some of the most powerful works in Western art, Pater steadily attempts to elucidate the personality of the artist through the expressive traces left in the work. Moreover, he follows a particular romantic historiography in seeing the period concentrated into single, intense 'moments' of expression which epitomize the whole, a theme explicitly announced in 'The School of Giorgione' (q.v.). Perhaps most important of all is the Hegelian notion of cultural development which underlies the argument of *The Renaissance*. Implicit in the book is a theory which regards cultural evolution as a series of renascences or rebirths, and which connects the 'outbreak of spirit' in the Renaissance back through the High Middle Ages to ancient Greece, as well as forward to the Romantic Revival of Pater's own century. This theory received its most important expression in the essay on 'Romanticism', which Pater placed as the 'Postscript' to his volume of literary criticism, *Appreciations*.

Pater's critical procedure rests on unabashedly romantic or subjective foundations: 'what is this poem or picture. . . to *me*?' he declares in the Preface to *The Renaissance*. In this practice Pater was following the trail blazed by his great predecessor, Ruskin, who also trusted the sensitiveness of his own mind in responding to a work of art, and who likewise moved from a preoccupation with the imagination in literature to its expression in the visual arts. At this point, however, the difference between the two men, and Pater's importance, begin to emerge. In contrast to Ruskin's strident, overwhelming, prophetic style, Pater developed a restrained, subtle, elusive one where, as Ian Fletcher puts it, 'the reader must construe as he reads'. More importantly, the substance of Ruskin's rhetoric was overtly moralistic, insisting upon the necessary link between a virtuous soul and good art. In contrast, the Preface to *The Renaissance* casually passes such metaphysical questions as being 'of no interest' to the 'aesthetic' critic;

later, detailing Leonardo's sojourn amid the 'brilliant sins and exquisite amusements' of Milan, Pater unobtrusively cuts free the production of great art from any moral constraint. This understated dissent from the heavy moralizing of the Victorians was an immense liberation to the rising generation, and though the extent of the rebellion alarmed the timid and conventional don, the 'aesthetic' movement in England was one from which Pater could not be dissociated. One after another, George Moore, Oscar Wilde, W. B. Yeats and Arthur Symons paid homage to the master who had first taught them the art of true perception (qq.v.).

In this light it becomes clear that Pater's importance finally rests on the transformation in imaginative thought which he helped to effect, turning romantic concepts into a late romantic formulation. Ultimately Ruskin shares with the High Romantics a belief in some eternally existing Absolute, to which man's imagination links him; but for Pater, who felt the full impact of Darwinian ideas, such a faith was not possible. His first published essay, on Coleridge, attacks the yearning for such an Absolute which eventually ruined the imaginative poet – though by the time he came to revise the essay in 1880 it is clear that Pater himself shared much the same desire. Exalting the creative imagination, Pater was ultimately unable to take the final romantic step of faith, to a belief in what William Blake called 'Eternity'. Thus, like his hero, Marius the Epicurean, Pater is left on the brink of belief but holding at the last to the material negation of 'what his eyes really saw'. This position is given its intensest and most desperate expression in the notorious 'Conclusion' to *The Renaissance* (q.v.), a few pages charged with all the consequences of a late romantic position – an immersion in the ceaseless flux of sensations, a devotion to self-culture and its attendant isolation, and a horrific fear of death. So Pater could offer a régimen of reaching for 'any exquisite passion, or any contribution to knowledge that seems by a lifted horizon to set the spirit free for a moment', and suggest that art provided the intensest and most meaningful 'moments' of perception as they passed. So, too, he became especially sensitive to the exponents of late romantic art in his day, such as Rossetti, the Pre-Raphaelites and William Morris.

Pater's most crucial link with later figures emerges in his detailed, perceptive analyses of such artistic components as form, language and style, which steadily advance the claim that good art is self-conscious and deliberately crafted. Following the doctrines of Poe and Baudelaire, Pater rejects Coleridge's romantic notion of *organic* form as giving too much credit to some exterior shaping spirit (whether God or Nature) and not enough to the artist's own imaginative mastery. (Here again Pater directly contradicts Ruskin, who believed implicitly in this organic theory.) This strain of thought reaches its climax in the celebrated essay, 'Style' (q.v.), which both Wilde and Symons took to heart later in the century. Praising the powers of *mind*, the deliberate shaping and refinement with which an artist crafts his work, Pater heralds the later extreme of complete self-consciousness, evident in Wilde's extravagant celebration of artifice and Symons's theories of wilfully non-natural symbolization. At the same time, the essay on 'Style' turns away from the Romantic celebration of common humanity which runs through Ruskin, Morris and the P.R.B., by distancing the aloof and aesthetically preoccupied artist from the ordinary concerns of mankind. Thus the aristocratic notion of the artist, entrenched in France since the time of Gautier and Baudelaire, entered the English tradition with Pater and has remained ever since.

Pater's position in this anthology is unique. In many ways the inheritor of a romantic tradition, he extended elements of that romanticism to a late and extreme form whose influence extends to our own day. Ironically, in the end Pater went much the same way as the Coleridge he attacked in his early essay, turning from the exhausting effort of holding to what his eyes really saw to the comfort of established religion and doctrinal absolutes. He ended his days in regular attendance at the College chapel and working with a small Christian community in London. This may have been only a final mask, however, for late essays such as 'Pascal' and 'Prosper Mérimée' suggest that he never fully embraced the faith, and that the comfort he derived was the aesthetic attraction to ritual which absorbed so many of Yeats's companions in the 'Tragic Generation'. Indeed the essay on Mérimée is remarkable for the accuracy with which it portrays the sort of existential irony that has supported the modern literary imagination, echoing through the poetry, drama and fiction of our own day. This is perhaps a last proof of Pater's position not only as a key to past sensibility, but as one of the earliest guideposts to the present.

I. Diaphaneitè[1]

There are some unworldly types of character which the world is able to estimate. It recognises certain moral types, or categories, and regards whatever falls within them as having a right to exist. The saint, the artist, even the speculative thinker, out of the world's order as they are, yet work, so far as they work at all, in and by means of the main current of the world's energy.[2]

Often it gives them late, or scanty, or mistaken acknowledgment; still it has room for them in its scheme of life, a place made ready for them in its affections. It is also patient of doctrinaires of every degree of littleness. As if dimly conscious of some great sickness and weariness of heart in itself, it turns readily to those who theorise about its unsoundness. To constitute one of these categories, or types, a breadth and generality of character is required. There is another type of character, which is not broad and general, rare, precious above all to the artist, a character which seems to have been the supreme moral charm in the Beatrice of the Commedia. It does not take the eye by breadth of colour; rather it is that fine edge of light, where the elements of our moral nature refine themselves to the burning point.[3] It crosses rather than follows the main current of the world's life. The world has no sense fine enough for those evanescent shades, which fill up the blanks between contrasted types of character – delicate provision in the organisation of the moral world for the transmission to every part of it of the life quickened at single points! For this nature there is no place ready in its affections. This colourless, unclassified purity of life it can neither use for its service, nor contemplate as an ideal.

"Sibi unitus et simplificatus esse," that is the long struggle of the Imitatio Christi.[4] The spirit which it forms is the very opposite of that which regards life as a game of skill, and values things and persons as marks or counters of something to be gained, or achieved, beyond them. It seeks to value everything at its eternal worth, not adding to it, or taking from it, the amount of influence it may have for or against its own special scheme of life. It is the spirit that sees external circumstances as they are, its own power and tendencies as they are, and realises the given conditions of its life, not disquieted by the desire for change, or the preference of one part in life rather than another, or passion, or opinion. The character we mean to indicate achieves this perfect life by a happy gift of nature, without any struggle at all. Not the saint only, the artist also, and the speculative thinker, confused, jarred, disintegrated in the world, as sometimes they inevitably are, aspire for this simplicity to the last. The struggle of this aspiration with a lower practical aim in the mind of Savonarola has been subtly traced by the author of Romola.[5] As language, expression, is the function of intellect, as art, the supreme expression, is the highest product of intellect, so this desire for simplicity is a kind of indirect self-assertion of the intellectual part of such natures. Simplicity in purpose and act is a kind of determinate expression in dexterous outline of one's personality. It is a kind of moral expressiveness; there is an intellectual triumph implied in it. Such a simplicity is characteristic of the repose of perfect intellectual culture.[6] The artist and he who has treated life in the spirit of art desires only to be shown to the world as he really is; as he comes nearer and nearer to perfection, the veil of an outer life not simply expressive of the inward becomes thinner and thinner. This intellectual throne is rarely won. Like the religious life, it is a paradox in the world, denying the first conditions of man's ordinary existence, cutting obliquely the spontaneous order of things. But the character we have before us is a kind of prophecy of this repose and simplicity, coming as it were in the order of grace, not of nature, by some happy gift, or accident of birth or constitution, showing that it is indeed within the limits of man's destiny. Like all the higher forms of inward life this character is a subtle blending and interpenetration of intellectual, moral and spiritual elements. But it is as a phase of intellect, of culture, that it is most striking and forcible. It is a mind of taste lighted up by some spiritual ray within. What is meant by taste is an imperfect intellectual state; it is but a sterile kind of culture. It is the mental attitude, the intellectual manner of perfect culture, assumed by a happy instinct. Its beautiful way of handling everything that appeals to the senses and the intellect is really directed by the laws of the higher intellectual life, but while culture is able to trace those laws, mere taste is unaware of them. In the character before us, taste, without ceasing to be instructive, is far more than a mental attitude or manner. A magnificent intellectual force is latent within it. It is like the reminiscence of a forgotten culture that once adorned the mind; as if the mind of one *φιλοσοφήσας ποτε μετ'ἔρωτος*,* fallen into a new cycle, were beginning its spiritual

* 'Having once philosophized with passion' – a paraphase (made up by Pater?) of Platonic thought.

progress over again, but with a certain power of anticipating its stages. It has the freshness without the shallowness of taste, the range and seriousness of culture without its strain and over-consciousness. Such a habit may be described as wistfulness of mind, the feeling that there is 'so much to know,' rather as a longing after what is unattainable, than as a hope to apprehend. Its ethical result is an intellectual guilelessness, or integrity, that instinctively prefers what is direct and clear, lest one's own confusion and intransparency should hinder the transmission from without of light that is not yet inward. He who is ever looking for the breaking of a light he knows not whence about him, notes with a strange heedfulness the faintest paleness in the sky. That truthfulness of temper, that receptivity, which professors often strive in vain to form, is engendered here less by wisdom than by innocence. Such a character is like a relic from the classical age, laid open by accident to our alien modern atmosphere. It has something of the clear ring, the eternal outline of the antique. Perhaps it is nearly always found with a corresponding outward semblance. The veil or mask of such a nature would be the very opposite of the 'dim blackguardism' of Danton, the type Carlyle has made too popular for the true interest of art.[7] It is just this sort of entire transparency of nature that lets through unconsciously all that is really lifegiving in the established order of things; it detects without difficulty all sorts of affinities between its own elements, and the nobler elements in that order. But then its wistfulness and a confidence in perfection it has makes it love the lords of change. What makes revolutionists is either self-pity, or indignation for the sake of others, or a sympathetic perception of the dominant undercurrent of progress in things. The nature before us is revolutionist from the direct sense of personal worth, that *χλιδή*, that pride of life, which to the Greek was a heavenly grace.[8] How can he value what comes of accident, or usage, or convention, whose individual life nature itself has isolated and perfected? Revolution is often impious. They who prosecute revolution have to violate again and again the instinct of reverence. That is inevitable, since after all progress is a kind of violence. But in this nature revolutionism is softened, harmonised, subdued as by distance. It is the revolutionism of one who has slept a hundred years. Most of us are neutralised by the play of circumstances. To most of us only one chance is given in the life of the spirit and the intellect, and circumstances prevent our dexterously seizing that one chance. The one happy spot in our nature has no room to burst into life. Our collective life, pressing equally on every part of every one of us, reduces nearly all of us to the level of a colourless uninteresting existence. Others are neutralised, not by suppression of gifts, but by just equipoise among them. In these no single gift, or virtue, or idea, has an unmusical predominance. The world easily confounds these two conditions. It sees in the character before us only indifferentism. Doubtless the chief vein of the life of humanity could hardly pass through it. Not by it could the progress of the world be achieved. It is not the guise of Luther or Spinoza; rather it is that of Raphael, who in the midst of the Reformation and the Renaissance, himself lighted up by them, yielded himself to neither, but stood still to live upon himself, even in outward form a youth, almost an infant, yet surprising all the world. The beauty of the Greek statues was a sexless beauty; the statues of the gods had the least traces of sex. Here there is a moral sexlessness, a kind of importance, an ineffectual wholeness of nature, yet with a divine beauty and significance of its own.

Over and over again the world has been surprised by the heroism, the insight, the passion, of this clear crystal nature. Poetry and poetical history have dreamed of a crisis, where it must needs be that some human victim be sent down into the grave. These are they whom in its profound emotion humanity might choose to send. "What," says Carlyle, of Charlotte Corday, "What if she had emerged from her secluded stillness, suddenly like a star; cruel-lovely, with half-angelic, half-daemonic splendour; to gleam for a moment, and in a moment be extinguished; to be held in memory, so bright complete was she, through long centuries!"[9]

Often the presence of this nature is felt like a sweet aroma in early manhood. Afterwards, as the adulterated atmosphere of the world assimilates us to itself, the savour of it faints away. Perhaps there are flushes of it in all of us; recurring moments of it in every period of life. Certainly this is so with every man of genius. It is a thread of pure white light that one might disentwine from the tumultuary richness of Goethe's nature. It is a natural prophecy of what the next generation will appear, renerved, modified by the ideas of this. There is a violence, an impossibility about men who have ideas, which makes one suspect that they could never be the type of any widespread life. Society could not be conformed to their image but by an unlovely straining from its true order. Well, in this nature the idea appears softened, harmonised as by distance, with an engaging naturalness, without the noise of axe or hammer.

People have often tried to find a type of life that might serve as a basement type. The philosopher, the saint, the artist, neither of them can be this type; the order of nature itself makes them exceptional. It cannot be the pedant, or the conservative, or anything rash and irreverent. Also the type must be one discounted with society as it is. The nature here indicated alone is worthy to be this type. A majority of such would be the regeneration of the world.

July, 1864.

II. From *The Renaissance*

Preface

Many attempts have been made by writers on art and poetry to define beauty in the abstract, to express it in the most general terms, to find a universal formula for it. The value of such attempts has most often been in the suggestive and penetrating things said by the way. Such discussions help us very little to enjoy what has been well done in art or poetry, to discriminate between what is more and what is less excellent in them, or to use words like beauty, excellence, art, poetry, with a more precise meaning than they would otherwise have. Beauty, like all other qualities presented to human experience, is relative; and the definition of it becomes unmeaning and useless in proportion to its abstractness. To define beauty, not in the most abstract, but in the most concrete terms possible, to find, not a universal formula for it, but the formula which expresses most adequately this or that special manifestation of it, is the aim of the true student of aesthetics.[1]

"To see the object as in itself it really is," has been justly said to be the aim of all true criticism whatever; and in aesthetic criticism the first step towards seeing one's object as it really is, is to know one's own impression as it really is, to discriminate it, to realise it distinctly.[2] The objects with which aesthetic criticism deals – music, poetry, artistic and accomplished forms of human life – are indeed receptacles of so many powers or forces: they possess, like the products of nature, so many virtues or qualities. What is this song or picture, this engaging personality presented in life or in a book, to *me*? What effect does it really produce on me? Does it give me pleasure? and if so, what sort or degree of pleasure? How is my nature modified by its presence, and under its influence? The answers to these questions are the original facts with which the aesthetic critic has to do; and, as in the study of light, of morals, of number, one must realise such primary data for oneself, or not at all. And he who experiences these impressions strongly, and drives directly at the discrimination and analysis of them, has no need to trouble himself with the abstract question what beauty is in itself, or what its exact relation to truth or experience – metaphysical questions, as unprofitable as metaphysical questions elsewhere. He may pass them all by as being, answerable or not, of no interest to him.

The aesthetic critic, then, regards all the objects with which he has to do, all works of art, and the fairer forms of nature and human life, as powers or forces producing pleasurable sensations, each of a more or less peculiar and unique kind. This influence he feels, and wishes to explain, analysing it, and reducing it to its elements. To him, the picture, the landscape, the engaging personality in life or in a book, *La Gioconda*, the hills of Carrara, Pico of Mirandola, are valuable for their virtues, as we say, in speaking of a herb, a wine, a gem; for the property each has of affecting one with a special, a unique, impression of pleasure.[3] Our education becomes complete in proportion as our susceptibility to these impressions increases in depth and variety. And the function of the aesthetic critic is to distinguish, analyse, and separate from its adjuncts, the virtue by which a picture, a landscape, a fair personality in life or in a book, produces this special impression of beauty or pleasure, to indicate what the source of that impression is, and under what conditions it is experienced. His end is reached when he has disengaged that virtue, and noted it, as a chemist notes some natural element, for himself and others; and the rule for those who would reach this end is stated with great exactness in the words of a recent critic of Sainte-Beuve: – *De se borner à connaître de près les belles choses, et à s'en nourrir en exquis amateurs, en humanistes accomplis.*[4]

What is important, then, is not that the critic should possess a correct abstract definition of beauty for the intellect, but a certain kind of temperament, the power of being deeply moved by the presence of beautiful objects. He will remember always that beauty exists in many forms. To him all periods, types, schools of taste, are in themselves equal. In all ages there have been some excellent workmen, and some excellent work done. The question he asks is always: – In whom did the stir, the genius, the sentiment of the period find itself? who was the receptacle of its refinement, its elevation, its taste? "The ages are all equal," says William Blake, "but genius is always above its age."[5]

Often it will require great nicety to disengage this virtue from the commoner elements with which it may be found in combination. Few artists, not Goethe or Byron even, work quite cleanly, casting off all *débris*, and leaving us only what the heat of their imagination has wholly fused and transformed.[6] Take, for instance, the writings of Wordsworth. The heat of his genius, entering into the substance of his work, had crystallised a part, but only a part, of it; and in that great mass of verse there is much which might well be forgotten.[7] But scattered up and down it, sometimes fusing and transforming entire compositions, like the Stanzas on *Resolution and Independence*, and the Ode on the *Recollections of Childhood*, sometimes, as if at random, depositing a fine crystal here or there, in a matter it does not wholly search through and transform, we trace the action of his unique, incommunicable faculty, that strange, mystical sense of a life in natural things, and of man's life as a part of nature, drawing strength and colour and character from local influences, from the hills and streams, and from natural sights and sounds. Well! that is the *virtue*, the active principle in

Wordsworth's poetry; and then the function of the critic of Wordsworth is to trace that active principle, to disengage it, to mark the degree in which it penetrates his verse.

The subjects of the following studies are taken from the history of the *Renaissance*, and touch what I think the chief points in that complex, many-sided movement. I have explained in the first of them what I understand by the word, giving it a much wider scope than was intended by those who originally used it to denote only that revival of classical antiquity in the fifteenth century which was but one of many results of a general excitement and enlightening of the human mind, and of which the great aim and achievements of what, as Christian art, is often falsely opposed to the Renaissance, were another result. This outbreak of the human spirit may be traced far into the middle age itself, with its qualities already clearly pronounced, the care for physical beauty, the worship of the body, the breaking down of those limits which the religious system of the middle age imposed on the heart and the imagination. I have taken as an example of this movement, this earlier Renaissance within the middle age itself, and as an expression of its qualities, two little compositions in early French; not because they constitute the best possible expression of them, but because they help the unity of my series, inasmuch as the Renaissance ends also in France, in French poetry, in a phase of which the writings of Joachim du Bellay are in many ways the most perfect illustration; the Renaissance thus putting forth in France an aftermath, a wonderful later growth, the products of which have to the full that subtle and delicate sweetness which belongs to a refined and comely decadence; just as its earliest phases have the freshness which belongs to all periods of growth in art, the charm of *ascêsis*, of the austere and serious girding of the loins in youth.[8]

But it is in Italy, in the fifteenth century, that the interest of the Renaissance mainly lies, in that solemn fifteenth century which can hardly be studied too much, not merely for its positive results in the things of the intellect and the imagination, its concrete of art, its special and prominent personalities, with their profound aesthetic charm, but for its general spirit and character, for the ethical qualities of which it is a consummate type.

The various forms of intellectual activity which together make up the culture of an age, move for the most part from different starting-points, and by unconnected roads. As products of the same generation they partake indeed of a common character, and unconsciously illustrate each other; but of the producers themselves, each group is solitary, gaining what advantage or disadvantage there may be in intellectual isolation. Art and poetry, philosophy and religious life, and that other life of refined pleasure and action in the open places of the world, are each of them confined to its own circle of ideas, and those who prosecute either of them are generally little curious of the thoughts of others. There come, however, from time to time, eras of more favourable conditions, in which the thoughts of men draw nearer together than is their wont, and the many interests of the intellectual world combine in one complete type of general culture. The fifteenth century in Italy is one of these happier eras; and what is sometimes said of the age of Pericles is true of that of Lorenzo: – it is an age productive in personalities, many-sided, centralised, complete.[9] Here, artist and philosophers and those whom the action of the world has elevated and made keen, do not live in isolation, but breathe a common air, and catch light and heat from each other's thoughts. There is a spirit of general elevation and enlightenment in which all alike communicate. It is the unity of this spirit which gives unity to all the various products of the Renaissance; and it is to this intimate alliance with mind, this participation in the best thoughts which that age produced, that the art of Italy in the fifteenth century owes much of its grave dignity and influence.

I have added an essay on Winckelmann, as not incongruous with the studies which precede it, because Winckelmann, coming in the eighteenth century, really belongs in spirit to an earlier age. By his enthusiasm for the things of the intellect and the imagination for their own sake,[10] by his Hellenism, his life-long struggle to attain to the Greek spirit, he is in sympathy with the humanists of an earlier century. He is the last fruit of the Renaissance, and explains in a striking way its motive and tendencies.

1873.

Luca della Robbia

Allgemeinheit – breadth, generality, universality – is the word chosen by Winckelmann, and after him by Goethe and many German critics, to express that law of the most excellent Greek sculptors, of Pheidias and his pupils, which prompted them constantly to seek the type in the individual, to abstract and express only what is structural and permanent, to purge from the individual all that belongs only to him, all the accidents, the feeling and actions of the special moment, all that (because in its own nature it endures but for a moment) is apt to look like a frozen thing if one arrests it.

In this way their works came to be like some subtle extract or essence, or almost like pure thoughts or ideas: and hence the breadth of humanity in them, that detachment from the conditions of a particular place or people, which has carried their influence far beyond the age which produced them, and insured them universal acceptance.

That was the Greek way of relieving the hardness and unspirituality of pure form. But it involved to a certain degree the sacrifice of what we call *expression*;[11] and a system of abstraction which aimed always at the broad and general type, at the purging away from the individual of what belonged only to him, and of the mere accidents of a particular time and place, imposed upon the range of effects open to the Greek sculptor limits somewhat narrowly defined; and when Michelangelo came, with a genius spiritualised by the reverie of the middle age, penetrated by its spirit of inwardness and introspection, living not a mere outward life like the Greek, but a life full of inward experiences, sorrows, consolations, a system which sacrificed so much of what was inward and unseen could not satisfy him. To him, lover and student of Greek sculpture as he was, work which did not bring what was inward to the surface, which was not concerned with individual expression, with individual character and feeling, the special history of the special soul, was not worth doing at all.[12]

And so, in a way quite personal and peculiar to himself, which often is, and always seems, the effect of accident, he secured for his work individuality and intensity of expression, while he avoided a too hard realism, that tendency to harden into caricature which the representation of feeling in sculpture must always have. [. . .]

I said that the work of Luca della Robbia possessed in an unusual measure that special characteristic which belongs to all the workmen of his school, a characteristic which, even in the the absence of much positive information about their actual history, seems to bring those workmen themselves very near to us – the impress of a personal quality, a profound expressiveness, what the French call *intimité*, by which is meant some subtler sense of originality – the seal of a man's work of what is most inward and peculiar in his moods and manner of apprehension: it is what we call *expression*, carried to its highest intensity of degree. That characteristic is rare in poetry, rarer still in art, rarest of all in the abstract art of sculpture; yet essentially, perhaps, it is the quality which alone makes works in the imaginative and moral order really worth having at all. It is because the works of the artists of the fifteenth century possess this quality in an unmistakable way that one is anxious to know all that can be known about them, and explain to oneself the secret of their charm.

1872.

Leonardo da Vinci
Homo minister et interpres naturae[13]

In Vasari's life of Leonardo da Vinci as we now read it there are some variations from the first edition. There, the painter who has fixed the outward type of Christ for succeeding centuries was a bold speculator, holding lightly by other men's beliefs, setting philosophy above Christianity. Words of his, trenchant enough to justify this impression, are not recorded, and would have been out of keeping with a genius of which one characteristic is the tendency to lose itself in a refined and graceful mystery. The suspicion was but the time-honoured mode in which the world stamps its appreciation of one who has thoughts for himself alone, his high indifference, his intolerance of the common forms of things; and in the second edition the image was changed into something fainter and more conventional. But it is still by a certain mystery in his work, and something enigmatical beyond the usual measure of great men, that he fascinates, or perhaps half repels. His life is one of sudden revolts, with intervals in which he works not at all, or apart from the main scope of his work. By a strange fortune the works on which his more popular fame rested disappeared early from the world, as the *Battle of the Standard*; or are mixed obscurely with the work of meaner hands, as the *Last Supper*. His type of beauty is so exotic it fascinates a larger number than it delights, and seems more than that of any other artist to reflect ideas and views and some scheme of the world within; so that he seemed to his contemporaries to be the possessor of some unsanctified and secret wisdom; as to Michelet and other to have anticipated modern ideas.[14] He trifles with his genius, and crowds all his chief work into a few tormented years of later life; yet he is so possessed by his genius that he passes unmoved through the most tragic events, overwhelming his country and friends, like one who comes across them by chance on some secret errand.[. . .]

And because it [his early Florentine art] was the perfection of that style, it awoke in Leonardo some seed of discontent which lay in the secret places of his nature. For the way to perfection is through a series of disgusts; and [. . .] all that he had done so far in his life at Florence – was after all in the old slight manner. His art, if it was to be something in the world, must be weighted with more of the meaning of nature and purpose of humanity. Nature was "the true mistress of higher intelligences." So he plunged into the study of nature. And in doing this he followed the manner of the older students; he brooded over the hidden virtues of plants and crystals, the lines traced by the stars as they moved in the sky, over the correspondences which exist between the different orders of living things, through which, to eyes opened, they interpret each other; and for years he seemed to those about him as one listening to a voice, silent for other men.

He learned here the art of going deep, of tracking the sources of expression to their subtlest retreats, the power of an intimate presence in the things he handled. He did not at once or entirely desert his art; only he was no longer the cheerful, objective painter, through whose soul, as through clear glass, the bright figures of Florentine life, only made a little mellower and more pensive by the transit, passed on to the white wall. [. . .]

And in such studies some interfusion of the extremes of beauty and terror shaped itself, as an image that might be seen and touched, in the mind of this gracious youth, so fixed that for the rest of his life it never left him; [. . .] It was not in play that he painted that other Medusa, the one great picture which he left behind him in Florence. The subject has been treated in various ways; Leonardo alone cuts to its centre; he alone realises it as the head of a corpse, exercising its powers through all the circumstances of death. What may be called the fascination of corruption penetrates in every touch its exquisitely finished beauty. About the dainty lines of the cheek the bat flits unheeded. The delicate snakes seem literally strangling each other in terrified struggle to escape from the Medusa brain. The hue which violent death always brings with it is in the features: features singularly massive and grand, as we catch them inverted, in a dexterous foreshortening, sloping upwards, almost sliding down upon us, crown foremost, like a great calm stone against which the wave of serpents breaks. But it is a subject that may well be left to the beautiful verses of Shelley.[15] [. . .]

Curiosity and the desire of beauty – these are the two elementary forces in Leonardo's genius; curiosity often in conflict with the desire of beauty, but generating, in union with it, a type of subtle and curious grace.[16] [. . .]

Sometimes this curiosity came in conflict with the desire of beauty; it tended to make him go too far below that outside of things in which art begins and ends. This struggle between the reason and its ideas, and the senses, the desire of beauty, is the key to Leonardo's life at Milan – his restlessness, his endless re-touchings, his odd experiments with colour. How much must he leave unfinished, how much recommence! His problem was the transmutation of ideas into images. What he had attained so far had been the mastery of that earlier Florentine style, with its naïve and limited sensuousness. Now he was to entertain in this narrow medium those divinations of a humanity too wide for it, that larger vision of the opening world, which is only not too much for the great, irregular art of Shakspere; and everywhere the effort is visible in the work of his hands. This agitation, this perpetual delay, give him an air of weariness and *ennui*. To others he seems to be aiming at an impossible effect, to do something that art, that painting, can never do. Often the expression of physical beauty at this or that point seems strained and marred in the effort, as in those heavy German foreheads – too German and heavy for perfect beauty.

For there was a touch of Germany in that genius which, as Goethe said, had "thought itself weary" – *müde sich gedacht*. What an anticipation of modern Germany, for instance, in that debate on the question whether sculpture or painting is the nobler art.[17] But there is this difference between him and the German, that, with all that curious science, the German would have thought nothing more was needed; and the name of Goethe himself reminds one how great for the artist may be the danger of over-much science; how Goethe, who, in the *Elective Affinities* and the first part of *Faust*, does transmute ideas into images, who wrought many such transmutations, did not invariably find the spell-word, and in the second part of *Faust* presents us with a mass of science which has almost no artistic character at all. But Leonardo will never work till the happy moment comes – that moment of *bien-être*, which to imaginative men is a moment of invention. On this moment he waits; other moments are but a preparation, or after-taste of it.[18] Few men distinguish between them as jealously as he did. Hence, so many flaws even in the choicest work. But for Leonardo the distinction is absolute, and, in the moment of *bien-être*, the alchemy complete: the idea is stricken into colour and imagery: a cloudy mysticism is refined to a subdued and graceful mystery, and painting pleases the eye while it satisfies the soul [. . .] Other artists have been as careless of present or future applause, in self-forgetfulness, or because they set moral or political ends above the ends of art; but in him this solitary culture of beauty seems to have hung upon a kind of self-love, and a carelessness in the work of art of all but art itself. Out of the secret places of a unique temperament he brought strange blossoms and fruits hitherto unknown; and for him, the novel impression conveyed, the exquisite effect woven, counted as an end in itself – a perfect end.[19] [. . .]

La Gioconda is, in the truest sense, Leonardo's masterpiece, the revealing instance of his mode of thought and work. In suggestiveness, only the *Melancholia* of Dürer is comparable to it; and no crude symbolism disturbs the effect of its subdued and graceful mystery. We all know the face and hands of the figure, set in its marble chair, in that cirque of fantastic rocks, as in some faint light under sea. Perhaps of all ancient pictures time has chilled it least.[20] As often happens with works in which invention seems to reach its limit, there is an element in it given to, not invented by, the master. In that inestimable folio of drawings, once in the possession of Vasari, were certain designs by Verrocchio, faces of such impressive beauty that Leonardo in his boyhood copied them many times. It is hard not to connect with these designs of the elder, by-past master, as with its germinal principle, the unfathomable smile, always with a touch of something sinister in it, which plays over all Leonardo's work. Besides, the picture is a portrait. From childhood we see this image defining itself on the fabric of his dreams; and but for express historical testimony, we might fancy that this was but his ideal lady, embodied and beheld at last. What was the relationship of a living Florentine to this creature of his thought? By means of what strange affinities had the person and the dream grown up thus apart, and yet so closely together? Present from the first incorporeally in Leonardo's thought, dimly traced in the designs of Verrocchio, she is found present at last in *Il Giocondo's* house. That there is much of mere portraiture in the picture is attested by the legend that by artificial means, the presence of mimes and flute-players, that subtle expression was protracted on the face. Again, was it in four years and by renewed labour never really completed, or in four months and as by stroke of magic, that the image was projected?

The presence that thus rose so strangely beside the waters, is expressive of what in the ways of a thousand years men had come to desire. Hers is the head upon which all "the ends of the world are come," and the eyelids are a little weary. It is a beauty wrought out from within upon the flesh, the deposit, little cell by cell, of strange thoughts and fantastic reveries and exquisite passions. Set it for a moment beside one of those white Greek goddesses or beautiful women of antiquity, and how would they be troubled by this beauty, into which the soul with all its maladies has passed![21] All the thoughts and experience of the world have etched and moulded there, in that which they have of power to refine and make expressive the outward form, the animalism of Greece, the lust of Rome, the reverie of the middle age with its spiritual ambition and imaginative loves, the return of the Pagan world, the sins of the Borgias. She is older than the rocks among which she sits; like the vampire, she has been dead many times, and learned the secrets of the grave; and has been a diver in deep seas, and keeps their fallen day about her; and trafficked for strange webs with Eastern merchants: and, as Leda, was the mother of Helen of Troy, and, as Saint Anne, the mother of Mary; and all this has been to her but as the sound of lyres and flutes, and lives only in the delicacy with which it has moulded the changing lineaments, and tinged the eyelids and the hands.[22] The fancy of a perpetual life, sweeping together ten thousand experiences, is an old one; and modern thought has conceived the idea of humanity as wrought upon by, and summing up in itself, all modes of thought and life. Certainly Lady Lisa might stand as the embodiment of the old fancy, the symbol of the modern idea.

The School of Giorgione[23]

It is the mistake of much popular criticism to regard poetry, music, and painting – all the various products of art – as but translations into different languages of one and the same fixed quantity of imaginative thought, supplemented by certain technical qualities of colour, in painting – of sound, in music – of rhythmical words, in poetry. In this way, the sensuous element in art, and with it almost everything in art that is essentially artistic, is made a matter of indifference; and a clear apprehension of the opposite principle – that the sensuous material of each art brings with it a special phase or quality of beauty, untranslatable into the forms of any other, an order of impressions distinct in kind – is the beginning of all true æsthetic criticism. For, as art addresses not pure sense, still less the pure intellect, but the "imaginative reason," through the senses, there are differences of kind in æsthetic beauty, corresponding to the differences in kind of the gifts of sense themselves. Each art, therefore, having its own peculiar and incommunicable sensuous charm, has its own special mode of reaching the imagination, its own special responsibilities to its material.[24] One of the functions of æsthetic criticism is to define these limitations; to estimate the degree in which a given work of art fulfils its responsibilities to its special material; to note in a picture that true pictorial charm, which is neither a mere poetical thought or sentiment, on the one hand, nor a mere result of communicable technical skill in colour or design, on the other; to define in a poem that true poetical quality, which is neither descriptive nor meditative merely, but comes of an inventive handling of rhythmical language – the element of song in the singing; to note in music the musical charm – that essential music which presents no words, no matter of sentiment of thought, separable from the special form in which it is conveyed to us.

To such a philosophy of the variations of the beautiful, Lessing's analysis of the spheres of sculpture and poetry, in the *Laocoon*, was a very important contribution.[25] But a true appreciation of these things is possible only in the light of a whole system of such art-casuistries. And it is in the criticism of painting that this truth most needs enforcing, for it is in popular judgments on pictures that that false generalisation of all art into forms of poetry is most prevalent. To suppose that all is mere technical acquirement in delineation or touch, working through and addressing itself to the intelligence, on the one side, or a merely poetical, or what may be called literary interest, addressed also to the pure intelligence, on the other; – this is the way of most spectators, and of many critics, who have never caught sight, all the time, of that true pictorial quality which lies between (unique pledge of the possession of the pictorial gift) the inventive or creative handling of pure line and colour, which, as almost always in Dutch painting, as often also in the works of Titian or Veronese, is quite independent of anything definitely poetical in the subject it accompanies. It is the *drawing* – the design projected from that peculiar pictorial temperament or constitution, in which, while it may possibly be ignorant of true anatomical proportions, all things whatever, all poetry, every idea however abstract or obscure, floats up as a visible scene or image: it is the *colouring* – that weaving as of just perceptible gold threads of light through the dress, the flesh, the atmosphere, in Titian's *Lace-girl* – the staining of the whole fabric of the thing with a new, delightful physical quality. This *drawing*, then – the arabesque traced in the air by Tintoret's flying figures, by Titian's forest branches; this colouring – the magic conditions of light and hue in the atmosphere of Titian's *Lace-girl*, or Rubens's *Descent from the Cross:* – these essential pictorial qualities must first of all delight the sense, delight it as directly and sensuously as a fragment of Venetian glass; and through this delight only be the medium of whatever poetry or science may lie beyond them, in the intention of the composer. In its primary aspect, a great picture has no more definite message for us than an accidental play of sunlight and shadow for a moment, on the wall or floor: is itself, in truth, a space of such fallen light, caught as the colours are caught in an Eastern carpet, but refined upon, and dealt with more subtly and exquisitely than by nature itself.[26] And this primary and essential condition fulfilled, we may trace the coming of poetry into painting, by fine gradations upwards; from Japanese fan-painting, for instance, where we get, first, only abstract colour; then, just a little interfused sense of the poetry of flowers; then, sometimes, perfect flower-painting; [. . .] But although each art has thus its own specific order of impressions, and an untranslatable charm, while a just apprehension of the ultimate differences of the arts is the beginning of aesthetic criticism; yet it is noticeable that, in its special mode of handling its given material, each art may be observed to pass into the condition of some other art, by what German critics term an *Anders-streben* – a partial alienation from its own limitations, by which the arts are able, not indeed to supply the place of each other, but reciprocally to lend each other new forces.[27]

Thus some of the most delightful music seems to be always approaching to figure, to pictorial definition. Architecture, again, though it has its own laws – laws esoteric enough, as the true architect knows only too well – yet sometimes aims at fulfilling the conditions of a picture, as in the *Arena* chapel; or of sculpture, as in the flawless unity of Giotto's tower at Florence; and often finds a true poetry, as in those strangely twisted staircases of the *châteaux* of the country of the Loire, as if it were intended that among their odd turnings the actors in a wild life might pass each other unseen: there being a poetry also of memory and of the mere effect of time, by which it often profits greatly. Thus, again, sculpture aspires out of the hard limitation of pure form towards colour, or its equivalent; poetry also, in many ways, finding guidance from the other arts, the analogy between a Greek tragedy and a work of Greek sculpture, between a sonnet and a relief, of French poetry generally with the art of engraving, being more than mere figures of speech; and all the arts in common aspiring towards the principle of music; music being the typical, or ideally consummate art, the object of the great *Anders-streben* of all art, of all that is artistic, or partakes of artistic qualities.

All art constantly aspires towards the condition of music. For while in all other works of art it is possible to distinguish the matter from the form, and the understanding can always make this distinction, yet it is the constant effort of art to obliterate it. That the mere matter of a poem, for instance – its subject, its given incidents or situation; that the mere matter of a picture – the actual circumstances of an event, the actual topography of a landscape – should be nothing without the form, the spirit, of the handling; that this form, this mode of handling, should become an end in itself, should penetrate every part of the matter: – this is what all art constantly strives after, and achieves in different degrees. [. . .] Poetry, again, works with words addressed in the first instance to the mere intelligence; and it deals, most often, with a definite subject or situation. Sometimes it may find a noble and quite legitimate function in the expression of moral or political aspiration, as often in the poetry of Victor Hugo. In such instances it is easy enough for the understanding to distinguish between the matter and the form, however much the matter, the subject, the element which is addressed to the mere intelligence, has been penetrated by the informing, artistic spirit. But the ideal types of poetry are those in which this distinction is reduced to its *minimum;* so that lyrical poetry, precisely because in it we are least able to detach the matter from the form, without a deduction of something from that matter itself, is, at least artistically, the highest and most complete form of poetry.[28] And the very perfection of such poetry often seems to depend, in part, on a certain suppression or vagueness of mere subject, so that the meaning reaches us through ways not distinctly traceable by the understanding, as in some of the most imaginative compositions of William Blake, and often in Shakspere's songs, as pre-eminently in that song of Mariana's page in *Measure for Measure*, in which the kindling force and poetry of the whole play seems to pass for a moment into an actual strain of music.[29]

And this principle holds good of all things that partake in any degree of artistic qualities, of the furniture of our houses, and of dress, for instance, of life itself, of gesture and speech, and the details of daily intercourse; these also, for the wise, being susceptible of a suavity and charm, caught from the way in which they are done, which gives them a worth in themselves; in which, indeed, lies what is valuable and justly attractive, in what is called the fashion of a time, which elevates the trivialities of speech, and manner, and dress, into "ends in themselves," and gives them a mysterious grace and attractiveness in the doing of them.[30]

Art, then, is thus always striving to be independent of the mere intelligence, to become a matter of pure perception, to get rid of its responsibilities to its subject or material; the ideal examples of poetry and painting being those in which the constituent elements of the composition are so welded together, that the material or subject no longer strikes the intellect only; nor the form, the eye or the ear only; but form and matter, in their union or identity, present one single effect to the "imaginative reason," that complex faculty for which every thought and feeling is twin-born with its sensible analogue or symbol.

It is the art of music which most completely realises this artistic ideal, this perfect identification of form and matter. In its ideal, consummate moments, the end is not distinct from the means, the form from the matter, the subject from the expression; they inhere in and completely saturate each other;

and to it, therefore, to the condition of its perfect moments, all the arts may be supposed constantly to tend and aspire. [. . .]

I have spoken of a certain interpenetration of the matter or subject of a work of art with the form of it, a condition realised absolutely only in music, as the condition to which every form of art is perpetually aspiring. In the art of painting, the attainment of this ideal condition, this perfect interpenetration of the subject with colour and design, depends, of course, in great measure, on dexterous choice of that subject, or phase of subject; and such choice is one of the secrets of Giorgione's school. It is the school of *genre*, and employs itself mainly with "painted idylls," but, in the production of this pictorial poetry, exercises a wonderful tact in the selecting of such matter as lends itself most readily and entirely to pictorial form, to complete expression by drawing and colour. For although its productions are painted poems, they belong to a sort of poetry which tells itself without an articulated story. The master is pre-eminent for the resolution, the ease and quickness, with which he reproduces instantaneous motion – the lacing-on of armour, with the head bent back so stately – the fainting lady – the embrace, rapid as the kiss caught, with death itself, from dying lips – the momentary conjunction of mirrors and polished armour and still water, by which all the sides of solid image are presented at once, solving that casuistical question whether painting can present an object as completely as sculpture. The sudden act, the rapid transition of thought, the passing expression – this, he arrests with that vivacity which Vasari has attributed to him, *il fuoco Giorgionesco*, as he terms it. Now it is part of the ideality of the highest sort of dramatic poetry, that it presents us with a kind of profoundly significant and animated instants, a mere gesture, a look, a smile, perhaps – some brief and wholly concrete moment – into which, however, all the motives, all the interests and effects of a long history, have condensed themselves, and which seem to absorb past and future in an intense consciousness of the present. Such ideal instants the school of Giorgione selects, with its admirable tact, from that feverish, tumultuously coloured life of the old citizens of Venice – exquisite pauses in time, in which, arrested thus, we seem to be spectators of all the fulness of existence, and which are like some consummate extract or quintessence of life.[31]

Conclusion[32]

*Λέγει που Ἡράκλειτος ὅτι πάντα χωρεί καὶ οὐδὲν μένει**

To regard all things and principles of things as inconstant modes or fashions has more and more become the tendency of modern thought. Let us begin with that which is without – our physical life. Fix upon it in one of its more exquisite intervals, the moment, for instance, of delicious recoil from the flood of water in summer heat. What is the whole physical life in that moment but a combination of natural elements to which science gives their names? But these elements, phosphorus and lime and delicate fibres, are present not in the human body alone: we detect them in places most remote from it. Our physical life is a perpetual motion of them – the passage of the blood, the wasting and repairing of the lenses of the eye, the modification of the tissues of the brain by every ray of light and sound – processes which science reduces to simpler and more elementary forces. Like the elements of which we are composed, the action of these forces extends beyond us; it rusts iron and ripens corn. Far out on every side of us those elements are broadcast, driven by many forces; and birth and gesture and death and the springing of violets from the grave are but a few out of ten thousand resultant combinations. That clear, perpetual outline of face and limb is but an image of ours, under which we group them – a design in a web, the actual threads of which pass out beyond it. This at least of flame-like our life has, that it is but the concurrence, renewed from moment to moment, of forces parting sooner or later on their ways.[33]

Or if we begin with the inward world of thought and feeling, the whirlpool is still more rapid, the flame more eager and devouring. There it is no longer the gradual darkening of the eye and fading of colour from the wall, – the movement of the shore-side, where the water flows down indeed, though in apparent rest, – but the race of the mid-stream, a drift of

* 'Heraclitus says that all things give way and nothing remains': Plato, *Cratylus* 402A.

momentary acts of sight and passion and thought. At first sight experience seems to bury us under a flood of external objects, pressing upon us with a sharp and importunate reality, calling us out of ourselves in a thousand forms of action. But when reflexion begins to act upon those objects they are dissipated under its influence; the cohesive force seems suspended like a trick of magic; each object is loosed into a group of impressions – colour, odour, texture – in the mind of the observer. And if we continue to dwell in thought on this world, not of objects in the solidity with which language invests them, but of impressions unstable, flickering, inconsistent, which burn and are extinguished with our consciousness of them, it contracts still further; the whole scope of observation is dwarfed to the narrow chamber of the individual mind. Experience, already reduced to a swarm of impressions, is ringed round for each one of us by that thick wall of personality through which no real voice has ever pierced on its way to us, or from us to that which we can only conjecture to be without.[34] Every one of those impressions is the impression of the individual in his isolation, each mind keeping as a solitary prisoner its own dream of a world. Analysis goes a step farther still, and assures us that those impressions of the individual mind to which, for each one of us, experience dwindles down, are in perpetual flight; that each of them is limited by time, and that as time is infinitely divisible, each of them is infinitely divisible also; all that is actual in it being a single moment, gone while we try to apprehend it, of which it may ever be more truly said that it has ceased to be than that it is. To such a tremulous wisp constantly reforming itself on the stream, to a single sharp impression, with a sense in it, a relic more or less fleeting, of such moments gone by, what is real in our life fines itself down. It is with this movement, with the passage and dissolution of impressions, images, sensations, that analysis leaves off – that continual vanishing away, that strange, perpetual, weaving and unweaving of ourselves.

Philosophiren, says Novalis, *ist dephlegmatisiren vivificiren.*[35] The service of philosophy, of speculative culture, towards the human spirit is to rouse, to startle it into sharp and eager observation. Every moment some form grows perfect in hand or face; some tone on the hills or the sea is choicer than the rest; some mood of passion or insight or intellectual excitement is irresistibly real and attractive for us, – for that moment only. Not the fruit of experience, but experience itself, is the end. A counted number of pulses only is given to us of a variegated, dramatic life. How may we see in them all that is to be seen in them by the finest senses?[36] How shall we pass most swiftly from point to point, and be present always at the focus where the greatest number of vital forces unite in their purest energy?

To burn always with this hard, gemlike flame, to maintain this ecstasy, is success in life. In a sense it might even be said that our failure is to form habits: for, after all, habit is relative to a stereotyped world, and meantime it is only the roughness of the eye that makes any two persons, things, situations, seem alike. While all melts under our feet, we may well catch at any exquisite passion, or any contribution to knowledge that seems by a lifted horizon to set the spirit free for a moment, or any stirring of the senses, strange dyes, strange colours, and curious odours, or work of the artist's hands, or the face of one's friend. Not to discriminate every moment some passionate attitude in those about us, and in the brilliancy of their gifts some tragic dividing of forces on their ways, is, on this short day of frost and sun, to sleep before evening. With this sense of the splendour of our experience and of its awful brevity, gathering all we are into one desperate effort to see and touch, we shall hardly have time to make theories about the things we see and touch. What we have to do is to be for ever curiously testing new opinions and courting new impressions, never acquiescing in a facile orthodoxy of Comte, or of Hegel, or of our own.[37] Philosphical theories or ideas, as points of view, instruments of criticism, may help us to gather up what might otherwise pass unregarded by us. "Philosophy is the microscope of thought." The theory or idea or system which requires of us the sacrifice of any part of this experience, in consideration of some interest into which we cannot enter, or some abstract theory we have not identified with ourselves, or what is only conventional, has no real claim upon us.

One of the most beautiful passages in the writings of Rousseau is that in the sixth book of the *Confessions*, where he describes the awakening in him of the literary sense. An undefinable taint of death had always clung about him, and now in early manhood he believed himself smitten by mortal disease. He asked himself how he might make as much as possible of the interval that remained; and he was not biassed by anything in his previous life when he decided that it must be by intellectual excitement, which he found just then in the clear, fresh writings of Voltaire. Well! we are all *condamnés*, as Victor Hugo says: we are all under sentence of death but with a sort of indefinite reprieve – *les hommes sont tous condamnés à mort avec des sursis indéfinis:* we have an interval, and then our place knows us no more. Some spend this interval in listlessness, some in high passions, the wisest, at least among 'the children of this world,' in art and song. For our one chance lies in expanding that interval, in getting as many pulsations as possible into the given time. Great passions may give us this quickened sense of life, ecstasy and sorrow of love, the various forms of enthusiastic activity, disinterested or otherwise, which come naturally to many of us. Only be sure it is passion – that it does yield you this fruit of a quickened, multiplied consciousness. Of this wisdom, the poetic passion, the desire of beauty, the love of art for art's sake, has most; for art comes to you professing frankly to give nothing but the highest quality to your moments as they pass, and simply for those moments' sake.[38]

1868.

III. From 'The Child in the House'[1]

[. . .] So the child of whom I am writing lived on there quietly; things without thus ministering to him, as he sat daily at the window with the birdcage hanging below it, and his mother taught him to read, wondering at the ease with which he learned, and at the quickness of his memory. The perfume of the little flowers of the lime-tree fell through the air upon them like rain; while time seemed to move ever more slowly to the murmur of the bees in it, till it almost stood still on June afternoons. How insignificant, at the moment, seem the influences of the sensible things which are tossed and fall and lie about us, so, or so, in the environment of early childhood. How indelibly, as we afterwards discover, they affect us; with what capricious attractions and associations they figure themselves on the white paper, the smooth wax, of our ingenuous souls, as "with lead in the rock forever," [. . .] And so for Florian that general human instinct was reinforced by this special home-likeness in the place his wandering soul had happened to light on, as, in the second degree, its body and earthly tabernacle; the sense of harmony between his soul and its physical environment became, for a time at least, like perfectly played music, and the life led there singularly tranquil and filled with a curious sense of self-possession. The love of security, of an habitually undisputed standing-ground or sleeping-place, came to count for much in the generation and correcting of his thoughts, and afterwards as a salutary principle of restraint in all his wanderings of spirit. The wistful yearning towards home, in absence from it, as the shadows of evening deepened, and he followed in thought what was doing there from hour to hour, interpreted to him much of a yearning and regret he experienced afterwards, towards he knew not what, out of strange ways of feeling and thought in which, from time to time, his spirit found itself alone; and in the tears shed in such absences there seemed always to be some soul-subduing foretaste of what his last tears might be.

And the sense of security could hardly have been deeper, the quiet of the child's soul being one with the quiet of its home, a place "inclosed" and "sealed." But upon this assured place, upon the child's assured soul which resembled it, there came floating in from the larger world without, as at windows left ajar unknowingly, or over the high garden walls, two streams of impressions, the sentiments of beauty and pain – recognitions of the visible, tangible, audible loveliness of things, as a very real and somewhat tyrannous element in them – and of the sorrow of the world, of grown people and children and animals, as a thing not to be put by in them. From this point he could trace two predominant processes of mental change in him – the growth of an almost diseased sensibility to the spectacle of suffering, and, parallel with this, the rapid growth of a certain capacity of fascination by bright colour and choice form – the sweet curvings, for instance, of the lips of those who seemed to him comely persons, modulated in such delicate unison to the things they said or sang, – marking early the activity in him of a more than customary sensuousness, "the lust of the eye," as the Preacher says, which might lead him, one day, how far! Could he have foreseen the weariness of the way! [. . .]

I have remarked how, in the process of our brain-building, as the house of thought in which we live gets itself together, like some airy bird's-nest of floating thistle-down and chance straws, compact at last, little accidents have their consequence; and thus it happened that, as he walked one evening, a garden gate, usually closed, stood open; and lo! within, a great red hawthorn in full flower, embossing heavily and bleached and twisted trunk and branches, so aged that there were but few green leaves thereon – a plumage of tender, crimson fire out of the heart of the dry wood. The perfume of the tree had now and again reached him, in the currents of the wind, over the wall, and he had wondered what might be behind it, and was now allowed to fill his arms with the flowers – flowers enough for all the old blue-china pots along the chimney-piece, making *fête* in the children's room. Was it some periodic moment in the expansion of soul within him, or mere trick of heat in the heavily-laden summer air? But the beauty of the thing struck home to him feverishly; and in dreams all night he loitered along a magic roadway of crimson flowers, which seemed to open ruddily in thick, fresh masses about his feet, and fill softly all the little hollows in the banks on either side. Always afterwards, summer by summer, as the flowers came on, the blossom of the red hawthorn still seemed to him absolutely the reddest of all things; and the goodly crimson, still alive in the works of old Venetian masters or old Flemish tapestries, called out always from afar the recollection of the flame in those perishing little petals, as it pulsed gradually out of them, kept long in the drawers of an old cabinet. Also then, for the first time, he seemed to experience a passionateness in his relation to fair outward objects, an inexplicable excitement in their presence, which disturbed him, and from which he half longed to be free. A touch of regret or desire mingled all night with the remembered presence of the red flowers, and their perfume in the darkness about him; and the longing for some undivined, entire possession of them was the beginning of a revelation to him, growing ever clearer, with the coming of the gracious summer guise of fields and trees and persons in each succeeding year, of a certain, at times seemingly exclusive, predominance in his interests, of beautiful physical things, a kind of tyranny of the senses over him.

In later years he came upon philosophies which occupied him much in the estimate of the proportion of the sensuous and the ideal elements in human knowledge, the relative parts they bear in it; and, in his intellectual scheme, was led to assign very little to the abstract thought, and much to its sensible vehicle or occasion. Such metaphysical speculation did but reinforce what was instinctive in his way of receiving the world, and for him, everywhere, that sensible vehicle or occasion became, perhaps only too surely, the necessary concomitant of any perception of things, real enough to be of any weight or reckoning, in his house of thought. [. . .]

So he yielded himself to these things, to be played upon by them like a musical instrument, and began to note with deepening watchfulness, but always with some puzzled, unutterable longing in his enjoyment, the phases of the seasons and of the growing or waning day, down even to the shadowy changes wrought on bare wall or ceiling – the light cast up from the snow, bringing out their darkest angles; the brown light in the cloud, which meant rain; that almost too austere clearness, in the protracted light of the lengthening day, before warm weather began, as if it lingered but to make a severer workday, with the school-books opened earlier and later; that beam of June sunshine, at last, as he lay awake before the time, a way of gold-dust across the darkness; all the humming, the freshness, the perfume of the garden seemed to lie upon it – and coming in one afternoon in September, along the red gravel walk, to look for a basket of yellow crab-apples left in the cool, old parlour, he remembered it the more, and how the colours struck upon him, because a wasp on one bitten apple stung him, and he felt the passion of sudden, severe pain. For this too brought its curious reflexions; and, in relief from it, he would wonder over it – how it had then been with him – puzzled at the depth of the charm or spell over him, which lay, for a little while at least, in the mere absence of pain; once, especially, when an older boy taught him to make flowers of sealing-wax, and he had burnt his hand badly at the lighted taper, and been unable to sleep. He remembered that also afterwards, as a sort of typical thing – a white vision of heat about him, clinging closely, through the languid scent of the ointments put upon the place to make it well.

Also, as he felt this pressure upon him of the sensible world, then, as often afterwards, there would come another sort of curious questioning how the last impressions of eye and ear might happen to him, how they would find him – the scent of the last flower, the soft yellowness of the last morning, the last recognition of some object of affection, hand or voice; it could not be but that the latest look of the eyes, before their final closing, would be strangely vivid; one would go with the hot tears, the cry, the touch of the wistful bystander, impressed how deeply on one! or would it be, perhaps a mere frail retiring of all things, great or little, away from one, into a level distance?

For with this desire of physical beauty mingled itself early the fear of death – the fear of death intensified by the desire of beauty. [. . .] Afterwards he came to think of those poor, home-returning ghosts, which all men have fancied to themselves – the *revenants* – pathetically, as crying, or beating with vain hands at the doors, as the wind came, their cries distinguishable in it as a wilder inner note. But, always making death more unfamiliar still, that old experience would ever, from time to time, return to him; even in the living he sometimes caught its likeness; at any time or place, in a moment, the faint atmosphere of the chamber of death would be breathed around him, and the image with the bound chin, the quaint smile, the straight, stiff feet, shed itself across the air upon the bright carpet, amid the gayest company, or happiest communing with himself.

To most children the sombre questionings to which impressions like these attach themselves, if they come at all, are actually suggested by religious books, which therefore they often regard with much secret distaste, and dismiss, as far as possible, from their habitual thoughts as a too depressing element in life. To Florian such impressions, these misgivings as to the ultimate tendency of the years, of the relationship between life and death, had been suggested spontaneously in the natural course of his mental growth by a strong innate sense for the soberer tones in things, further strengthened by actual circumstances; and religious sentiment, that system of biblical ideas in which he had been brought up, presented itself to him as a thing that might soften and dignify, and light up as with a "lively hope," a melancholy already deeply settled in him. So he yielded himself easily to religious impressions, and with a kind of mystical appetite for sacred things; the more as they came to him through a saintly person who loved him tenderly, and believed that this early pre-occupation with them already marked the child out for a saint. He began to love, for their own sakes, church lights, holy days, all that belonged to the comely order of the sanctuary, the secrets of its white linen, and holy vessels, and fonts of pure water; and its hieratic purity and simplicity became the type of something he desired always to have about him in actual life. [. . .] His way of conceiving religion came then to be in effect what it ever afterwards remained – a sacred history indeed, but still more a sacred ideal, a transcendent version or representation, under intenser and more expressive light and shade, of human life and its familiar or exceptional incidents, birth, death, marriage, youth, age, tears, joy, rest, sleep, waking – a mirror, towards which men might turn away their eyes from vanity and dullness, and see themselves therein as angels, [. . .] A place adumbrated itself in his thoughts, wherein those sacred personalities, which are at once the reflex and the pattern of our nobler phases of life, housed themselves; and this region in his intellectual scheme all subsequent experience did but tend still further to realise and define. Some ideal, hieratic persons he would always need to occupy it and keep a warmth there. And he could hardly understand those who felt no such need at all, finding themselves quite happy without such heavenly companionship, and sacred double of their life, beside them. [. . .]

Sensibility – the desire of physical beauty – a strange biblical awe, which made any reference to the unseen act on him like solemn music – these qualities the child took away with him, when, at about the age of twelve years, he left the old house, and was taken to live in another place.

IV. From *Appreciations*

Romanticism[1]

*αἰνει δὲ παλαιὸν μὲν οἶνον, ἄνθεα δ' ὕμνων νεωτέρων**

The words, *classical* and *romantic*, although, like many other critical expressions, sometimes abused by those who have understood them too vaguely or too absolutely, yet define two real tendencies in the history of art and literature. Used in an exaggerated sense, to express a greater opposition between those tendencies than really exists, they have at times tended to divide people of taste into opposite camps. But in that *House Beautiful*, which the creative minds of all generations – the artists and those who have treated life in the spirit of art – are always building together, for the refreshment of the human spirit, these oppositions cease;[2] and the *Interpreter* of the *House Beautiful*, the true aesthetic critic, uses these divisions, only so far as they enable him to enter into the peculiarities of the objects with which he has to do. The term *classical*, fixed, as it is, to a well-defined literature, and a well-defined group in art, is clear, indeed; but then it has often been used in a hard, and merely scholastic sense, by the praisers of what is old and accustomed, at the expense of what is new, by critics who would never have discovered for themselves the charm of any work, whether new or old, who value what is old, in art or literature, for its accessories, and chiefly for the conventional authority that has gathered about it – people who would never really have been made glad by any Venus fresh-risen from the sea, and who praise the Venus of old Greece and Rome, only because they fancy her grown now into something staid and tame.

And as the term, *classical*, has been used in a too absolute, and therefore in a misleading sense, so the term, *romantic*, has been used much too vaguely, in various accidental senses. The sense in which Scott is called a romantic writer is chiefly this; that, in opposition to the literary tradition of the last century, he loved strange adventure, and sought it in the Middle Age. Much later, in a Yorkshire village, the spirit of romanticism bore a

* 'When you praise the wine that is old, you should also praise the flowers of new songs' (Pindar, IX Olympian, ll. 48–9).

more really characteristic fruit in the work of a young girl, Emily Brontë, the romance of *Wuthering Heights*; the figures of Hareton Earnshaw, of Catherine Linton, and of Heathcliffe – tearing open Catherine's grave, removing one side of her coffin, that he may really lie beside her in death – figures so passionate, yet woven on a background of delicately beautiful, moorland scenery, being typical examples of that spirit.[3] [. . .]

But the romantic spirit is, in reality, an ever-present, an enduring principle, in the artistic temperament; and the qualities of thought and style which that, and other similar uses of the word *romantic* really indicate, are indeed but symptoms of a very continuous and widely working influence.[4] [. . .]

It is the addition of strangeness to beauty, that constitutes the romantic character in art; and the desire of beauty being a fixed element in every artistic organisation, it is the addition of curiosity to this desire of beauty, that constitutes the romantic temper.[5] Curiosity and the desire of beauty, have each their place in art, as in all true criticism. When one's curiosity is deficient, when one is not eager enough for new impressions, and new pleasures, one is liable to value mere academical proprieties too highly, to be satisfied with worn-out or conventional types, with the insipid ornament of Racine, or the prettiness of that later Greek sculpture, which passed so long for true Hellenic work; to miss those places where the handiwork of nature, or of the artist, has been most cunning; to find the most stimulating products of art a mere irritation. And when one's curiosity is in excess, when it overbalances the desire of beauty, then one is liable to value in works of art what is inartistic in them; to be satisfied with what is exaggerated in art, with productions like some of those of the romantic school in Germany; [. . .]

But, however falsely those two tendencies may be opposed by critics, or exaggerated by artists themselves, they are tendencies really at work at all times in art, moulding it, with the balance sometimes a little on one side, sometimes a little on the other, generating, respectively, as the balance inclines on this side or that, two principles, two traditions, in art, and in literature so far as it partakes of the spirit of art. If there is a great overbalance of curiosity, then, we have the grotesque in art: if the union of strangeness and beauty, under very difficult and complex conditions, be a successful one, if the union be entire, then the resultant beauty is very exquisite, very attractive. With a passionate care for beauty, the romantic spirit refuses to have it, unless the condition of strangeness be first fulfilled. Its desire is for a beauty born of unlikely elements, by a profound alchemy, by a difficult initiation, by the charm which wrings it even out of terrible things; and a trace of distortion, of the grotesque, may perhaps linger, as an additional element of expression, about its ultimate grace.[6] Its eager, excited spirit will have strength, the grotesque, first of all – the trees shrieking as you tear off the leaves; for Jean Valjean, the long years of convict life; for Redgauntlet, the quicksands of Solway Moss;[7] then, incorporate with this strangeness, and intensified by restraint, as much sweetness, as much beauty, as is compatible with that. [. . .]

Few, probably, now read Madame de Staël's *De l'Allemagne*, though it has its interest, the interest which never quite fades out of work really touched with the enthusiasm of the spiritual adventurer, the pioneer in culture. It was published in 1810, to introduce to French readers a new school of writers – the romantic school, from beyond the Rhine; and it was followed, twenty-three years later, by Heine's *Romantische Schule*, as at once a supplement and a correction. Both these books, then, connect romanticism with Germany, with the names especially of Goethe and Tieck; and, to many English readers, the idea of romanticism is still inseparably connected with Germany – that Germany which, in its quaint old towns, under the spire of Strasburg or the towers of Heidelberg, was always listening in rapt inaction to the melodious, fascinating voices of the Middle Age,[8] [. . .] But neither Germany, with its Goethe and Tieck, nor England, with its Byron and Scott, is nearly so representative of the romantic temper as France, with Murger, and Gautier, and Victor Hugo. It is in French literature that its most characteristic expression is to be found; and that, as most closely derivative, historically, from such peculiar conditions, as ever reinforce it to the utmost. [. . .]

It is in the terrible tragedy of Rousseau, in fact, that French romanticism, with much else, begins: reading his *Confessions* we seem actually to assist at the birth of this new, strong spirit in the French mind.[9] The wildness which has shocked so many, and the fascination which has influenced almost every one, in the squalid, yet eloquent figure, we see and hear so clearly in that book, wandering under the apple-blossoms and among the vines of Neuchâtel or Vevey actually give it the quality of a very successful romantic invention. His strangeness or distortion, his profound subjectivity, his passionateness – the *cor laceratum* – Rousseau makes all men in love with these. *Je ne suis fait comme aucun de ceux que j'ai sus. Mais si je ne vaux pas mieux, au moins je suis autre.* – "I am not made like any one else I have ever known: yet, if I am not better, at least I am different." These words, from the first page of the *Confessions*, anticipate all the Werthers, Renés, Obermanns, of the last hundred years.[10] For Rousseau did but anticipate a trouble in the spirit of the whole world; and thirty years afterwards, what in him was a pecularity, became part of the general consciousness. A storm was coming: Rousseau, with others, felt it in the air, and they helped to bring it down: they introduced a disturbing element into French literature, then so trim and formal, like our own literature of the age of Queen Anne.

In 1815 the storm had come and gone, but had left, in the spirit of "young France," the *ennui* of an immense disillusion.[11] In the last chapter of Edgar Quinet's *Révolution Française*, a work itself full of irony, of disillusion, he distinguishes two books, Senancour's *Obermann* and Chateaubriand's *Génie du Christianisme*, as characteristic of the first decade of the present century. In those two books we detect already the disease and the cure – in *Obermann* the irony, refined into a plaintive philosophy of "indifference" – in Chateaubriand's *Génie du Christianisme*, the refuge from a tarnished actual present, a present of disillusion, into a world of strength and beauty in the Middle Age, as at an earlier period – in *René* and *Atala* – into the free play of them in savage life. It is to minds in this spiritual situation, weary of the present, but yearning for the spectacle of beauty and strength, that the works of French romanticism appeal.[12] They set a positive value on the intense, the exceptional; and a certain distortion is sometimes noticeable in them, as in conceptions like Victor Hugo's *Quasimodo*, or *Gwynplaine*, something of a terrible grotesque, of the *macabre*, as the French themselves call it; though always combined with perfect literary execution, [. . .] Stendhal, a writer whom I have already quoted, and of whom English readers might well know much more than they do, stands between the earlier and later growths of the romantic spirit.[13] His novels are rich in romantic quality; and his other writings – partly criticism, partly personal reminiscences – are a very curious and interesting illustration of the needs out of which romanticism arose. In his book on *Racine and Shakespeare*, Stendhal argues that all good art was romantic in its day; and this is perhaps true in Stendhal's sense. That little treatise, full of "dry light"[14] and fertile ideas, was published in the year 1823, and its object is to defend an entire independence and liberty in the choice and treatment of subject, both in art and literature, against those who upheld the exclusive authority of precedent. In pleading the cause of romanticism, therefore, it is the novelty, both of form and of motive, in writings like the *Hernani* of Victor Hugo (which soon followed it, raising a storm of criticism) that he is chiefly concerned to justify. To be interesting and really stimulating, to keep us from yawning even, art and literature must follow the subtle movements of that nimbly-shifting *Time-Spirit*, or *Zeit-Geist*, understood by French not less than by German criticism, which is always modifying men's taste, as it modifies their manners and their pleasures.[15] This, he contends, is what all great workmen had always understood. Dante, Shakespeare, Molière, had exercised an absolute independence in their choice of subject and treatment. To turn always with that ever-changing spirit, yet to retain the flavour of what was admirably done in past generations, in the classics, as we say – is the problem of true romanticism. [. . .]

Romanticism, then, although it has its epochs, is in its essential characteristics rather a spirit which shows itself at all times, in various degrees, in individual workmen and their work, and the amount of which criticism has to estimate in them taken one by one, than the peculiarity of a time or a school. Depending on the varying proportion of curiosity and the desire of beauty, natural tendencies of the artistic spirit at all times, it must always be partly a matter of individual temperament. The eighteenth century in England has been regarded as almost exclusively a classical period; yet William Blake, a type of so much which breaks through what are conventionally thought the influences of that century, is still a noticeable phenomenon in it, and the reaction in favour of naturalism in poetry begins in that century, early. There are, thus, the born romanticists and the born classicists. There are the born classicists who start with *form*, to whose minds the comeliness of the old, immemorial, well-recognised types in art and literature, have revealed themselves impressively; who will entertain no matter which will not go easily and flexibly into them; whose work aspires only to be a variation upon, or study from, the older masters. "'Tis art's decline, my son!" they are always saying, to the progressive element in their own generation; to those who care for that which in fifty years' time everyone will be caring for. On the other hand, there are the born romanticists, who start with an original, untried *matter*, still in fusion; who conceive this vividly, and hold by it as the essence of their work; who, by the very vividness and heat of their conception, purge away, sooner or later, all that is not organically appropriate to it, till the whole effect adjusts itself in clear, orderly, proportionate form;[16] which form, after a very little time, becomes classical in its turn. [. . .]

Material for the artist, motives of inspiration, are not yet exhausted: our curious, complex, aspiring age still abounds in subjects for aesthetic manipulation by the literary as well as by other forms of art. For the literary art, at all events, the problem just now is, to induce order upon the contorted, proportionless accumulation of our knowledge and experience, our science and history, our hopes and disillusion, and, in effecting this, to do consciously what has been done hitherto for the most part too unconsciously, to write our English language as the Latins wrote theirs, as the French write, as scholars should write. Appealing, as he may, to precedent in this matter, the scholar will still remember that if "the style is the man" it is also the age;[17] that the nineteenth century too will be found to have had its style, justified by necessity – a style very different, alike from the baldness of an impossible "Queen Anne" revival, and an incorrect, incondite exuberance, after the mode of Elizabeth: that we can only return to either at the price of an impoverishment of form or matter, or both, although, an intellectually rich age such as ours being necessarily an eclectic one, we may well cultivate some of the excellences of literary types so different as those: that in literature as in other matters it is well to unite as many diverse elements as may be: that the individual writer or artist, certainly, is to be estimated by the number of graces he combines, and his power of interpenetrating them in a given work. To discriminate schools, of art, of literature, is, of course, part of the obvious business of literary criticism: but, in the work of literary production, it is easy to be overmuch occupied concerning them. For, in truth, the legitimate contention is, not of one age or school of literary art against another, but of all successive schools alike, against the stupidity which is dead to the substance, and the vulgarity which is dead to form.

1876.

Coleridge[18]

Forms of intellectual and spiritual culture sometimes exercise their subtlest and most artful charm when life is already passing from them.[19] Searching and irresistible as are the changes of the human spirit on its way to perfection, there is yet so much elasticity of temper that what must pass away sooner or later is not disengaged all at once, even from the highest order of minds. Nature, which by one law of development evolves ideas, hypotheses, modes of inward life, and represses them in turn, has in this way provided that the earlier growth should propel its fibres into the later, and so transmit the whole of its forces in an unbroken continuity of life. Then comes the spectacle of the reserve of the elder generation exquisitely refined by the antagonism of the new. That current of new life chastens them while they contend against it.[20] Weaker minds fail to perceive the change: the clearest minds abandon themselves to it. To feel the change everywhere, yet not abandon oneself to it, is a situation of difficulty and contention. Communicating, in this way, to the passing stage of culture, the charm of what is chastened, high-strung, athletic, they yet detach the highest minds from the past, by pressing home its difficulties and finally proving it impossible. Such has been the charm of many leaders of lost causes in philosophy and in religion. It is the special charm of Coleridge, in connexion with those older methods of philosphic inquiry, over which the empirical philosphy of our day has triumphed.

Modern thought is distinguished from ancient by its cultivation of "relative" spirit in place of the "absolute." Ancient philosophy sought to arrest every object in an eternal outline, to fix thought in a necessary formula, and the varieties of life in a classification by "kinds," or *genera*. To the modern spirit nothing is, or can be rightly known, except relatively and under conditions. The philosophical conception of the relative has been developed in modern times through the influence of the sciences of observation. Those sciences reveal types of life evanescing into each other by inexpressible refinements of change. Things pass into their opposites by accumulation of undefinable quantities. The growth of those sciences consists in a continual analysis of facts of rough and general observation into groups of facts more precise and minute. The faculty for truth is recognised as a power of distinguishing and fixing delicate and fugitive detail. The moral world is ever in contact with the physical, and the relative spirit has invaded moral philosophy from the ground of the inductive sciences. There it has started a new analysis of the relations of body and mind, good and evil, freedom and necessity. Hard and abstract moralities are yielding to a more exact estimate of the subtlety and complexity of our life.[21] [. . .] It is the truth of these relations that experience gives us, not the truth of eternal outlines ascertained once for all, but a world of fine gradations and subtly linked conditions, shifting intricately as we ourselves change – and bids us, by a constant clearing of the organs of observation and perfecting of analysis, to make what we can of these. To the intellect, the critical spirit, just these subtleties of effect are more precious than anything else. What is lost in precision of form is gained in intricacy of expression. It is no vague scholastic abstraction that will satisfy the speculative instinct in our modern minds. Who would change the colour or curve of a rose-leaf for that *οὐσία ἀχρώματος, ἀσχημάτιστος, ἀναφὴς* – that colourless, formless, intangible, being – Plato put so high?[22] For the true illustration of the speculative temper is not the Hindoo mystic, lost to sense, understanding, individuality, but one such as Goethe, to whom every moment of life brought its contribution of experimental, individual knowledge; by whom no touch of the world of form, colour, and passion was disregarded.

Now the literary life of Coleridge was a disinterested struggle against the relative spirit. With a strong native bent towards the tracking of all questions, critical or practical, to first principles, he is ever restlessly scheming to 'apprehend the absolute,' to affirm it effectively, to get it acknowledged. It was an effort, surely, an effort of sickly thought, that saddened his mind, and limited the operation of his unique poetic gift. [. . .] Perhaps the chief offence in Coleridge is an excess of seriousness, a seriousness arising not from any moral principle, but from a misconception of the perfect manner. There is a certain shade of unconcern, the perfect manner of the eighteenth century, which may be thought to make complete culture in the handling of abstract questions. The humanist, the possessor of that complete culture, does not "weep" over the failure of "a theory of the quantification of the predicate," nor "shriek" over the fall of a philosophical formula. A kind of humour is, in truth, one of the conditions of the just mental attitude, in the criticism of by-past stages of thought.[23] [. . .] But on Coleridge lies the whole weight of the sad reflection that has since come into the world, with which for us the air is full, which the "children in the market-place" repeat to each other. His very language is forced and broken lest some saving formula should be lost – *distinctities, enucleation, pentad of operative Christianity;* he has a whole armoury of these terms, and expects to turn the tide of human thought by fixing the sense of such expressions as "reason," "understanding," "idea." Again, he lacks the jealousy of a true artist in excluding all associations that have no colour, or charm, or gladness in them; and everywhere allows the impress of a somewhat inferior theological literature. [. . .]

Coleridge's intellectual sorrows were many; but he had one singular intellectual happiness. With an inborn taste for transcendental philosophy, he lived just at the time when that philosophy took an immense spring in Germany, and connected itself with an impressive literary movement. He had the good luck to light upon it in its freshness, and introduce it to his countrymen. What an opportunity for one reared on the colourless analytic English philosophies of the last century, but who feels an irresistible attraction towards bold metaphysical synthesis! How rare are such occasions of intellectual contentment! This transcendental philosophy, chiefly as systematised by the mystic Schelling, Coleridge applied with an eager, unwearied subtlety, to the questions of theology, and poetic or artistic criticism.[24] It is in his theory of poetry, of art, that he comes nearest to principles of permanent truth and importance: that is the least fugitive part of his prose work. What, then, is the essence of his philosophy of art – of imaginative production?

Generally, it may be described as an attempt to reclaim the world of art as a world of fixed laws, to show that the creative activity of genius and the simplest act of thought are but higher and lower products of the laws of a universal logic. Criticism, feeling its own inadequacy in dealing with the greater works of art, is sometimes tempted to make too much of those dark and capricious suggestions of *genius*, which even the intellect possessed by them is unable to explain or recall. It has seemed due to the half-sacred character of those works to ignore all analogy between the productive process by which they had their birth, and the simpler processes of mind. Coleridge, on the other hand, assumes that the highest phases of thought must be more, not less, than the lower, subject to law. [. . .]

It is natural that Shakespeare should be the favourite illustration of such criticism, whether in England or Germany. The first suggestion in Shakespeare is that of capricious detail, of a waywardness that plays with the parts careless of the impression of the whole; what supervenes is the constraining unity of effect, the ineffaceable impression, of Hamlet or Macbeth. His hand moving freely is curved round as if by some law of gravitation from within: an energetic unity or identity makes itself visible amid an abounding variety. This unity or identity Coleridge exaggerates into something like the identity of a natural organism, and the associative act which effected it into something closely akin to the primitive power of nature itself. "In the Shakespearian drama," he says, "there is a vitality which grows and evolves itself from within."

Again –

"He, too, worked in the spirit of nature, by evolving the germ from within, by the imaginative power, according to the idea. For as the power of seeing is to light, so is an idea in mind to a law in nature. They are correlatives which suppose each other."

Again –

"The organic form is innate: it shapes, as it develops, itself from within, and the fulness of its development is one and the same with the perfection of its outward form. Such as the life is, such is the form. Nature, the prime, genial artist, inexhaustible in diverse powers, is equally inexhaustible in forms: each exterior is the physiognomy of the being within, and even such is the appropriate excellence of Shakespeare, himself a nature humanised, a genial understanding, directing self-consciously a power and an implicit wisdom deeper even than our consciousness."[25]

In this late age we are become so familiarised with the greater works of art as to be little sensitive of the act of creation in them: they do not impress us as a new presence in the world. Only sometimes, in productions which realise immediately a profound influence and enforce a change in taste, we are actual witnesses of the moulding of an unforeseen type by some new principle of association; and to that phenomenon Coleridge wisely recalls our attention. What makes his view a one-sided one is, that in it the artist has become almost a mechanical agent: instead of the most luminous and self-possessed phase of consciousness, the associative act in art or poetry is made to look like some blindly organic process of assimilation. The work of art is likened to a living organism. That expresses truly the sense of a self-delighting, independent life which, the finished work of art gives us: it hardly figures the process by which such work was produced. Here there is no blind ferment of lifeless elements towards the realisation of a type. By exquisite analysis the artist attains clearness of idea; then, through many stages of refining, clearness of expression. He moves slowly over his work, calculating the tenderest tone, and restraining the subtlest curve, never letting hand or fancy move at large, gradually enforcing flaccid spaces to the higher degree of expressiveness. The philosophic critic, at least, will value, even in works of imagination, seemingly the most intuitive, the power of the understanding in them, their logical process of construction, the spectacle of a supreme intellectual dexterity which they afford.[26] [. . .]

Coleridge's prose writings on philosophy, politics, religion, and criticism, were, in truth, but one element in a whole lifetime of endeavours to present the then recent metaphysics of Germany to English readers, as a legitimate expansion of the older, classical and native masters of what has been variously called the *a priori*, or absolute, or spiritual, or Platonic, view of things. His criticism, his challenge for recognition in the concrete, visible, finite work of art, of the dim, unseen, comparatively infinite, soul or power of the artist, may well be remembered as part of the long pleading of German culture for the things "behind the veil." To introduce that spiritual philosophy, as represented by the more transcendental parts of Kant, and by Schelling, into all subjects, as a system of reason in them, one and ever identical with itself, however various the matter through which it was diffused, became with him the motive of an unflagging enthusiasm, which seems to have been the one thread of continuity in a life otherwise singularly wanting in unity of purpose, and in which he was certainly far from uniformly at his best. Fragmentary and obscure, but often eloquent, and always at once earnest and ingenious, those writings, supplementing his remarkable gift of conversation, were directly and indirectly influential, even on some the furthest removed from Coleridge's own masters; on John Stuart Mill, for instance, and some of the earlier writers of the "high-church" school. Like his verse, they display him also in two other characters – as a student of words, and as a psychologist, that is, as a more minute observer or student than other men of the phenomena of mind. [. . .] The latter gift, that power of the "subtle-souled psychologist," as Shelley calls him, seems to have been connected with some tendency to disease in the physical temperament, something of a morbid want of balance in those parts where the physical and intellectual elements mix most closely together, with a kind of languid visionariness, deep-seated in the very constitution of the "narcotist," who had quite a gift for "plucking the poisons of self-harm," and which the actual habit of taking opium, accidentally acquired, did but reinforce. This morbid languor of nature, connected both with his fitfulness of purpose and his rich delicate dreaminess, qualifies Coleridge's poetic composition even more than his prose; his verse, with the exception of his avowedly political poems, being, unlike that of the "Lake School," to which in some respects he belongs, singularly unaffected by any moral, or professional, or personal effort or ambition, – "written," as he says, "after the more violent emotions of sorrow, to give him pleasure, when perhaps nothing else could;" but coming thus, indeed, very close to his own most intimately personal characteristics, and having a certain languidly soothing grace or cadence, for its most fixed quality, from first to last.[27] [. . .] *Kubla Khan*, the fragment of a poem actually composed in some certainly not quite healthy sleep, is perhaps chiefly of interest as showing, by the mode of its composition, how physical, how much of a diseased or valetudinarian temperament, in its moments of relief, Coleridge's happiest gift really was; and side by side with *Kubla Khan* should be read, as Coleridge placed it, the *Pains of Sleep*, to illustrate that retarding physical burden in his temperament, that "unimpassioned grief," the source of which lay so near the source of those pleasures. Connected also with this, and again in contrast with Wordsworth, is the limited quantity of his poetical performance, as he himself regrets so eloquently in the lines addressed to Wordsworth after his recitation of *The Prelude*.[28] It is like some exotic plant, just managing to blossom a little in the somewhat un-english air of Coleridge's own south-western birthplace, but never quite well there.

In 1798 he joined Wordsworth in the composition of a volume of poems – the *Lyrical Ballads*. What Wordsworth then wrote already vibrates with that blithe impulse which carried him to final happiness and self-possession. In Coleridge we feel already that faintness and obscure dejection which clung like some contagious damp to all his work.[29] Wordsworth was to be distinguished by a joyful and penetrative conviction of the existence of certain latent affinities between nature and the human mind, which reciprocally gild the mind and nature with a kind of "heavenly alchemy."

> "My voice proclaims
> How exquisitely the individual mind
> (And the progressive powers, perhaps, no less
> Of the whole species) to the external world
> Is fitted; and how exquisitely, too,
> The external world is fitted to the mind;
> And the creation, by now lower name
> Can it be called, which they with blended might
> Accomplish."[30]

In Wordsworth this took the form of an unbroken dreaming over the aspects and transitions of nature – a reflective, though altogether unformulated, analysis of them.

There are in Coleridge's poems expressions of this conviction as deep as Wordsworth's. But Coleridge could never have abandoned himself to the dream, the vision, as Wordsworth did, because the first condition of such abandonment must be an unvexed quietness of heart. No one can read the *Lines composed above Tintern* without feeling how potent the physical element was among the conditions of Wordsworth's genius – "felt in the blood and felt along the heart."

> "My whole life I have lived in quiet thought!"

The stimulus which most artists require of nature he can renounce. He leaves the ready-made glory of the Swiss mountains that he may reflect glory on a mouldering leaf. He loves best to watch the floating thistledown, because of its hint at an unseen life in the air. Coleridge's temperament, *ἀεί ἐν σφοδρᾷ ὀρέξει*,* with its faintness, its grieved dejection, could never have been like that.

> "My genial spirits fail;
> And what can these avail
> To lift the smothering weight from off my breast?
> It were a vain endeavour,
> Though I should gaze for ever
> On that green light that lingers in the west:

* 'Engaged in excessive longing'.

> I may not hope from outward forms to win
> The passion and the life whose fountains are within."[31]

Wordsworth's flawless temperament, his fine mountain atmosphere of mind, that calm, sabbatic, mystic, well-being which De Quincey, a little cynically, connected with worldly (that is to say, pecuniary) good fortune, kept his conviction of a latent intelligence in nature within the limits of sentiment or instinct, and confined it to those delicate and subdued shades of expression which alone perfect art allows. In Coleridge's sadder, more purely intellectual, cast of genius, what with Wordsworth was sentiment or instinct became a philosophical idea, or philosophical formula, developed, as much as possible, after the abstract and metaphysical fashion of the transcendental schools of Germany. [. . .]

The student of empirical science asks, 'Are absolute principles attainable? What are the limits of knowledge?' The answer he receives from science itself is not ambiguous. What the moralist asks is, 'Shall we gain or lose by surrendering human life to the relative spirit?' Experience answers that the dominant tendency of life is to turn ascertained truth into a dead letter, to make us all the phlegmatic servants of routine. The relative spirit, by its constant dwelling on the more fugitive conditions or circumstances of things, breaking through a thousand rough and brutal classifications, and giving elasticity to inflexible principles, begets an intellectual *finesse* of which the ethical result is a delicate and tender justice in the criticism of human life. Who would gain more than Coleridge by criticism in such a spirit? We know how his life has appeared when judged by absolute standards. We see him trying to "apprehend the absolute", to stereotype forms of faith and philosophy, to attain, as he says, "fixed principles" in politics, morals, and religion, to fix one mode of life as the essence of life, refusing to see the parts as parts only; and all the time his own pathetic history pleads for a more elastic moral philosophy than his, and cries out against every formula less living and flexible than life itself.

"From his childhood he hungered for eternity." There, after all, is the incontestable claim of Coleridge. The perfect flower of any elementary type of life must always be precious to humanity, and Coleridge is a true flower of the *ennuyé*, of the type of René. More than Childe Harold, more than Werther, more than René himself, Coleridge, by what he did, what he was, and what he failed to do, represents that inexhaustible discontent, languor, and home-sickness, that endless regret, the chords of which ring all through our modern literature. It is to the romantic element in literature that those qualities belong. One day, perhaps, we may come to forget the distant horizon, with full knowledge of the situation, to be content with "what is here and now"; and herein is the essence of classical feeling. But by us of the present moment, certainly – by us for whom the Greek spirit, with its engaging naturalness, simple, chastened, debonair, *τρυφῆς, ἁβρότητος, χλιδῆς, χαρίτων, ἱμέρου, πόθου πατήρ,** is itself the Sangrail of an endless pilgrimage, Coleridge, with his passion for the absolute, for something fixed where all is moving, his faintness, his broken memory, his intellectual disquiet, may still be ranked among the interpreters of one of the constituent elements of our life.

1865, 1880.

Style[32]

Dryden, with the characteristic instinct of his age, loved to emphasise the distinction between poetry and prose, the protest against their confusion with each other, coming with somewhat diminished effect from one whose poetry was so prosaic. In truth, his sense of prosaic excellence affected his verse rather than his prose, which is not only fervid, richly figured, poetic, as we say, but vitiated, all unconsciously, by many a scanning line. Setting up correctness, that humble merit of prose, as the central literary excellence, he is really a less correct writer than he may seem, still with an imperfect mastery of the relative pronoun. It might have been foreseen that, in the rotations of mind, the province of poetry in prose would find its assertor; and, a century after Dryden, amid very different intellectual needs, and with the need therefore of great modifications in literary form, the range of the poetic force in literature was

* 'Of wantonness, daintiness, luxury, grace, desire, and longing the sire' (Plato, *Symposium* 197D).

effectively enlarged by Wordsworth. The true distinction between prose and poetry he regarded as the almost technical or accidental one of the absence or presence of metrical beauty, or, say! metrical restraint; and for him the opposition came to be between verse and prose of course; but, as the essential dichotomy in this matter, between imaginative and unimaginative writing, parallel to De Quincey's distinction between "the literature of power and the literature of knowledge," in the former of which the composer gives us not fact, but his peculiar sense of fact, whether past or present.[33]

Dismissing then, under sanction of Wordsworth, that harsher opposition of poetry to prose, as savouring in fact of the arbitrary psychology of the last century, and with it the prejudice that there can be but one only beauty of prose style, I propose here to point out certain qualities of all literature as a fine art, which, if they apply to the literature of fact, apply still more to the literature of the imaginative sense of fact, while they apply indifferently to verse and prose, so far as either is really imaginative. [. . .]

The line between fact and something quite different from external fact is, indeed, hard to draw. In Pascal, for instance, in the persuasive writers generally, how difficult to define the point where, from time to time, argument which, if it is to be worth anything at all, must consist of facts or groups of facts, becomes a pleading – a theorem no longer, but essentially an appeal to the reader to catch the writer's spirit, to think with him, if one can or will – an expression no longer of fact but of his sense of it, his peculiar intuition of a world, prospective, or discerned below the faulty conditions of the present, in either case changed somewhat from the actual world. [. . .] For just in proportion as the writer's aim, consciously or unconsciously, comes to be the transcribing, not of the world, not of mere fact, but of his sense of it, he becomes an artist, his work *fine* art; and good art (as I hope ultimately to show) in proportion to the truth of his presentment of that sense; [. . .] Truth! there can be no merit, no craft at all, without that. And further, all beauty is in the long run only *fineness* of truth, or what we call expression, the finer accommodation of speech to that vision within.[34] [. . .]

Such is the matter of imaginative or artistic literature – this transcript, not of mere fact, but of fact in its infinite variety, as modified by human preference in all its infinitely varied forms. It will be good literary art not because it is brilliant or sober, or rich, or impulsive, or severe, but just in proportion as its representation of that sense, that soul-fact, is true, verse being only one department of such literature, and imaginative prose, it may be thought, being the special art of the modern world. That imaginative prose should be the special and opportune art of the modern world results from two important facts about the latter: first, the chaotic variety and complexity of its interests, making the intellectual issue, the really master currents of the present time incalculable – a condition of mind little susceptible of the restraint proper to verse form, so that the most characteristic verse of the nineteenth century has been lawless verse; and secondly, an all-pervading naturalism, a curiosity about everything whatever as it really is, involving a certain humility of attitude, cognate to what must, after all, be the less ambitious form of literature. And prose thus asserting itself as the special and privileged artistic faculty of the present day, will be, however critics may try to narrow its scope, as varied in its excellence as humanity itself reflecting on the facts of its latest experience.[35] [. . .]

The literary artist is of necessity a scholar, and in what he proposes to do will have in mind, first of all, the scholar and the scholarly conscience [. . .]. For the material in which he works is no more a creation of his own than the sculptor's marble. Product of a myriad various minds and contending tongues, compact of obscure and minute association, a language has its own abundant and often recondite laws, in the habitual and summary recognition of which scholarship consists. [. . .] In a somewhat changed sense, we might say that the art of the scholar is summed up in the observance of those rejections demanded by the nature of his medium, the material he must use. Alive to the value of an atmosphere in which every term finds its utmost degree of expression, and with all the jealousy of a lover of words, he will resist a constant tendency on the part of the majority of those who use them to efface the distinctions of language, the facility of writers often reinforcing in this respect the work of the vulgar. [. . .] His appeal, again, is to the scholar, who has great experience in literature, and will show no favour to short-cuts, or hackneyed illustration, or an affectation of learning designed for the unlearned. Hence a contention, a sense of self-restraint and renunciation, having for the susceptible reader the effect of a challenge for minute consideration; the attention of the writer, in every minutest detail, being a pledge that it is worth the reader's while to be attentive too, that the writer is dealing scrupulously with his instrument, and therefore, indirectly, with the reader himself also, that he has the science of the instrument he plays on, perhaps, after all, with a freedom which in such case will be the freedom of a master. [. . .]

A scholar writing for the scholarly, he will of course leave something to the willing intelligence of his reader. "To go preach to the first passer-by," says Montaigne, "to become tutor to the ignorance of the first I meet, is a thing I abhor;" a thing, in fact, naturally distressing to the scholar, who will therefore ever be shy of offering uncomplimentary assistance to the reader's wit. To really strenuous minds there is a pleasurable stimulus in the challenge for a continuous effort on their part, to be rewarded by securer and more intimate grasp of the author's sense. Self-restraint, a skilful economy of means, *ascêsis*, that too has a beauty of its own; and for the reader supposed there will be an æsthetic satisfaction in that frugal closeness of style which makes the most of a word, in the exaction from every sentence of a precise relief, in the just spacing out of word to thought, in the logically filled space connected always with the delightful sense of difficulty overcome.

Different classes of persons, at different times, make, of course, very various demands upon literature. Still, scholars, I suppose, and not only scholars, but all disinterested lovers of books, will always look to it, as to all other fine art, for a refuge, a sort of cloistral refuge, from a certain vulgarity in the actual world. A perfect poem like *Lycidas*, a perfect fiction like *Esmond*, the perfect handling of a theory like Newman's *Idea of a University*, has for them something of the uses of a religious "retreat."[36] [. . .]

So far I have been speaking of certain conditions of the

literary art arising out of the medium or material in or upon which it works, the essential qualities of language and its aptitudes for contingent ornamentation, matters which define scholarship as science and good taste respectively. They are both subservient to a more intimate quality of good style: more intimate, as coming nearer to the artist himself. The otiose, the facile, surplusage: why are these abhorrent to the true literary artist, except because, in literary as in all other art, structure is all-important, felt, or painfully missed, everywhere? – that architectural conception of work, which foresees the end in the beginning and never loses sight of it, and in every part is conscious of all the rest, till the last sentence does but, with undiminished vigour, unfold and justify the first – a condition of literary art, which, in contradistinction to another quality of the artist himself, to be spoken of later, I shall call the necessity of *mind* in style.

An acute philosophical writer, the late Dean Mansel (a writer whose works illustrate the literary beauty there may be in closeness, and with obvious repression or economy of a fine rhetorical gift) wrote a book, of fascinating precision in a very obscure subject, to show that all the technical laws of logic are but means of securing, in each and all of its apprehensions, the unity, the strict identity with itself, of the apprehending mind.[37] All the laws of good writing aim at a similar unity or identity of the mind in all the processes by which the word is associated to its import. The term is right, and has its essential beauty, when it becomes, in a manner, what it signifies, as with the names of simple sensations. To give the phrase, the sentence, the structural member, the entire composition, song, or essay, a similar unity with its subject and with itself: – style is in the right way when it tends towards that. All depends upon the original unity, the vital wholeness and identity, of the initiatory apprehension or view.[38] With some strong and leading sense of the world, the tight hold of which secures true *composition* and not mere loose accretion, the literary artist, I suppose, goes on considerately, setting joint to joint, sustained by yet restraining the productive ardour, retracing the negligences of his first sketch, repeating his steps only that he may give the reader a sense of secure and restful progress, readjusting mere assonances even, that they may soothe the reader, or at least not interrupt him on his way; and then, somewhere before the end comes, is burdened, inspired, with his conclusion, and betimes delivered of it, leaving off, not in weariness and because he finds *himself* at an end, but in all the freshness of volition.[39] His work now structurally complete, with all the accumulating effect of secondary shades of meaning, he finishes the whole up to the just proportion of that ante-penultimate conclusion, and all becomes expressive. The house he has built is rather a body he has informed.

Aesthetic Poetry[40]

The "aesthetic" poetry is neither a mere reproduction of Greek or medieval poetry, nor only an idealisation of modern life and sentiment. The atmosphere on which its effect depends belongs to no simple form of poetry, no actual form of life.[41] Greek poetry, medieval or modern poetry, projects, above the realities of its time, a world in which the forms of things are transfigured. Of that transfigured world this new poetry takes possession, and sublimates beyond it another still fainter and more spectral, which is literally an artificial or "earthly paradise." It is a finer ideal, extracted from what in relation to any actual world is already an ideal. Like some strange second flowering after date, it renews on a more delicate type the poetry of a past age, but must not be confounded with it. The secret of the enjoyment of it is that inversion of home-sickness known to some, that incurable thirst for the sense of escape, which no actual form of life satisfies, no poetry even, if it be merely simple and spontaneous.

The writings of the "romantic school," of which the aesthetic poetry is an afterthought, mark a transition not so much from the pagan to the medieval ideal, as from a lower to a higher degree of passion in literature. The end of the eighteenth century, swept by vast disturbing currents, experienced an excitement of spirit of which one note was a reaction against an outworn classicism severed not more from nature than from the genuine motives of ancient art; and a return to true Hellenism was as much a part of this reaction as the sudden preoccupation with things medieval.[42] The medieval tendency is in Goethe's *Goetz von Berlichingen*, the Hellenic in his *Iphigenie*. At first this medievalism was superficial, or at least external. Adventure, romance in the frankest sense, grotesque individualism – that is one element in medieval poetry, and with it alone Scott and Goethe dealt. Beyond them were the two other elements of the medieval spirit: its mystic religion at its apex in Dante and Saint Louis, and its mystic passion, passing here and there into the great romantic loves of rebellious flesh, of Lancelot and Abelard. That stricter, imaginative medievalism which re-creates the mind of the Middle Age, so that the form, the presentment grows outward from within, came later with Victor Hugo in France, with Heine in Germany.[43]

In the *Defence of Guenevere: and Other Poems*, published by Mr. William Morris now many years ago, the first typical specimen of aesthetic poetry, we have a refinement upon this later, profounder medievalism. The poem which gives its name to the volume is a thing tormented and awry with passion, like the body of Guenevere defending herself from the charge of adultery, and the accent falls in strange, unwonted places with the effect of a great cry. In truth these Arthurian legends, in their origin prior to Christianity, yield all their sweetness only in a Christian atmosphere. What is characteristic in them is the strange suggestion of a deliberate choice between Christ and a rival lover. That religion, monastic religion at any rate, has its sensuous side, a dangerously sensuous side, has been often seen: it is the experience of Rousseau as well as of the Christian mystics. The Christianity of the Middle Age made way among a people whose loss was in the life of the senses partly by its aesthetic beauty, a thing so profundly felt by the Latin hymn-writers, who for one moral or spiritual sentiment have a hundred sensuous images. And so in those imaginative loves, in their highest expression, the Provençal poetry, it is a rival religion with a new rival *cultus* that we see.[44] Coloured through and through with Christian sentiment, they are rebels against it. The rejection of one worship for another is never lost sight of. The jealousy of that other lover, for whom these words and images and refined ways of sentiment were first devised, is the secret here of a borrowed, perhaps factitious colour and heat. It is the mood of the cloister taking a new direction, and winning so a later space of life it never anticipated.

Hereon, as before in the cloister, so now in the *château*, the reign of reverie set in. The devotion of the cloister knew that mood thoroughly, and had sounded all its stops. For the object of this devotion was absent or veiled, not limited to one supreme plastic form like Zeus at Olympia or Athena in the Acropolis, but distracted, as in a fever dream, into a thousand symbols and reflections. But then, the Church, that new Sibyl, had a thousand secrets to make the absent near. Into this kingdom of reverie, and with it into a paradise of ambitious refinements, the earthly love enters, and becomes a prolonged somnambulism. Of religion it learns the art of directing towards an unseen object sentiments whose natural direction is towards objects of sense. Hence a love defined by the absence of the beloved, choosing to be without hope, protesting against all lower uses of love, barren, extravagant, antinomian. It is the love which is incompatible with marriage, for the chevalier who never comes, of the serf for the *châtelaine*, of the rose for the nightingale, of Rudel for the Lady of Tripoli. Another element of extravagance came in with the feudal spirit: Provençal love is full of the very forms of vassalage. To be the servant of love, to have offended, to taste the subtle luxury of chastisement, of reconciliation – the religious spirit, too, knows that, and meets just there, as in Rousseau, the delicacies of the earthly love. Here, under this strange complex of conditions, as in some medicated air, exotic flowers of sentiment expand, among people of a remote and unaccustomed beauty, somnambulistic, frail, androgynous, the light almost shining through them. Surely, such loves were too fragile and adventurous to last more than for a moment.[45]

That monastic religion of the Middle Age was, in fact, in many of its bearings, like a beautiful disease or disorder of the senses: and a religion which is a disorder of the senses must always be subject to illusions. Reverie, illusion, delirium: they are the three stages of a fatal descent both in the religion and the loves of the Middle Age. Nowhere has the impression of this delirium been conveyed as by Victor Hugo in *Notre Dame de Paris*. The strangest creations of sleep seem here, by some appalling licence, to cross the limit of the dawn. The English poet too has learned the secret. He has diffused through *King Arthur's Tomb* the maddening white glare of the sun, and tyranny of the moon, not tender and far-off, but close down – the sorcerer's moon, large and feverish. The colouring is intricate and delirious, as of "scarlet lilies." The influence of summer is like a poison in one's blood, with a sudden bewildered sickening of life and all things. In *Galahad: a Mystery*, the frost of Christmas night on the chapel stones acts as a strong narcotic: a sudden shrill ringing pierces through the numbness: a voice proclaims that the Grail has gone forth through the great forest. It is in the *Blue Closet* that this delirium reaches its height with a singular beauty, reserved perhaps for the enjoyment of the few.

A passion of which the outlets are sealed, begets a tension of nerve, in which the sensible world comes to one with a reinforced brilliancy and relief – all redness is turned into blood, all water into tears.[46] Hence a wild, convulsed sensuousness in the poetry of the Middle Age, in which the things of nature begin to play a strange delirious part. Of the things of nature the medieval mind had a deep sense; but its sense of them was not objective, no real escape to the world without us. The aspects and motions of nature only reinforced its prevailing mood, and were in conspiracy with one's own brain against one. A single sentiment invaded the world: everything was infused with a motive drawn from the soul. The amorous poetry of Provence, making the starling and the swallow its messengers, illustrates the whole attitude of nature in this electric atmosphere, bent as by miracle or magic to the service of human passion. [. . .]

The *Defence of Guenevere* was published in 1858; the *Life and Death of Jason* in 1867; to be followed by *The Earthly Paradise*; and the change of manner wrought in the interval, entire, almost a revolt, is characteristic of the aesthetic poetry. Here there is no delirium or illusion, no experiences of mere soul while the body and the bodily senses sleep, or wake with convulsed intensity at the prompting of imaginative love; but rather the great primary passions under broad daylight as of the pagan Veronese. This simplification interests us, not merely for the sake of an individual poet – full of charm as he is – but chiefly because it explains through him a transition which, under many forms, is one law of the life of the human spirit, and of which what we call the Renaissance is only a supreme instance. Just so the monk in his cloister, through the "open vision," open only to the spirit, divined, aspired to, and at last apprehended, a better daylight, but earthly, open only to the senses. Complex and subtle interests, which the mind spins for itself many occupy art and poetry or our own spirits for a time; but sooner or later they come back with a sharp rebound to the simple elementary passions – anger, desire, regret, pity, and fear: and what corresponds to them in the sensuous world – bare, abstract fire, water, air, tears, sleep, silence, and what De Quincey has called the "glory of motion."

This reaction from dreamlight to daylight gives, as always happens, a strange power in dealing with morning and the things of the morning. Not less is this Hellenist of the Middle Age master of dreams, of sleep and the desire of sleep – sleep in which no one walks, restorer of childhood to men – dreams, not like Galahad's or Guenevere's, but full of happy, childish wonder as in the earlier world. It is a world in which the centaur and the ram with the fleece of gold are conceivable. The song sung always claims to be sung for the first time. There are hints at a language common to birds and beasts and men. Everywhere there is an impression of surprise, as of people first waking from the golden age, at fire, snow, wine, the touch of water as one swims, the salt taste of the sea. And this simplicity at first hand is a strange contrast to the sought-out simplicity of Wordsworth. Desire here is towards the body of nature for its own sake, not because a soul is divined through it.[47] [. . .]

One characteristic of the pagan spirit the aesthetic poetry has, which is on its surface – the continual suggestion, pensive or passionate, of the shortness of life. This is contrasted with the bloom of the world, and gives new seduction to it – the sense of death and the desire of beauty: the desire of beauty quickened by the sense of death. But that complexion of sentiment is at its height in another "aesthetic" poet of whom I have to speak next, Dante Gabriel Rossetti.

1868.

Dante Gabriel Rossetti[48]

It was characteristic of a poet who had ever something about him of mystic isolation, and will still appeal perhaps, though with a name it may seem now established in English literature, to a special and limited audience, that some of his poems had won a kind of exquisite fame before they were in the full sense published. *The Blessed Damozel*, although actually printed twice before the year 1870, was eagerly circulated in manuscript; and the volume which it now opens came at last to satisfy a long-standing curiosity as to the poet, whose pictures also had become an object of the same peculiar kind of interest. For those poems were the work of a painter, understood to belong to, and to be indeed the leader, of a new school then rising into note;[49] and the reader of to-day may observe already, in *The Blessed Damozel*, written at the age of eighteen, a prefigurement of the chief characteristics of that school, as he will recognise in it also, in proportion as he really knows Rossetti, many of the characteristics which are most markedly personal and his own. Common to that school and to him, and in both alike of primary significance, was the quality of sincerity, already felt as one of the charms of that earliest poem – a perfect sincerity, taking effect in the deliberate use of the most direct and unconventional expression, for the conveyance of a poetic sense which recognised no conventional standard of what poetry was called upon to be. At a time when poetic originality in England might seem to have had its utmost play, here was certainly one new poet more, with a structure and music of verse, a vocabulary, an accent, unmistakably novel, yet felt to be no mere tricks of manner adopted with a view to forcing attention – an accent which might rather count as the very seal of reality on one man's own proper speech; as that speech itself was the wholly natural expression of certain wonderful things he really felt and saw.[50] Here was one, who had a matter to present to his readers, to himself at least, in the first instance, so valuable, so real and definite, that his primary aim, as regards form or expression in his verse, would be but its exact equivalence to those *data* within. That he had this gift of transparency in language – the control of a style which did but obediently shift and shape itself to the mental motion, as a well-trained hand can follow on the tracing-paper the outline of an original drawing below it, was proved afterwards by a volume of typically perfect translations from the delightful but difficult "early Italian poets": such transparency being indeed the secret of all genuine style, of all such style as can truly belong to one man and not to another. His own meaning was always personal and even recondite, in a certain sense learned and casuistical, sometimes complex or obscure; but the term was always, one could see, deliberately chosen from many competitors, as the just transcript of that peculiar phase of soul which he alone knew, precisely as he knew it.

One of the peculiarities of *The Blessed Damozel* was a definiteness of sensible imagery, which seemed almost grotesque to some, and was strange, above all, in a theme so profoundly visionary.[51] The gold bar of heaven from which she leaned, her hair yellow like ripe corn, are but examples of a general treatment, as naively detailed as the pictures of those early painters contemporary with Dante, who has shown a similar care for minute and definite imagery in his verse; there, too, in the very midst of profoundly mystic vision. Such definition of outline is indeed one among many points in which Rossetti resembles the great Italian poet, of whom, led to him at first by family circumstances, he was ever a lover – a "servant and singer," faithful as Dante, "of Florence and of Beatrice" – with some close inward conformities of genius also, independent of any mere circumstances of education. It was said by a critic of the last century, not wisely though agreeably to the practice of his time, that poetry rejoices in abstractions. For Rossetti, as for Dante, without question on his part, the first condition of the poetic way of seeing and presenting things is particularisation. "Tell me now," he writes, for Villon's

"Dictes-moy oú, n'en quel pays,
Est Flora, la belle Romaine" –

"Tell me now, in what hidden way is
Lady Flora the lovely Roman:"[52]

– "way," in which one might actually chance to meet her; the unmistakably poetic effect of the couplet in English being dependent on the definiteness of that single word (though actually lighted on in the search after a difficult double rhyme) for which every one else would have written, like Villon himself, a more general one, just equivalent to place or region.

And this delight in concrete definition is allied with another of his conformities to Dante, the really imaginative vividness, namely, of his personifications – his hold upon them, or rather their hold upon him, with the force of a Frankenstein, when once they have taken life from him. Not Death only and Sleep, for instance, and the winged spirit of Love, but certain particular aspects of them, a whole "populace" of special hours and places, "the hour" even "which might have been, yet might not be," are living creatures, with hands and eyes and articulate voices.

"Stands it not by the door –
Love's Hour – till she and I shall meet;
With bodiless form and unapparent feet
That cast no shadow yet before,
Though round its head the dawn begins to pour
The breath that makes day sweet?" –

"Nay, why
Name the dead hours? I mind them well:
Their ghosts in many darkened doorways dwell
With desolate eyes to know them by."[53]

Poetry as a *mania* – one of Plato's two higher forms of "divine" mania – has, in all its species, a mere insanity incidental to it, the "defect of its quality," into which it may lapse in its moment of weakness; and the insanity which follows a vivid poetic anthropomorphism like that of Rossetti may be noted here and there in his work, in a forced and almost grotesque materialising of abstractions, as Dante also became at times a mere subject of the scholastic realism of the Middle Age. [. . .]

With him indeed, as in some revival of the old mythopoeic age, common things – dawn, noon, night – are full of human or personal expression, full of sentiment. The lovely little sceneries scattered up and down his poems, glimpses of a landscape, not indeed of broad open-air effects, but rather that of a painter concentrated upon the picturesque effect of one or two selected objects at a time – the "hollow brimmed with mist," or the "ruined weir," as he sees it from one of the windows, or reflected in one of the mirrors of his "house of life" (the vignettes for instance seen by Rose Mary in the magic beryl) attest, by their very freshness and simplicity, to a pictorial or descriptive power in dealing with the inanimate world, which is certainly also one half of the charm, in that other, more remote and mystic, use of it. For with Rossetti this sense of lifeless nature, after all, is translated to a higher service, in which it does but incorporate itself with some phase of strong emotion. Every one understands how this may happen at critical moments of life; what a weirdly expressive soul may have crept, even in full noonday, into "the white-flower'd elder-thicket," when Godiva saw it "gleam through the Gothic archways in the wall," at the end of her terrible ride. To Rossetti it is so always, because to him life is a crisis at every moment. A sustained impressibility towards the mysterious conditions of man's everyday life, towards the very mystery itself in it, gives a singular gravity to all his work: those matters never became trite to him.[54] But throughout, it is the ideal intensity of love – of love based upon a perfect yet peculiar type of physical or material beauty – which is enthroned in the midst of those mysterious powers; Youth and Death, Destiny and Fortune, Fame, Poetic Fame, Memory, Oblivion, and the like. Rossetti is one of those who, in the words of Mérimée, *se passionnent pour la passion*, one of Love's lovers.

And yet, again as with Dante, to speak of his ideal type of beauty as material, is partly misleading. Spirit and matter, indeed, have been for the most part opposed, with a false contrast or antagonism by schoolmen, whose artificial creation those abstractions really are. In our actual concrete experience, the two trains of phenomena which the words *matter* and *spirit* do but roughly distinguish, play inextricably into each other. Practically, the church of the Middle Age by its aesthetic worship, its sacramentalism, its real faith in the resurrection of the flesh, had set itself against that Manichean opposition of spirit and matter, and its results in men's way of taking life; and in this, Dante is the central representative of its spirit. To him, in the vehement and impassioned heat of his conceptions, the material and the spiritual are fused and blent: if the spiritual attains the definite visibility of a crystal, what is material loses its earthiness and impurity. And here again, by force of instinct, Rossetti is one with him. His chosen type of beauty is one,

> "Whose speech Truth knows not from her thought,
> Nor Love her body from her soul."[55]

Like Dante, he knows no region of spirit which shall not be sensuous also, or material. The shadowy world, which he realises so powerfully, has still the ways and houses, the land and water, the light and darkness, the fire and flowers, that had so much to do in the moulding of those bodily powers and aspects which counted for so large a part of the soul, here.

V. Prosper Mérimée[1]

For one born in eighteen hundred and three much was recently become incredible that had at least warmed the imagination even of the sceptical eighteenth century. Napoleon, sealing the tomb of the Revolution, had foreclosed many a problem, extinguished many a hope, in the sphere of practice. And the mental parallel was drawn by Heine. In the mental world too a great outlook had lately been cut off. After Kant's criticism of the mind, its pretensions to pass beyond the limits of individual experience seemed as dead as those of old French royalty.[2] And Kant did but furnish its innermost theoretic force to a more general criticism, which had withdrawn from every department of action, underlying principles once thought eternal. A time of disillusion followed. The typical personality of the day was Obermann, the very genius of *ennui*, a Frenchman disabused even of patriotism, who has hardly strength enough to die.[3] More energetic souls, however, would recover themselves, and find some way of making the best of a changed world. Art: the passions, above all, the ecstasy and sorrow of love: a purely empirical knowledge of nature and man: these still remained, at least for pastime, in a world of which it was no longer proposed to calculate the remoter issues: – art, passion, science, however, in a somewhat novel attitude towards the practical interests of life. The *désillusionné*, who had found in Kant's negations the last word concerning an unseen world, and is living, on the morrow of the Revolution, under a monarchy made out of hand, might seem cut off from certain ancient natural hopes, and will demand, from what is to interest him at all, something in the way of artificial stimulus. He has lost that sense of large proportion in things, that all-embracing prospect of life as a whole (from end to end of time and space, it had seemed), the utmost expanse of which was afforded from a cathedral tower of the Middle Age: by the church of the thirteenth century, that is to say, with its consequent aptitude for the co-ordination of human effort. Deprived of that exhilarating yet pacific outlook, imprisoned now in the narrow cell of its own subjective experience, the action of a powerful nature will be intense, but exclusive and peculiar. It will come to art, or science, to the experience of life itself, not as to portions of human nature's daily food, but as to something that must be, by the circumstances of the case, exceptional; almost as men turn in despair to gambling or narcotics, and in a little while the narcotic, the game of chance or skill, is valued for its own sake.[4] The vocation of the artist, of the student of life or books, will be realised with something – say! of fanaticism, as an end in itself, unrelated, unassociated. The science he turns to will be a science of crudest fact; the passion extravagant, a passionate love of passion, varied through all the exotic phases of French fiction as inaugurated by Balzac; the art exaggerated, in matter of form, or both, as in Hugo or Baudelaire. The development of these conditions is the mental story of the nineteenth century, especially as exemplified in France.

In no century would Prosper Mérimée have been a theologian or metaphysician. But that sense of negation, of theoretic insecurity, was in the air, and conspiring with what was of like tendency in himself made of him a central type of disillusion. In him the passive *ennui* of Obermann became a satiric, aggressive, almost angry conviction of the littleness of the world around; it was as if man's fatal limitations constituted a kind of stupidity in him, what the French call *bêtise*. Gossiping friends, indeed, linked what was constitutional in him and in the age with an incident of his earliest years. Corrected for some childish fault, in passionate distress, he overhears a half-pitying laugh at his expense, and has determined, in a moment, never again to give credit – to be for ever on his guard, especially against his own instinctive movements. Quite unreserved, certainly, he never was again. Almost everywhere he could detect the hollow ring of fundamental nothingness under the apparent surface of things. Irony surely, habitual irony, would be the proper complement thereto, on his part.[5] In his infallible self-possession, you might even fancy him a mere man of the world, with a special aptitude for matters of fact. Though indifferent in politics, he rises to social, to political eminence; but all the while he is feeding all his scholarly curiosity, his imagination, the very eye, with the, to him ever delightful, relieving, reassuring spectacle, of those straightforward forces in human nature, which are also matters of fact. There is the formula of Mérimée! the enthusiastic amateur of rude, crude, naked force in men and women wherever it could be found; himself carrying ever, as a mask, the conventional attire of the modern world – carrying it with an infinite, contemptuous grace, as if that, too, were an all-sufficient end in itself. With a natural gift for words, for expression, it will be his literary function to draw back the veil of time from the true greatness of old Roman character; the veil of modern habit from the primitive energy of the creatures of his fancy, as the *Lettres à une Inconnue* discovered to general gaze, after his death, a certain depth of passionate force which had surprised him in himself. And how forcible will be their outlines in an otherwise insignificant world! Fundamental belief gone, in almost all of us, at least some relics of it remain – queries, echoes, reactions, afterthoughts; and they help to make an atmosphere, a mental atmosphere, hazy perhaps, yet with many secrets of soothing light and shade, associating more definite objects to each other by a perspective pleasant to the inward eye against a hopefully receding background of remoter and ever remoter possibilities. Not so with Mérimée! For him the fundamental criticism has nothing more than it can do; and there are no half-lights. The last traces of hypothesis, of supposition, are evaporated. Sylla, the false Demetrius, Carmen, Colomba, that impassioned self within himself, have no atmosphere.[6] Painfully distinct in outline, inevitable to sight, unrelieved, there they stand, like solitary mountain forms on some hard, perfectly transparent day. What Mérimée gets around his singularly sculpturesque creations is neither more nor less than empty space. [. . .]

JAMES WHISTLER (1834–1903)

James Abbot McNeill Whistler is perhaps an odd figure to be represented in a book such as this, for as one of the most talented painters of the nineteenth century his care was primarily for his art and he wasted little time in aesthetic theorizing. Yet in his case his art extended to more than his canvases, and he has a significant place here simply because he cannot be ignored: he was too vigorous, and too effective, at putting himself in the public mind to be passed over. This was a talent promptly absorbed by his studious disciple, Oscar Wilde, and indeed, to a lesser extent than with Wilde, one is tempted to regard Whistler's life as his greatest work of art; throughout his career he sought to be, and was, a phenomenon, and his enduring legend is in some sense his success. His rare artistic gifts were combined with an aggressive temper, a keen wit, and a flair for self-advertisement which few celebrities before or since have equalled. Like the skyrocket in one of his famous paintings, Whistler burst upon the late Victorian art scene, dazzling spectators with a succession of brilliant works, audacious ploys, and tart remarks which turned the conventional aesthetic upside down. In so doing he turned the corner of transition and paved the way for the acceptance in England of what we now call 'modern' art.

Whistler claimed that the artist's power of aesthetic arrangement extended even to his own life, and he 'declined' his real birth-place of Lowell, Massachusetts, 'choosing' instead to be born in the more appropriate milieu of Baltimore or St. Petersburg. There is a sense in which this exaggeration is true, for Whistler was exposed to cosmopolitan influences from an early age. In 1842 the Czar of Russia selected his father to oversee the building of the Moscow to St. Petersburg railway, and at the tender age of nine Whistler found himself in the sumptuous Russian capital. It was here that he had his first systematic training in art, and where he acquired his excellent French – accomplishments which, after the death of his father, helped him to persuade his pious and puritannical mother to let him go to Paris and pursue a career as an artist.

It would be hard to overrate the impact France had on Whistler. At the time he arrived in 1855 his conception of Paris had been formed by Henri Murger's *Scènes de la Vie de Bohème*, and he soon plunged into the attractive, dissolute, hilarious life of the Latin Quarter. Though originally in the same hotel as Du Maurier and the set immortalized in *Trilby*, Whistler spurned the athletic clique of the English colony and sought out the genuine artists of the time. During these Paris years he became familiar with Courbet, Manet, Legros, and Fantin-Latour, and though never diligent in his studies he absorbed a good deal of the reigning French aesthetic, then undergoing the transition from Realism to Impressionism. His instinctive bent as a Baudelairean dandy blossomed as well, and he wandered everywhere in black patent-leather pumps, sporting a straw hat with long blue silk ribbons trailing behind. Soon enough he was a distinct and recognized figure. Hence, though he lived most of his life in England, Whistler spoke a vital truth about himself when he told a would-be biographer: 'First of all, I am not English.' His close links with French art and ideas remained throughout his life, providing him with a solid framework from which he could do battle with aesthetic orthodoxy in England.

That orthodoxy, by the 1870s, resided in one man: John Ruskin. Though the British public were reluctant to follow his political ideas, Ruskin had, by and large, carried the day in aesthetics; not only was 'truth to nature' considered a canonical value, but most of the educated public believed it was proper for the artist to address himself to social and moral issues, and more proper still for him to take direction from the art critic. Whistler flatly contradicted all these beliefs. With the aesthetic principles of Gautier and Baudelaire, he steadily maintained that the artist only selected crude materials from nature and then rearranged them into higher states of imaginative significance. More importantly, Whistler held that the true artist was concerned, not with extraneous moral or social matters but solely with the aesthetic perfection of his art, and that neither critic nor populace (unfamiliar with the long process and difficult skills involved) could make any relevant comment on that art. Thus the notion of the aristocracy of the artist came to full flower in England with Whistler, transforming the prevailing romantic aesthetic: where Ruskin and Morris followed Wordsworth in positing the artist as differing only in degree from other men, Whistler asserted that the difference was in kind, thus opening a breach between the artist and the rest of humanity which has remained ever since.

No doubt Ruskin sensed the antithesis to his teaching that Whistler represented, for leaving behind the generous sensitivity which had led him to defend Turner's not dissimilar late style, he violently attacked one of Whistler's Nocturnes in print (q.v.). Whistler sued for libel, bringing the two notions of aesthetics to a head-on clash in one of the nineteenth century's most notorious court cases. Unfortunately the promised collision all but disappeared when Ruskin's mental breakdown prevented him from attending the hearings. Whistler conducted his case with great wit and spirit and was eventually awarded the derisory sum of one farthing's damages. But though he was made bankrupt by the court costs, Whistler had nevertheless won a tremendous psychological victory: he had shown that Ruskin was not infallible and impressed upon the world the fact that he too had something to say. And when he reappeared in London a few years later he found a public more than ready to listen to him say it.

The most important delivery of his message occurred in 1885, in the famous 'Ten O'Clock Lecture'. Prompted by growing jealousy of Wilde – then enjoying considerable success as a lecturer – Whistler determined to make a sudden, dramatic impact on the public mind, to have the artist appear as Emperor. The occasion was a triumph of the performing self, stage-managed and calculated down to the last detail. The venue was St. James's Hall, Piccadilly, and the late hour was chosen to ensure that there would be no latecomers, giving the wealthy and the fashionable plenty of time for after-dinner port and cigars. To this glittering audience Whistler launched his barbed talk, propounding doctrines directly opposed to the familiar Ruskinian lines and attacking by implication nearly every major figure in the English aesthetic tradition – the social preaching of Ruskin and Morris behind him as well as Wilde and the 'aesthetes' looming on the horizon. The lecture was not without peculiarities. Whistler's disdain for 'literature' left him without the solid literary background that strengthened the writings of Ruskin and Pater, Swinburne and Baudelaire. Moreover, his facility as a wit led him naturally to terse, epigrammatic forms (most of his *bon mots* were made in telegrams). As a result the lecture never builds to any sustained climax or peroration, but rather makes its points in an abrupt, lapidary style. Nonetheless, the attack on current beliefs was clearly felt, and henceforth it became increasingly difficult to see art as a social duty or hieratic penance rather than as a means of mandarin authority and prestige.

Whistler was certainly an original phenomenon, and yet it is easy to exaggerate his novelty. It has often been noted that Whistler capitalized on the new climate of interest in art and artists which had been awakened by Ruskin. Indeed, much of Whistler's doctrine was a development of seeds already contained within the Pre-Raphaelite movement: the disdain for the heavy weight of ethical concern art had been made to carry was implicit in Rossetti's more symbolist canvases, and it is not surprising that the two men became friends for a time.

Whistler's advance, however, was to make this rejection explicit by giving it sparkling articulation. In the same way the use of musical titles for his paintings – 'Symphony', 'Harmony', 'Variations', etc. – can be traced back through Baudelaire and Gautier to Poe (one of Whistler's favourite authors), and the notion of a musical analogy for the intense states of mind depicted on canvas lurks throughout Rossetti's work. Once again, Whistler's bold gestures achieved a publicity which crystallized the point in the public mind.

Even so, one cannot ignore the fact that Whistler did break free of his contemporary context and altered the direction of English art. He was devoid of any exaggerated homage to an earlier historical era and thus free from the idealized medieval or classical sentiment which clogs so much nineteenth-century art. Among other things this freedom could make Whistler a better judge of art than Ruskin, since he appreciated the genius of such figures as Rembrandt and Velasquez, both of whom were shunted aside in Ruskin's condemnation of all post-medieval art. Perhaps even more important is the fact that Whistler's lack of any yearning for a bygone age makes his paintings fresh and vital today, where those of the Pre-Raphaelites appear hopelessly dated. Rather than shut himself up in a dream-world, Whistler met the life of his age with zest and flair, painting contemporary subjects with complete ease. Like Baudelaire, his confidence in the artist's powers of imaginative transformation led him to find a distinctly 'modern' beauty in the urban environment, painting the cluttered commercial piers of the East End, from which any of the Pre-Raphaelites would have recoiled in horror. Finally, Whistler was in the vanguard of appreciation for Japanese art and artists, whose powerful simplification became the hallmark of his aesthetic 'arrangements', and led him to develop ideas of restrained and harmonized effects in decoration – both in domestic interiors and art galleries – that have since become standard. When ideas of Oriental precision, conciseness and intensity were making their way through modernist poetics it was perhaps too little recognized that much of the original impetus had come through Whistler.

In the end Whistler, with all his bristling pugnacity, arch pride, and artistic elegance, brought the conceptions underlying modern art firmly to the fore, crystallizing a movement which had been latent throughout the century. The modern art world, whether acknowledging him or not, owes Whistler a considerable debt, and perhaps the new aesthetic could not have had a better spokesman than the small stinging butterfly who moved so masterfully through the last decades of the nineteenth century.

The Ten O'Clock Lecture[1]

Ladies and Gentlemen:

It is with great hesitation and much misgiving that I appear before you, in the character of The Preacher.

If timidity be at all allied to the virtue modesty, and can find favour in your eyes, I pray you, for the sake of that virtue, accord me you utmost indulgence.

I would plead for my want of habit, did it not seem preposterous, judging from precedent, that aught save the most efficient effrontery could be ever expected in connection with my subject – for I will not conceal from you that I mean to talk about Art. Yes, Art – that has of late become, as far as much discussion and writing can make it, a sort of common topic for the tea-table.

Art is upon the Town! – to be chucked under the chin by the passing gallant – to be enticed within the gates of the householder – to be coaxed into company, as a proof of culture and refinement.

If familiarity can breed contempt, certainly Art – or what is currently taken for it – has been brought to its lowest stage of intimacy.

The people have been harassed with Art in every guise, and vexed with many methods as to its endurance. They have been told how they shall love Art, and live with it.[2] Their homes have been invaded, their walls covered with paper, their very dress taken to task – until, roused at last, bewildered and filled with the doubts and discomforts of senseless suggestion, they resent such intrusion, and cast forth the false prophets, who have brought the very name of the beautiful into disrepute, and derision upon themselves.

Alas! ladies and gentlemen, Art has been maligned. She has naught in common with such practices. She is a goddess of dainty thought – reticent of habit, abjuring all obtrusiveness, purposing in no way to better others.

She is, withal, selfishly occupied with her own perfection only – having no desire to teach – seeking and finding the beautiful in all conditions and in all times, as did her high priest, Rembrandt, when he saw picturesque grandeur and noble dignity in the Jews' quarter of Amsterdam, and lamented not that its inhabitants were not Greeks.[3]

As did Tintoret and Paul Veronese, among the Venetians, while not halting to change the brocaded silks for the classic draperies of Athens.

As did, at the Court of Philip, Velasquez, whose Infantas, clad in inaesthetic hoops, are, as works of Art, of the same quality as the Elgin marbles.[4]

No reformers were these great men – no improvers of the way of others! Their productions alone were their occupation, and, filled with the poetry of their science, they required not to alter their surroundings – for, as the laws of their Art were revealed to them they saw, in the development of their work, that real beauty which, to them, was as much a matter of certainty and triumph as is to the astronomer the verification of the result, foreseen with the light given to him alone. In all this, their world was completely severed from that of their fellow-creatures with whom sentiment is mistaken for poetry; and for whom there is no perfect work that shall not be explained by the benefit conferred upon themselves.

Humanity takes the place of Art, and God's creations are excused by their usefulness. Beauty is confounded with virtue, and, before a work of Art, it is asked: "What good shall it do?"

Hence it is that nobility of action, in this life, is hopelessly linked with the merit of the work that portrays it; and thus the people have acquired the habit of looking, as who should say, not *at* a picture, but *through* it, at some human fact, that shall, or shall not, from a social point of view, better their mental or moral state. So we have come to hear of the painting that elevates, and of the duty of the painter – of the picture that is full of thought, and of the panel that merely decorates.

A favourite faith, dear to those who teach, is that certain periods were especially artistic, and that nations, readily named, were notably lovers of Art.[5]

So we are told that the Greeks were, as a people, worshippers of the beautiful, and that in the fifteenth century Art was engrained in the multitude.

That the great masters lived in common understanding with

their patrons – that the early Italians were artists – and that the demand for the lovely thing produced it.

That we, of to-day, in gross contrast to this Arcadian purity, call for the ungainly, and obtain the ugly.

That, could we but change our habits and climate – were we willing to wander in groves – could we be roasted out of broadcloth – were we to do without haste, and journey without speed, we should again *require* the spoon of Queen Anne, and pick at our peas with the fork of two prongs. And so, for the flock, little hamlets grow near Hammersmith, and the steam horse is scorned.

Useless! quite hopeless and false is the effort! – built upon fable, and all because "a wise man has uttered a vain thing and filled his belly with the East wind."

Listen! There never was an artistic period.

There never was an Art-loving nation.

In the beginning, man went forth each day – some to do battle, some to the chase; others, again, to dig and to delve in the field – all that they might gain and live, or lose and die. Until there was found among them one, differing from the rest, whose pursuits attracted him not, and so he stayed by the tents with the women, and traced strange devices with a burnt stick upon a gourd.

This man, who took no joy in the ways of his brethren – who cared not for conquest, and fretted in the field – this designer of quaint patterns – this deviser of the beautiful – who perceived in Nature about him curious curvings, as faces are seen in the fire – this dreamer apart, was the first artist.

And when, from the field and from afar, there came back the people, they took the gourd – and drank from out of it.

And presently there came to this man another – and, in time, others – of like nature, chosen by the Gods – and so they worked together; and soon they fashioned, from the moistened earth, forms resembling the gourd. And with the power of creation, the heirloom of the artist, presently they went beyond the slovenly suggestion of Nature, and the first vase was born, in beautiful proportion.

And the toilers tilled, and were athirst; and the heroes returned from fresh victories, to rejoice and to feast; and all drank alike from the artists' goblets, fashioned cunningly, taking no note the while of the craftsman's pride, and understanding not his glory in his work; drinking at the cup, not from choice, not from a consciousness that it was beautiful, but because, forsooth, there was none other!

And time, with more state, brought more capacity for luxury, and it became well that men should dwell in large houses, and rest upon couches, and feast at tables; whereupon the artist, with his artificers, built palaces, and filled them with furniture, beautiful in proportion and lovely to look upon.

And the people lived in marvels of art – and ate and drank out of masterpieces – for there was nothing else to eat and to drink out of, and no bad building to live in; no article of daily life, of luxury, or of necessity, that had not been handed down from the design of the master, and made by his workmen.

And the people questioned not, *and had nothing to say in the matter.*

So Greece was in its splendour, and Art reigned supreme – by force of fact, not by election – and there was no meddling from the outsider. The mighty warrior would no more have ventured to offer a design for the temple of Pallas Athene than would the sacred poet have proffered a plan for constructing the catapult.

And the Amateur was unkown – and the Dilettante undreamed of!

And history wrote on, and conquest accompanied civilisation, and Art spread, or rather its products were carried by the victors among the vanquished from one country to another. And the customs of cultivation covered the face of the earth, so that all peoples continued to use what *the artist alone produced.*

And centuries passed in this using, and the world was flooded with all that was beautiful, until there arose a new class, who discovered the cheap, and foresaw fortune in the facture of the sham.

Then sprang into existence the tawdry, the common, the gewgaw.[6]

The taste of the tradesman supplanted the science of the artist, and what was born of the million went back to them, and charmed them, for it was after their own heart; and the great and the small, the statesman and the slave, took to themselves the abomination that was tendered, and preferred it – and have lived with it ever since!

And the artist's occupation was gone, and the manufacturer and the huckster took his place.

And now the heroes filled from the jugs and drank from the bowls – with understanding – noting the glare of their new bravery, and taking pride in its worth.

And the people – this time – had much to say in the matter – and all were satisfied. And Birmingham and Manchester arose in their might – and Art was relegated to the curiosity shop.

Nature contains the elements, in colour and form, of all pictures, as the keyboard contains the notes of all music.

But the artist is born to pick, and choose, and group with science, these elements, that the result may be beautiful – as the musician gathers his notes, and forms his chords, until he bring forth from chaos glorious harmony.

To say to the painter, that Nature is to be taken as she is, is to say to the player, that he may sit on the piano.[7]

That Nature is always right, is an assertion, artistically, as untrue, as it is one whose truth is universally taken for granted. Nature is very rarely right, to such an extent even, that it might almost be said that Nature is usually wrong: that is to say, the condition of things that shall bring about the perfection of harmony worthy a picture is rare, and not common at all.

This would seem, to even the most intelligent, a doctrine almost blasphemous. So incorporated with our education has the supposed aphorism become, that its belief is held to be part of our moral being, and the words themselves have, in our ear, the ring of religion. Still, seldom does Nature succeed in producing a picture.

The sun glares, the wind blows from the east, the sky is bereft of cloud, and without, all is of iron. The windows of the Crystal Palace are seen from all points of London. The holiday-maker rejoices in the glorious day, and the painter turns aside to shut his eyes.

How little this is understood, and how dutifully the casual in Nature is accepted as sublime, may be gathered from the unlimited admiration daily produced by a very foolish sunset.

The dignity of the snow-capped mountain is lost in distinctness, but the joy of the tourist is to recognise the traveller on the top. The desire to see, for the sake of seeing it, is, with the mass, alone the one to be gratified, hence the delight in detail.

And when the evening mist clothes the riverside with poetry, as with a veil, and the poor buildings lose themselves in the dim sky, and the tall chimneys become campanili, and the warehouses are palaces in the night, and the whole city hangs in the heavens, and fairy-land is before us – then the wayfarer hastens home; the working man and the cultured one, the wise man and the one of pleasure, cease to understand, as they have ceased to see, and Nature, who, for once, has sung in tune, sings her exquisite song to the artist alone, her son and her master – her son in that he loves her, her master in that he knows her.[8]

To him her secrets are unfolded, to him her lessons have become gradually clear. He looks at her flower, not with the enlarging lens, that he may gather facts for the botanist, but with the light of the one who sees in her choice selection of brilliant tones and delicate tints, suggestions of future harmonies.

He does not confine himself to purposeless copying, without thought, each blade of grass, as commended by the inconsequent, but, in the long curve of the narrow leaf, corrected by the straight tall stem, he learns how grace is wedded to dignity, how strength enhances sweetness, that elegance shall be the result.

In the citron wing of the pale butterfly, with its dainty spots of orange, he sees before him the stately halls of fair gold, with their slender saffron pillars, and is taught how the delicate drawing high upon the walls shall be traced in tender tones of orpiment, and repeated by the base in notes of graver hue.

In all that is dainty and lovable he finds hints for his own combinations, and *thus* is Nature ever his resource and always at his service, and to him is naught refused.

Through his brain, as through the last alembic, is distilled the refined essence of that thought which began with the Gods, and which they left him to carry out.

Set apart by them to complete their works, he produces that wondrous thing called the masterpiece, which surpasses in perfection all that they have contrived in what is called Nature; and the Gods stand by and marvel, and perceive how far away more beautiful is the Venus of Melos than was their own Eve.

For some time past, the unattached writer has become the middleman in this matter of Art, and his influence, while it has widened the gulf between the people and the painter, has brought about the most complete misunderstanding as to the aim of the picture.

For him a picture is more or less a hieroglyph or symbol of story.[9] Apart from a few technical terms, for the display of which he finds an occasion, the work is considered absolutely from a literary point of view; indeed, from what other can he consider it? And in his essays he deals with it as with a novel – a history – or an anecdote. He fails entirely and most naturally to see its excellences, or demerits – artistic – and so degrades Art, by supposing it a method of bringing about a literary climax.

It thus, in his hands, becomes merely a means of perpetrating something further, and its mission is made a secondary one, even as a means is second to an end.

The thoughts emphasised, noble or other, are inevitably attached to the incident, and become more or less noble, according to the eloquence or mental quality of the writer, who looks the while, with disdain, upon what he holds as "mere execution" – a matter belonging, he believes, to the training of the schools, and the reward of assiduity. So that, as he goes on with his translation from canvas to paper, the work becomes his own. He finds poetry where he would feel it were he himself transcribing the event, invention in the intricacy of the *mise en scène*, and noble philosophy in some detail of philanthropy, courage, modesty, or virtue, suggested to him by the occurrence.

All this might be brought before him, and his imagination be appealed to, by a very poor picture – indeed, I might safely say that it generally is.

Meanwhile, the *painter's* poetry is quite lost to him[10] – the amazing invention that shall have put form and colour into such perfect harmony, that exquisiteness is the result, he is without understanding – the nobility of thought, that shall have given the artist's dignity to the whole, says to him absolutely nothing.

So that his praises are published, for virtues we would blush to possess – while the great qualities, that distinguish the one work from the thousand, that make of the masterpiece the thing of beauty that it is – have never been seen at all.

That this is so, we can make sure of, by looking back at old reviews upon past exhibitions, and reading the flatteries lavished upon men who have since been forgotten altogether – but, upon whose works, the language has been exhausted, in rhapsodies – that left nothing for the National Gallery.

A curious matter, in its effect upon the judgment of these gentlemen, is the accepted vocabulary of poetic symbolism, that helps them, by habit, in dealing with Nature: a mountain, to them, is synonymous with height – a lake, with depth – the ocean, with vastness – the sun, with glory.

So that a picture with a mountain, a lake, and an ocean – however poor in paint – is inevitably "lofty," "vast," "infinite," and "glorious" – on paper.

There are those also, sombre of mien, and wise with the wisdom of books, who frequent museums and burrow in crypts; collecting – comparing – compiling – classifying – contradicting.

Experts these – for whom a date is an accomplishment – a hall-mark, success!

Careful in scrutiny are they, and conscientious of judgment – establishing, with due weight, unimportant reputations – discovering the picture, by the stain on the back – testing the torso, by the leg that is missing – filling folios with doubts on the way of that limb – disputatious and dictatorial, concerning the birthplace of inferior persons – speculating, in much writing, upon the great worth of bad work.

True clerks of the collection, they mix memoranda with ambition, and, reducing Art to statistics, they "file" the fifteenth century, and "pigeon-hole" the antique!

Then the Preacher "appointed"!

He stands in high places – harangues and holds forth.

Sage of the Universities – learned in many matters, and of much experience in all, save his subject.[11]

Exhorting – denouncing – directing.

Filled with wrath and earnestness.

Bringing powers of persuasion, and polish of language, to prove – nothing.

Torn with much teaching – having naught to impart.

Impressive – important – shallow.

Defiant – distressed – desperate.

Crying out, and cutting himself – while the gods hear not.

Gentle priest of the Philistine withal, again he ambles pleasantly from all points, and through many volumes, escaping scientific assertion – "babbles of green fields."

So Art has become foolishly confounded with education – that all should be equally qualified.

Whereas, while polish, refinement, culture, and breeding, are in no way arguments for artistic result, it is also no reproach to the most finished scholar or greatest gentleman in the land that he be absolutely without eye for painting or ear for music – that in his heart he prefers the popular print to the scratch of Rembrandt's needle, or the songs of the hall to Beethoven's "C minor Symphony."

Let him have but the wit to say so, and not feel the admission a proof of inferiority.

Art happens – no hovel is safe from it, no Prince may depend upon it, the vastest intelligence cannot bring it about, and puny efforts to make it universal end in quaint comedy, and coarse farce.

This is as it should be – and all attempts to make it otherwise are due to the eloquence of the ignorant, the zeal of the conceited.

The boundary-line is clear. Far from me to propose to bridge it over – that the pestered people be pushed across. No! I would save them from further fatigue. I would come to their relief, and would lift from their shoulders this incubus of Art.

Why, after centuries of freedom from it, and indifference to it, should it now be thrust upon them by the blind – until wearied and puzzled, they know no longer how they shall eat or drink – how they shall sit or stand – or wherewithal they shall clothe themselves – without afflicting Art.

But, lo! there is much talk without!

Triumphantly they cry, "Beware! This matter does indeed concern us. We also have our part in all true Art! – for, remember the 'one touch of Nature' that 'makes the whole world kin.'"

True, indeed. But let not the unwary jauntily suppose that Shakespeare herewith hands him his passport to Paradise, and thus permits him speech among the chosen. Rather, learn that, in this very sentence, he is condemned to remain without – to continue with the common.

This one chord that vibrates with all – this "one touch of Nature" that calls aloud to the response of each – that explains the popularity of the "Bull" of Paul Potter – that excuses the price of Murillo's "Conception" – this one unspoken sympathy that pervades humanity, is – Vulgarity!

Vulgarity – under whose fascinating influence "the many" have elbowed "the few," and the gentle circle of Art swarms with the intoxicated mob of mediocrity, whose leaders prate and counsel, and call aloud, where the Gods once spoke in whisper!

And now from their midst the Dilettante stalks abroad. The amateur is loosed. The voice of the æsthete is heard in the land, and catastrophe is upon us.[12]

The meddler beckons the vengeance of the Gods, and ridicule threatens the fair daughters of the land.

And there are curious converts to a weird *culte*, in which all instinct for attractiveness – all freshness and sparkle – all woman's winsomeness – is to give way to a strange vocation for the unlovely – and this desecration in the name of the Graces!

Shall this gaunt, ill-at-ease, distressed, abashed mixture of *mauvaise honte* and desperate assertion call itself artistic, and claim cousinship with the artist – who delights in the dainty, the sharp, bright gaiety of beauty?

No! – a thousand times no! Here are no connections of ours.

We will have nothing to do with them.

Forced to seriousness, that emptiness may be hidden, they dare not smile –

While the artist, in fulness of heart and head, is glad, and laughs aloud, and is happy in his strength, and is merry at the pompous pretension – the solemn silliness that surrounds him.

For Art and Joy go together, with bold openness, and high head, and ready hand – fearing naught, and dreading no exposure.

Know, then, all beautiful women, that we are with you. Pay no heed, we pray you, to this outcry of the unbecoming – this last plea for the plain.

It concerns you not.

Your own instinct is near the truth – your own wit far surer guide than the untaught ventures of thick-heeled Apollos.

What! will you up and follow the first piper that leads you down Petticoat Lane, there, on a Sabbath, to gather, for the week, from the dull rags of ages wherewith to bedeck yourselves? that, beneath your travestied awkwardness, we have trouble to find your own dainty selves? Oh, fie! Is the world, then, exhausted? and must we go back because the thumb of the mountebank jerks the other way?

Costume is not dress.

And the wearers of wardrobes may not be doctors of taste!

For by what authority shall these be pretty masters! Look well, and nothing have they invented – nothing put together for comeliness' sake.

Haphazard from their shoulders hang the garments of the hawker – combining in their person the motley of many manners with the medley of the mummers' closet.

Set up as a warning, and a finger-post of danger, they point to the disastrous effect of Art upon the middle classes.

Why this lifting of the brow in deprecation of the present – this pathos in reference to the past?

If Art be rare to-day, it was seldom heretofore.

It is false, this teaching of decay.

The master stands in no relation to the moment at which he occurs – a monument of isolation – hinting at sadness – having no part in the progress of his fellow-men.

He is also no more the product of civilisation than is the scientific truth asserted dependent upon the wisdom of a period. The assertion itself requires the *man* to make it. The truth was from the beginning.

So Art is limited to the infinite, and beginning there cannot progress.

A silent indication of its wayward independence from all extraneous advance, is in the absolutely unchanged condition and form of implement since the beginning of things.

The painter has but the same pencil – the sculptor the chisel of centuries.

Colours are not more since the heavy hangings of night were first drawn aside, and the loveliness of light revealed.

Neither chemist nor engineer can offer new elements of the masterpiece.

False again, the fabled link between the grandeur of Art and the glories and virtues of the State, for Art feeds not upon nations, and peoples may be wiped from the face of the earth, but Art *is*. It is indeed high time that we cast aside the weary weight of responsibility and co-partnership, and know that, in no way, do our virtues minister to its worth, in no way do our vices impede its triumph!

How irksome! how hopeless! how superhuman the self-imposed task of the nation! How sublimely vain the belief that it shall live nobly or art perish.

Let us reassure ourselves, at our own option is our virtue. Art we in no way affect.

A whimsical goddess, and a capricious, her strong sense of joy tolerates no dulness, and, live we never so spotlessly, still may she turn her back upon us.

As, from time immemorial, she has done upon the Swiss in their mountains.

What more worthy people! Whose every Alpine gap yawns with tradition, and is stocked with noble story; yet; the perverse and scornful one will none of it, and the sons of patriots are left with the clock that turns the mill, and the sudden cuckoo, with difficulty restrained in its box.

For this was Tell a hero! For this did Gessler die!

Art, the cruel jade, cares not, and hardens her heart, and hies her off to the East, to find, among the opium-eaters of Nankin, a favourite with whom she lingers fondly – caressing his blue porcelain, and painting his coy maidens, and marking his plates with her six marks of choice – indifferent in her companionship with him, to all save the virtue of his refinement!

He it is who calls her – he who holds her!

And again to the West, that her next lover may bring together the Gallery at Madrid, and show to the world how the Master towers above all;[13] and in their intimacy they revel, he and she, in this knowledge; and he knows the happiness untasted by other mortal.

She is proud of her comrade, and promises that in after-years, others shall pass that way, and understand.

So in all time does this superb one cast about for the man worthy her love – and Art seeks the Artist alone.[14]

Where he is, there she appears, and remains with him – loving and fruitful – turning never aside in moments of hope deferred – of insult – and of ribald misunderstanding; and when he dies she sadly takes her flight, though loitering yet in the land, from fond association, but refusing to be consoled.

With the man, then, and not with the multitude, are her intimacies; and in the book of her life the names inscribed are few – scant, indeed, the list of those who have helped to write her story of love and beauty.

From the sunny morning, when, with her glorious Greek relenting, she yielded up the secret of repeated line, as, with his hand in hers, together they, marked in marble, the measured rhyme of lovely limb and draperies flowing in unison, to the day when she dipped the Spaniard's brush in light and air, and made his people live within their frames, and *stand upon their legs*, that all nobility and sweetness, and tenderness, and magnificence should be theirs by right, ages had gone by, and few had been her choice.

Countless, indeed, the horde of pretenders! But she knew them not.

A teeming, seething, busy mass, whose virtue was industry, and whose industry was vice!

Their names go to fill the catalogue of the collection at home, of the gallery abroad, for the delectation of the bagman and the critic.

Therefore have we cause to be merry! – and to cast away all care – resolved that all is well – as it ever was – and that it is not meet that we should be cried at, and urged to take measures!

Enough have we endured of dulness! Surely are we weary of weeping, and our tears have been cozened from us falsely, for they have called out woe! when there was no grief – and alas! where all is fair!

We have then but to wait – until, with the mark of the Gods upon him – there come among us again the chosen – who shall continue what has gone before. Satisfied that, even were he never to appear, the story of the beautiful is already complete – hewn in the marbles of the Parthenon – and broidered, with the birds, upon the fan of Hokusai – at the foot of Fusiyama.[15]

GEORGE MOORE (1852–1933)

George Augustus Moore has always been a puzzle for literary historians, sometimes too simple to be taken seriously, yet overall too serious simply to be dismissed. He flung himself with great energy into literary activity, producing poetry, plays, fiction, criticism – most of it marred by imperfect gifts and too keen a desire for success. Yet his persistence was rewarded in the creation of one classic work of English fiction, *Esther Waters*, and at least two others (*Evelyn Innes* and *The Lake*) which merit more than their present neglect. In a similar way Moore's impulse for self-dramatization was as unfortunate as it was boundless, and he obtruded himself into his work with reckless naïveté and endless invention. But the strain of fictionalized reminiscence he developed became an art form in its own right, and his stylistic innovations in narration prefigure the work of Joyce. This duality informs our present purpose too, for Moore's egotism was matched by a strangely receptive temperament, which enabled him to soak up much that was most vital in the developing French culture of the day and to become one of its earliest and most forceful proponents in England.

In a sense Moore's life was his greatest creation, and deserved the attention he gave to it. The eldest son of a prominent Irish landowner, he resisted all attempts at formal education and passed his youth happily amid the drama and excitements of his father's racing stable. He was far from being a Philistine, however, and an early exposure to Shelley and the Romantic poets struck a deeply responsive chord in the young man which to some extent shaped his life thereafter. When Moore was eighteen his father died, leaving him a substantial yearly income, and upon reaching his majority he set off for Paris. He cherished a vague idea of becoming an artist, drawn more by the bohemian *ambiance* of the life than anything else. This was a doubly foolhardy gesture in view of the fact that he knew no French; but Moore was as hardy as he was foolish, and his receptive attention soon gave him sufficient command of the language to enroll in one of the leading studios of the day. Intermittently he struggled to master the techniques of painting, but what he really cultivated was experience, and Parisian life of the 1870s had plenty to offer the young Irishman.

Soon he had abandoned the idea of becoming a painter and moved into society, attentively gathering ideas and anecdotes which might serve a writer's needs.

Despite his awkwardness Moore was not without charm, a charm which came from his peculiar mixture of earnestness and self-deprecating humour. In 1877 began the phase of his so-called 'café education', when he began to know the important artists and writers of the day, sitting at their tables in the cafés of Montmartre, taking part in their discussions and counsels. In this way he absorbed a great deal of the aesthetic that was to triumph over the next twenty years, and he found his own cultural niche in exporting these ideas to England. His *Confessions of a Young Man* (q.v.) was thinly disguised autobiography recounting these Parisian adventures, and the book soon achieved the status of an English *Scènes de la Vie de Bohème*. Moore's experiences in France became the *desiderata* of any young person of imagination and talent during the nineties, and throughout the book one can hear the accents and tone which Oscar Wilde was shortly to make notorious. Indeed Wilde waggishly remarked that Moore conducted his education in public, but it is clear that he himself was one of the chief beneficiaries of the display. Perhaps more important is the fact that the book extended the romantic strain of fictionalized autobiography from the diffuse narrative form which Pater had evolved, to a more slangy, conversational article which Moore's compatriot, James Joyce, was to take to even greater heights.

The *Confessions* were also important in bringing to light several of the important artistic innovators in France, then almost unknown in England; and as such figures as Verlaine, Mallarmé, Degas and Manet became progressively established in the canon the book went through several editions. It must be admitted, however, that Moore's propagation of the new aesthetic ideas through formal criticism was less effective than that of Symons or Yeats. He lacked the scholarship of the former and the imagination of the latter, and his criticism is based mainly on reminiscence and personal impression. From 1891 he was the regular art critic of *The Speaker*, and his training meant that he could competently discuss the technical details of painting despite his inability to grasp broader trends. He was, moreover, possessed of sufficient taste to see the drawbacks of the nineteenth century's over-zealous devotion to anecdotal subjects, its passion for paintings of a 'literary' nature (q.v.). His greatest contributions to the criticism of art were to champion the Impressionists in England, to proselytize for Manet and Degas (q.v.), his two favourite French painters, and to offer some of the earliest sensitive appreciation of the art of Whistler (q.v.). Similarly, in the literary field his was virtually the first English voice to urge the claims of Verlaine, Rimbaud, Laforgue and Turgenev.

Moore helped to transform nineteenth-century aesthetics in one further way which we must take note of – that is, his fight against Victorian censorship. His first publication, *Flowers of Passion*, was a volume of poems almost entirely derived from Shelley and Baudelaire. The book was severely received and Moore, aware of its failings, let it drop quietly from sight. But a similar attack on the moral laxity of his first novel, *A Modern Lover*, was not left unanswered. The attack on the institution of circulating libraries, *Literature at Nurse* (q.v.), first brought the young Moore to prominence. At the time, these libraries were the chief means of obtaining new fiction, and thus its tacit moral and intellectual censors. Novels were printed in three volumes, a cumbersome and expensive form which precluded most individual purchasers but benefited the libraries, who would buy up virtually the whole edition for circulation to their subscribers throughout Britain. Refusal by these libraries (of which Charles Mudie's and W. H. Smith's were the largest) to take on a new work thus meant almost certain failure, and they exercised a considerable power of conformity over budding authors. When *A Modern Lover*, written along Zolaesque or Naturalist lines, was dropped by Mudie's, Moore took up the challenge and issued the pamphlet as a public protest in defence of literary freedom which echoed Swinburne's 'Notes on Poems and Reviews' (q.v.) twenty years before.

Moore lived on well into this century, but as he himself realized he was essentially a creature of the century before. He was unable to take much interest in the work of the modernists, and indeed after the turn of the century, with a few exceptions, he made his mark chiefly by his memory, spinning out long volumes of memoirs which elaborated but never exceeded the ideas absorbed in his youth. Still he had the good fortune to be in the right place at the right time, and to be a sensitive and attractive reporter; as a result his record of experiences and currents he had observed in France added considerable impetus to the growing 'aesthetic' wave in England.

Literature at Nurse, or Circulating Morals[1]

In an article contributed to the *Pall Mall Gazette* last December, I called attention to the fact that English writers were subject to the censorship of a tradesman who, although doubtless an excellent citizen and a worthy father, was scarcely competent to decide the delicate and difficult artistic questions that authors in their struggles for new ideals might raise [. . .].

The case, so far as I am individually concerned, stands thus: In 1883, I published a novel called "A Modern Lover." It met with the approval of the entire press; *The Athenaeum* and *The Spectator* declared emphatically that it was not immoral; but Mr. Mudie told me that two ladies in the country had written to him to say that they disapproved of the book and on that account he could not circulate it. I answered, "You are acting in defiance of the opinion of the press – you are taking a high position indeed, and one from which you will probably be overthrown. I, at least, will have done with you; for I shall find a publisher willing to issue my next book at a purchasable price, and so enable me to appeal direct to the public." Mr. Mudie tried to wheedle, attempted to dissuade me from my rash resolution; he advised me to try another novel in three volumes. Fortunately I disregarded his suggestion, and my next book, "A Mummer's Wife," was published at the price of six shillings. The result exceeded my expectations, for the book is now in its fourth edition. [. . .] Therefore it is not with a failing but with a firm heart that I return to the fight – a fight which it is my incurable belief must be won if we are again to possess a literature worthy of the name. [. . .]

It has been and will be again advanced that it is impossible to force a man to buy goods if he does not choose to do so: but with every privilege comes a duty. Mr. Mudie possesses a monopoly, and he cannot be allowed to use that monopoly to the detriment of all interests but his own. But even if this were not so, it is no less my right to point out to the public, that the character for strength, virility, and purpose, which our literature has always held, the old literary tradition coming down to us through a long line of glorious ancestors, is being gradually obliterated to suit the commercial views of a narrow-minded tradesman. Instead of being allowed to fight, with and amid, the thoughts and aspirations of men, literature is now rocked to an ignoble rest in the motherly arms of the librarian. [. . .] Into this nursery none can enter except in baby clothes; and the task of discriminating between a divided skirt and a pair of trousers is performed by the librarian. Deftly his fingers lift skirt and under-skirt, and if the examination prove satisfactory the sometimes decently attired dolls are packed in tin-cornered boxes, and scattered through ever drawing-room in the kingdom, to be in rocking-chairs fingered and fondled by the "young person" until she longs for some newer fashion in literary frills and furbelows. Mudie is the law we labour after; the suffrage of young women we are supposed to gain: the paradise of the English novelist is in the school-room: he is read there or nowhere. And yet it is certain that never in any age or country have writers been asked to write under such restricted conditions; if the same test by which modern writers are judged were applied to their forefathers, three-fourths of the contents of our libraries would have to be condemned as immoral publications. Now of the value of conventional innocence I don't pretend to judge, but I cannot help thinking that the cultivation of this curiosity is likely to run the nation into literary losses of some magnitude.

It will be said that genius triumphs over circumstances, but I am not sure that this is absolutely the case; and turning to Mr. Mathew Arnold, I find that he is of the same opinion. He says, [. . .] "but it must have the atmosphere, it must find itself in the order of ideas, to work freely, and this is not so easy to command. This is why the great creative epochs in literature are so rare . . . because for the creation of a master work of literature two powers must concur, the power of the man and the power of the moment; the creative has for its happy exercise appointed elements, and those elements are not in its own control."[2] I agree with Mr. Mathew Arnold. Genius is a natural production, just as are chickweed and roses; under certain conditions it matures, under others it dies; and the deplorable dearth of talent among the novelists of to-day is owing to the action of the circulating library, which for the last thirty years has been staying the current of ideas, and quietly opposing the development of fresh thought. [. . .] The struggle for existence, therefore, no longer exists; the librarian rules the roost; he crows, and every chanticleer pitches his note in the same key. He, not the ladies and gentlemen who place their names on the title-pages, is the author of modern English fiction. He models it, fashions it to suit his purpose, and the artistic individualities of his employees count for as little as that of the makers of the pill-boxes in which are sold certain well-known and mildly purgative medicines. And in accordance with his wishes English fiction now consists of either a sentimental misunderstanding, which is happily cleared up in the end, or of singular escapes over the edges of precipices, and miraculous recoveries of one or more of the senses of which the hero was deprived, until the time has come for the author to bring his tale to a close. The novel of observation, of analysis, exists no longer among us. Why? Because the librarian does not feel as safe in circulating a study of life and manners as a tale concerning a lost will.[3] [. . .]

It is doubtless a terrible thing to advocate the breaking down of the thirty-one and sixpenny safeguards, and to place it in the power of young girl to buy an immoral book if she chooses to do so; but I am afraid it cannot be helped. Important an element as she undoubtedly is in our sociological system, still we must not lose sight of everything but her; and that the nineteenth century should possess a literature characteristic of its nervous, passionate life, I hold is as desirable, and would be as far-reaching in its effects, as the biggest franchise bill ever planned.

Confessions of a Young Man[4]

I.

My soul, so far as I understand it, has very kindly taken colour and form from the many various modes of life that self-will and an impetuous temperament have forced me to indulge in. Therefore I may say that I am free from original qualities, defects, tastes, etc. What is mine I have acquired, or, to speak more exactly, chance bestowed, and still bestows, upon me. I came into the world apparently with a nature like a smooth sheet of wax, bearing no impress, but capable of receiving any; of being moulded into all shapes. Nor am I exaggerating when I say I think that I might equally have been a Pharaoh, an ostler, a pimp, an archbishop, and that in the fulfilment of the duties of each a certain measure of success would have been mine. I have felt the goad of many impulses, I have hunted many a trail; when one scent failed another was taken up, and pursued with the pertinacity of instinct, rather than the fervour of a reasoned conviction. Sometimes, it is true, there came moments of weariness, of despondency, but they were not enduring: a word spoken, a book read, or yielding to the attraction of environment, I was soon off in another direction, forgetful of past failures. Intricate, indeed, was the labyrinth of my desires; all lights were followed with the same ardour, all cries were eagerly responded to: they came from the right, they came from the left, from every side. But one cry was more persistent, and as the years passed I learned to follow it with increasing vigour, and my strayings grew fewer and the way wider.

I was eleven years old when I first heard and obeyed this cry, or, shall I say, echo-augury? [. . .] There was magic, there was revelation in the name, and Shelley became my soul's divinity. Why did I love Shelley? Why not attracted to Byron? Shelley! That crystal name, and his poetry also crystalline. I must see it, I must know him. Escaping from the schoolroom, I ransacked the library, and at last my ardour was rewarded. The book – a small pocket edition in red boards, no doubt long out of print – opened at the 'Sensitive Plant.' Was I disappointed? I think I had expected to understand better; but I had no difficulty in assuming that I was satisfied and delighted. And henceforth the little volume never left my pocket, and I read the dazzling stanzas by the shores of a pale green Irish lake, comprehending little, and loving a great deal. Byron, too, was often with me, and these poets were the ripening influence of years otherwise merely nervous and boisterous. [. . .] In London I made the acquaintance of a great blond man, who talked incessantly about beautiful women, and painted them sometimes larger than life, in somnolent attitudes, and luxurious tints.[5] His studio was a welcome contrast to the spitting and betting of the tobacco shop. His pictures – Doré-like improvisations, devoid of skill, and, indeed, of artistic perception, save a certain sentiment for the grand and noble – filled me with wonderment and awe. 'How jolly it would be to be a painter!' I once said, quite involuntarily. 'Why, would you like to be a painter?' he asked abruptly. I laughed, not suspecting that I had the slightest gift, as indeed was the case, but the idea remained in my mind, and soon after I began to make sketches in the streets and theatres. My attempts were not very successful, but they encouraged me to tell my father that I would go to the military tutor no more, and he allowed me to enter the Kensington Museum as an Art student. There, of course, I learned nothing, and, from the point of view of art merely, I had much better have continued my sketches in the streets; but the museum was a beautiful and beneficent influence, and one that applied marvellously well to the besetting danger of the moment; for in the galleries I met young men who spoke of other things than betting and steeplechase riding, who, I remember, it was clear to me then, looked to a higher ideal than mine, breathed a purer atmosphere of thought than I. [. . .]

'But if you want to be a painter you must go to France – France is the only school of Art.' I must again call attention to the phenomenon of echo-augury, that is to say, words heard in an unlooked-for quarter, that, without any appeal to our reason, impel belief. France! The word rang in my ears and gleamed in my eyes. France! All my senses sprang from sleep like a crew when the man on the look-out cries, 'Land ahead!' Instantly I knew that I should, that I must, go to France, that I would live there, that I would become as a Frenchman. I knew not when nor how, but I knew I should go to France. [. . .]

II.

The studio to which I had been recommended was perched high up in the Passage des Panoramas, and in it I found M. Julien, a typical meridional: dark eyes, crafty and watchful, a seductively mendacious manner, and a sensual mind.[6] We made friends at once – he consciously making use of me, I unconsciously making use of him. To him my forty francs, a month's subscription, were a godsend, nor were my invitations to dinner and to the theatre to be disdained, though to be sure it was a little tiresome to have to put up with a talkative person, whose knowledge of the French language had been acquired in three months; but the dinners were good, and I was quaint. No doubt Julien reasoned so; I did not reason at all, but I felt this crafty, clever man of the world was necessary to me. I had never met such a man before, and all my curiosity was awake. He spoke of art and literature, of the world and the flesh; he told me of the books he had read, he narrated thrilling incidents in his own life; and the moral reflections with which he sprinkled his conversation I thought very striking. Like every young man of twenty, I was on the look-out for something to set up that would do duty for an ideal. The world was to me, at this time, what a toy-shop had been fifteen years before: everything was spick and span, and every illusion was set out straight and smart in new paint and gilding. Julien threw open a door of Parisian life to me; all open doors were welcome to me at that time, and his society served to prepare my mind for the friendship which awaited me, and which was destined to absorb some years of my life. [. . .] And just as I had watched the chorus girls and mummers, three years ago, at the Globe Theare, now, excited by a nervous curiosity, I watched this world of Parisian adventures and lights-o'-love. And this craving for observation of manners, this instinct for the rapid notation of gestures and words that epitomize a state of feeling, of attitudes that mirror forth the soul, declared itself a main passion; and it grew and strengthened, to the detriment of the other Art still so dear to me. With the patience of a cat before a mouse-hole, I watched and listened, picking one characteristic phrase out of hours of vain chatter, interested and amused by an angry or loving glance. These men and women seemed to me like the midges that fret the surface of a shadowy stream, and though I laughed and danced, and made merry with them, I was not of them. [. . .] Why could I not live without an ever-present and acute consciousness of life? Why could I not love, forgetful of the ticking of the clock in the perfumed silence of the chamber?[7] [. . .]

V.

Then I took an *appartement* in one of the old houses in Rue de la Tour des Dames, for windows there overlooked a bit of tangled garden with a dilapidated statue. It was Marshall, of course, who undertook the task of furnishing, and he lavished on the rooms the fancies of an imagination that suggested the collaboration of a courtesan of high degree and a fifth-rate artist. Nevertheless, our salon was a pretty resort – English cretonne of a very happy design – vine leaves, dark green and golden, broken up by many fluttering jays. The walls were stretched with this colourful cloth, and the arm-chairs and the couches were to match. The drawing-room was in cardinal red, hung from the middle of the ceiling and looped up to give the appearance of a tent; a faun, in terra-cotta, laughed in the red gloom, and there were Turkish couches and lamps. In another room you faced an altar, a Buddhist temple, a statue of Apollo, and a bust of Shelley. The bedrooms were made unconventional with cushioned seats and rich canopies; and in picturesque corners there were censers, great church candlesticks, and palms; then think of the smell of burning incense and wax and you will have imagined the sentiment of our apartment in Rue de la Tour des Dames. I bought a Persian cat, and a python that made a monthly meal off guinea-pigs; Marshall, who did not care for pets, filled his rooms with flowers – he used to sleep beneath a tree of gardenias in full bloom. We were so, Henry Marshall and George Moore, when we went to live in 76, Rue de la Tour des Dames, we hoped for the rest of our lives. He was to paint, I was to write.[8] [. . .]

Books are like individuals; you know at once if they are going to create a sense within the sense, to fever, to madden you in blood and brain, or if they will merely leave you indifferent, or irritable, having unpleasantly disturbed sweet intimate musings as might a draught from an open window. Many are the reasons for love, but I confess I only love woman or book, when it is as a voice of conscience, never heard before, heard suddenly, a voice I am at once endearingly intimate with. This announces feminine depravities in my affections. I am feminine, morbid, perverse. But above all perverse; almost everything perverse interests, fascinates me. Wordsworth is the only simple-minded man I ever loved, if that great austere mind, chill even as the Cumberland year, can be called simple. But Hugo is not perverse, nor even personal. Reading him was like being in church with a strident-voiced preacher shouting from out of a terribly sonorous pulpit. [. . .] I still read and spoke of Shelley with a rapture of joy – he was still my 'pinnace.' But this craft, fashioned of mother-o'-pearl, with starlight at the helm and moonbeams for sails, suddenly ran on a reef and went down, not out of sight, but out of the agitation of actual life. The reef was Gautier; I read 'Mlle. de Maupin' at a moment when I was weary of spiritual passion, and this great exaltation of the visible above the invisible at once conquered and led me captive. [. . .] Shelley's teaching had been, while accepting the body, to dream of the soul as a star, and so preserve our ideal; but now I saw suddenly, with delightful clearness and with intoxicating conviction, that by looking without shame and accepting with love the flesh, I might raise it to as high a place within as divine a light as even the soul had been set in. [. . .]

I had shaken off all belief in Christianity early in life with Shelley's help. He had replaced faith by reason; I still suffered, but need suffer no more. Here was a new creed proclaiming the divinity of the body; and for a long time the reconstruction of all my theories of life on a purely pagan basis occupied my attention. [. . .] Never shall I open these books again, but were I to live for a thousand years, their power in my soul would remain unshaken. I am what they made me. Belief in humanity, pity for the poor, hatred of injustice, all that Shelley gave may never have been very deep or earnest; but I did love, I did believe. Gautier destroyed these illusions. He taught me that our boasted progress is but a pitfall into which the race is falling, and I learned that the correction of form is the highest ideal, and I accepted the plain, simple conscience of the pagan world as the perfect solution of the problem that had vexed me so long! [. . .]

The study of Baudelaire hurried the course of the disease. No longer is it the grand barbaric face of Gautier; now it is the clean-shaven face of the mock priest, the slow, cold eyes and the sharp, cunning sneer of the cynical libertine who will be tempted that he may better know the worthlessness of temptation. 'Les Fleurs du Mal!' beautiful flowers, beautiful in sublime decay. What a great record is yours, and were Hell a reality how many souls would we find wreathed with your poisonous blossoms! The village maiden goes to her Faust; the children of the nineteenth century go to you, O Baudelaire, and having tasted of your deadly delight all hope of repentance is vain. Flowers, beautiful in your sublime decay, I press you to my lips; [. . .]

For months I fed on the mad and morbid literature that the enthusiasm of 1830 called into existence.[9] [. . .]

There were for contrast Mallarmé's Tuesday evenings, a few friends sitting round the hearth, the lamp on the table. I have met none whose conversation was more fruitful, but I never enjoyed his poetry, his early verses of course excepted. When I know him he had published the celebrated 'L'Après-Midi d'un Faune': the first poem written in accordance with the theory of symbolism. But when it was given to me (this marvellous brochure furnished with strange illustrations and wonderful tassels), I thought it absurdly obscure. Since then, however, it has been rendered by force of contrast with the enigmas the author has since published a marvel of lucidity; I am sure if I were to read it now I should appreciate its many beauties. It bears the same relation to the author's later work as *Rienzi* to *The Walkyrie*. But what is symbolism? Vulgarly speaking, saying the opposite to what you mean. [. . .] We have heard a great deal in England of Browning obscurity. The 'Red Cotton Nightcap Country' is a child at play compared to a sonnet by such a determined symbolist as Mallarmé, or better still his disciple Ghil who has added to the infirmities of symbolism those of poetic instrumentation.[10] For according to M. Ghil and his organ *Les Ecrits pour l'Art*, it would appear that the syllables of the French language evoke in us the sensations of different colours; consequently the timbre of the different instruments. The vowel *u* corresponds to the colour yellow, and therefore to the sound of flutes. [. . .]

I laughed at these verbal eccentricities, but they were not without their effect, and that a demoralizing one; for in me they aggravated the fever of the unknown, and whetted my appetite for the strange, abnormal and unhealthy in art. Hence all pallidities of thought and desire were eagerly welcomed; Verlaine became my poet, and the terraces and colonnades of 'Les Fêtes Galantes' the chapel of my meditations,[11] [. . .] 'Les Fêtes Galantes' is lit with dresses, white, blue, yellow, green, mauve, and undecided purple; the voices? strange contraltos; the forms? not those of men or women, but mystic, hybrid creatures, with hands nervous and pale, and eyes charged with eager and fitful light. [. . .]

Gautier sang to his antique lyre praise of the flesh and contempt of the soul; Baudelaire on a mediaeval organ chanted his unbelief in goodness and truth and his hatred of life. But Verlaine advances one step further: hate is to him as commonplace as love, unfaith as vulgar as faith. The world is merely a doll to be attired to-day in eighteenth-century hoops, tomorrow in aureoles and stars. [. . .] And strangely enough, a withdrawing from all commerce with virtue and vice is, it would seem, a licentiousness more curiously subtle and penetrating than any other; and the licentiousness of the verse is equal to that of the emotion; every natural instinct of the language is violated, and the simple music native in French metre is replaced by falsetto notes sharp and intense. The charm is that of an odour of iris exhaled by some ideal tissues, or of a missal in a gold case, a precious relic of the pomp and ritual of an archbishop of Persepolis. [. . .] Not in Baudelaire nor even in Poe is there more beautiful poetry to be found. Poe, unread and ill-understood in America and England, here, thou art an integral part of our artistic life.

The Island o' Fay, Silence, Eleonore, were the familiar spirits of an apartment beautiful with Manets and tapestry;[12] Swinburne and Rossetti were the English poets I read there; and I, a unit in the generation they have enslaved, clanked fetters and trailed a golden chain, in a set of stories in many various metres, to be called 'Roses of Midnight.' One of the characteristics of the volume was banishment of daylight: from its pages terraces, gardens and orchards were held forbidden; and my fantastics lived out their loves in the lamplight of yellow boudoirs, and died with the dawn which was supposed to be an awakening to consciousness of reality.

VII.

A Japanese dressing-gown, the ideality of whose tissue delights me, some fresh honey and milk set by this couch hung with royal fringes; and having partaken of this odorous refreshment, I call to Jack, my great python crawling about after a two months' fast. I tie up a guinea-pig to the *tabouret*, pure Louis XV., the little beast struggles and squeaks, the snake, his black, bead-like eyes are fixed, how superb are the oscillations . . . now he strikes: and with what exquisite gourmandise he lubricates and swallows!

Marshall is at the organ in the hall, he is playing a Gregorian chant, that beautiful hymn, the 'Vexilla Regis,' by Saint Fortunatus, the great poet of the Middle Ages. And, having turned over the leaves of 'Les Fêtes Galantes,' I sit down to write.

My original intention was to write some thirty or forty stories varying from thirty to three hundred lines in length. The nature of these stories is easy to imagine: there was the youth who wandered by night into a witches' sabbath, and was disputed for by the witches, young and old. There was the light o' love who went into the desert to tempt the holy man; but he died as he yielded, his arms stiffening by some miracle about her, and she, unable to free herself, died while her bondage was loosening in decay. My difficulties were increased by adopting as part of my task the introduction of all sorts of elaborate, and in many cases extravagantly composed metres, and I began to feel that I was working in sand; the house I was raising crumbled and fell away on every side. My stories had one merit: they were all, as far as I can remember, perfectly constructed. The art of telling a story clearly and dramatically, *selon les procédés de M. Scribe*, had been learnt from M. Duval, the author of a hundred and sixty plays, written in collaboration with more than a hundred of the best writers of his day, including the master himself, Gautier. We used to meet at breakfast at a neighbouring *café*, and our conversation turned on *l'exposition de la pièce, préparer la situation, nous aurons des larmes*, etc. One day, as I sat waiting for him, I took up the *Voltaire*. It contained an article by M. Zola.[13] *Naturalisme, la vérité, la science*, were repeated some half-a-dozen times. Hardly able to believe my eyes, I read that one should write with as little imagination as possible, that plot in a novel or in a play was illiterate and puerile, and that the art of M. Scribe was an art of strings and wires, etc. I rose up from breakfast, ordered my coffee, and stirred the sugar, a little dizzy, like one who has received a violent blow on the head.

Echo-augury! Words heard in an unexpected quarter, but applying marvellously well to the besetting difficulty of the moment. [. . .]

And now for a third time I experienced the pain and joy of a sudden and inward light. Naturalism, truth, the new art, above all the phrase, 'The new art,' impressed me as with a sudden sense of light. I was dazzled, and I vaguely understood that my 'Roses of Midnight' were sterile eccentricities, dead flowers that could not be galvanized into any semblance of life, passionless in all their passion.

I had read a few chapters of the 'Assommoir,' as it appeared in *La République des Lettres*; I had cried, 'ridiculous, abominable,' only because it is characteristic of me to form an opinion instantly and assume at once a violent attitude. But now I bought up the back numbers of the *Voltaire*, and I look forward to the weekly exposition of the new faith with febrile eagerness. The great zeal with which the new master continued his propanganda, and the marvellous way in which subjects the most diverse, passing events, political, social, religious, were caught up and turned into arguments for, or proof of the truth of naturalism astonished me wholly. The idea of a new art based upon science, in opposition to the art of the old world that was based on imagination, an art that should explain all things and embrace modern life in its entirety, in its endless ramifications, be, as it were, a new creed in a new civilization, filled me with wonder, and I stood dumb before the vastness of the conception, and the towering height of the ambition. In my fevered fancy I saw a new race of writers that would arise, and with the aid of the novel would continue to a more glorious and legitimate conclusion the work that the prophets had begun; and at each development of the theory of the new art and its universal applicability, my wonder increased and my admiration choked me. [. . .]

But although I am apt to love too dearly the art of my day, and to the disparagement of that of other days, I did not fall into the stupid mistake of placing the realistic writers of 1877 side by side with and on the same plane of intellectual vision as the great Balzac; I felt that that vast immemorial mind rose above them all, like a mountain above the highest tower. [. . .]

Balzac was the great moral influence of my life, and my reading culminated in the 'Comédie Humaine.'[14] I no doubt fluttered through some scores of other books, of prose and verse, sipping a little honey, but he alone left any important or lasting impression upon my mind. The rest was like walnuts and wine, an agreeable after-taste.

But notwithstanding all this reading I can lay no claim to

scholarship of any kind; for save life I could never learn anything correctly. I am a student only of ballrooms, bar-rooms, streets, and alcoves. I have read very little; but all I read I can turn to account, and all I read I remember. To read freely, extensively, has always been my ambition, and my utter inability to study has always been to me a subject of grave inquietude – study as contrasted with a general and haphazard gathering of ideas taken in flight. But in me the impulse is so original to frequent the haunts of men that it is irresistible, conversation is the breath of my nostrils, I watch the movement of life, and my ideas spring from it uncalled for, as buds from branches. Contact with the world is in me the generating force; without this what invention I have is thin and sterile, and it grows thinner rapidly, until it dies away utterly, as it did in the composition of my unfortunate 'Roses of Midnight.' [. . .]

I did not go to either Oxford or Cambridge, but I went to the 'Nouvelle Athènes.' What is the 'Nouvelle Athènes'? He who would know anything of my life must know something of the academy of the fine arts. Not the official stupidity you read of in the daily papers, but the real French academy, the *café*. The 'Nouvelle Athènes' is a *café* on the Place Pigalle. Ah! the morning idlenesses and the long evening when life was but a summer illusion, the grey moonlights on the Place where we used to stand on the pavements, the shutters clanging up behind us, loath to separate, thinking of what we had left unsaid, and how much better we might have enforced our arguments. Dead and scattered are all those who used to assemble there, and those years and our home, for it was our home, live only in a few pictures and a few pages of prose. The same old story, the vanquished only are victorious; and though unacknowledged, though unknown, the influence of the 'Nouvelle Athènes' is inveterate in the artistic thought of the nineteenth century.

How magnetic, intense, and vivid are 'these memories of youth! With what strange, almost unnatural clearness do I see and hear – see the white face of that *café*, the white nose of that block of houses, stretching up to the Place, between two streets. I can see down the incline of those two streets, and I know what shops are there; I can hear the glass door of the *café* grate on the sand as I open it. I can recall the smell of every hour. In the morning that of eggs frizzling in butter, the pungent cigarette, coffee and bad cognac; at five o'clock the fragrant odour of absinthe; and soon after the steaming soup ascends from the kitchen; and as the evening advances, the mingled smells of cigarettes, coffee, and weak beer. A partition, rising a few feet or more over the hats, separates the glass front from the main body of the *café*. The usual marble tables are there, and it is there we sat and aestheticized till two o'clock in the morning.

XII.

But this book is not a course of literature, and I will tarry no longer with mere criticism, but go direct to the book to which I owe the last temple in my soul – 'Marius the Epicurean.'[15] Well I remember when I read the opening lines, and how they came upon me sweetly as the flowing breath of a bright spring. I knew that I was awakened a fourth time, that a fourth vision of life was to be given to me. Shelley had revealed to me the unimagined skies where the spirit sings of light and grace; Gautier had shown me how extravagantly beautiful is the visible world and how divine is the rage of the flesh; and with Balzac I had descended circle by circle into the nether world of the soul, and watched its afflictions. Then there were minor awakenings. Zola had enchanted me with decoration and inebriated me with theory; Flaubert had astonished with the wonderful delicacy and subtlety of his workmanship; Goncourt's brilliant adjectival effects had captivated me for a time, but all these impulses were crumbling into dust, these aspirations were etiolated, sickly as faces grown old in gaslight.

I had not thought of the simple and unaffected joy of the heart of natural things; the colour of the open air, the many forms of the country, the birds flying – that one making for the sea; the abandoned boat, the dwarf roses and the wild lavender; nor had I thought of the beauty of mildness in life, and how by a certain avoidance of the wilfully passionate, and the surely ugly, we may secure an aspect of temporal life which is abiding and soul-sufficing. A new dawn was in my brain, fresh and fair, full of wide temples and studious hours, and the lurking fragrance of incense; that such a vision of life was possible I had no suspicion, and it came upon me almost with the same strength, almost as intensely, as that divine song of the flesh, Mademoiselle de Maupin.

In my mind, these books will be always intimately associated; and when a few adventitious points of difference are forgotten, it is interesting to note how firm is the alliance, and how cognate and co-equal the sympathies on which it is based; the same glad worship of the visible world, and the same incurable belief that the beauty of material things is sufficient for all the needs of life. Mr. Pater can join hands with Gautier in saying – *je trouve la terre aussi belle que le ciel, et je pense que la correction de la forme est la vertu.*[16] And I too am of their company – in this at least I too love the great pagan world, its bloodshed, its slaves, its injustice, its loathing of all that is feeble.

But 'Marius the Epicurean' was more to me than a mere emotional influence, precious and rare though that may be, for this book was the first in English prose I had come across that procured for me any genuine pleasure in the language itself, in the combination of words for silver or gold chime, and unconventional cadence, and for all those lurking half-meanings, and that evanescent suggestion, like the odour of dead roses, that words retain to the last of other times and elder usage. Until I read 'Marius' the English language (English prose) was to me what French must be to the majority of English readers. I read for the sense and that was all; the language itself seemed to me coarse and plain, and awoke in me neither aesthetic emotion nor even interest. 'Marius' was the stepping-stone that carried me across the channel into the genius of my own tongue. The translation was not too abrupt; I found a constant and careful invocation of meaning that was a little aside of the common comprehension, and also a sweet depravity of ear for unexpected falls of phrase, and of eye for the less observed depths of colours, which although new was a sort of sequel to the education I had chosen, and a continuance of it in a foreign, but not wholly unfamiliar medium; and having saturated myself with Pater, the passage to De Quincey was easy. He, too, was a Latin in manner and in temper of mind; but he was truly English, and through him I passed to the study of the Elizabethan dramatists, the real literature of my race, and washed myself clean of France.

A Great Poet[17]

I write about a poet whose verse, whose name, and whose life are unknown in England – of one who even in his own country is known only to the *élite* – of one who, although he has published beautiful books for more than a quarter of a century, remains to this day unhonoured and unrecognised by the general reading public in the most distinguished literary centre in the world – in Paris. His name is Verlaine, and standing to-day on the last verge of life he sees glory rising out of the chasm beneath him. [. . .] In the meantime, he lives in poverty, if not in absolute hunger. [. . .] Among men of letters Verlaine is as well known as Victor Hugo; to the occasional reader his name is as unknown as that of *concierge* over the way, or the *cocher* turning the corner of the street. And this, because the general reading public cares little for poetry? No. But because Verlaine is of all men of genius I have ever met the least fitted to defend himself in the battle of life. He is able for nothing except the occasional writing of beautiful verses. And verses that have no other characteristic than beauty may be said to be an almost unsaleable commodity. His instincts are neither patriotic nor popular, but entirely aesthetical – the religious emotion of a monk painting the joys of heaven above the dim altar, and the sensuousness of the same monk delineating the tall adolescent angel. [. . .] But besides the disadvantage of being entirely and exclusively a poet, the disorder of his private life has reckoned heavily against Verlaine. For many years hardly any newspaper dared to print his name; only the ephemeral reviews that the ardour of enthusiasts called into existence for a season published his verse. He has lived the prey of strange passions that have ruined and dishonoured him. He has been in prison, and has lived many years in exile, sometimes gaining a precarious livelihood as a French teacher in English schools. Of late years sickness has not left him; from hospital to hospital he has dragged a pitiful body, and when discharged partly cured he has found shelter only in distant quarters of the town, among the working folk that herd together, *dans le quartier du Temple.* [. . .]

In speaking of Verlaine, in my book *Confessions of a Young*

Man, I spoke of his devotional poems as being the result of poetic calculations; their originality I said was attained, as Edgar Poe puts it, negatively rather than affirmatively. Perhaps this is not quite clear. In one of his essays Edgar Poe says that no one is original by temperament; that we become original by a deliberate effort of reason, by desiring originality, and declining to write in this way and that way, because these methods have been appropriated by other writers, and not because they are unnatural to us. When I wrote the *Confessions* I was only slightly acquainted with Verlaine's later work, and being at a loss to reconcile beautiful, pitiful pleas for pardon addressed to Jesus Christ and His Holy Mother with the well-known disorder of his life, I hastily concluded that Verlaine was a striking exemplification of Poe's theory of originality and how it may be acquired. I have since discovered that I was mistaken. Nature is more subtle than our logic, even more subtle than Poe's. Verlaine believes in the Roman Catholic Church as earnestly as the Pope himself, but in Verlaine there is only belief – practice is wholly wanting in him. Nor do I think he ever quite realises how he lives or how he writes. [. . .]

The whole man – his poetry, his life, his literary success, and his failure – is contained in an all-embracing sense of his own unworthiness; he keeps it continually before you; he tells you of it in a hundred different ways, for he is the most personal of poets. He writes of nothing but himself; his own life is his only theme. Sometimes he confides it by a personal narrative, sometimes it assumes some slight and obvious disguisement. His unworthiness is all he has to tell you, and it is most affecting, for it is the whole man.

Degas[18]

One evening, after a large dinner party, given in honour of the publication of *L'Oeuvre*, when most of the guests had done, and the company consisted of *les intimes de la maison*, a discussion arose as to whether Claude Lantier was or was not a man of talent. Madame Charpentier, by dint of much provocative asseveration that he was undistinguished by even any shred of the talent which made Manet a painter for painters, forced

Emile Zola to take up the cudgels and defend his hero. Seeing that all were siding with Madame Charpentier, Zola plunged like a bull into the thick of the fray, and did not hesitate to affirm that he had gifted Claude Lantier with infinitely larger qualities than those which nature had bestowed upon Edouard Manet.[19] This statement was received in mute anger by those present, all of whom had been personal friends and warm admirers of Manet's genius, and cared little to hear any word of disparagement spoken of their dead friend. It must be observed that M. Zola intended no disparagement of M. Manet, but he was concerned to defend the theory of his book – namely, that no painter working in the modern movement had achieved a result equivalent to that which had been achieved by at least three or four writers working in the same movement, inspired by the same ideas, animated by the same aestheticism. And, in reply to one who was anxiously urging Degas' claim to the highest consideration, he said, "I cannot accept a man who shuts himself up all his life to draw a ballet-girl as ranking co-equal in dignity and power with Flaubert, Daudet, and Goncourt."

Some four, or perhaps five, years after, one morning in May, a friend tried the door of Degas' studio. It is always strictly fastened, and when shaken vigorously a voice calls from some loophole; if the visitor be an intimate friend, a string is pulled and he is allowed to stumble his way up the cork-screw staircase into the studio. There are neither Turkey carpets nor Japanese screens, nor indeed any of those signs whereby we know the dwelling of the modern artist. Only at the further end, where the artist works, is there daylight. In perennial gloom and dust the vast canvases of his youth are piled up in formidable barricades. Great wheels belonging to lithographic presses – lithography was for a time one of Degas' avocations – suggest a printing-office. There is much decaying sculpture – dancing-girls modelled in red wax, some dressed in muslin skirts, strange dolls – dolls if you will, but dolls modelled by a man of genius. [. . .]

As they entered the apartment the eye of the visitor was caught by a faint drawing in red chalk, placed upon a sideboard; he went straight to it. Degas said, "Ah! look at it, I bought it only a few days ago; it is a drawing of a female hand by Ingres;

look at those finger-nails, see how they are indicated. That's my idea of genius, a man who finds a hand so lovely, so wonderful, so difficult to render, that he will shut himself up all his life, content to do nothing else but indicate finger-nails."

The collocation of these remarks by Zola and Degas – two men of genius, working in the same age, floating in the same stream of tendency, although in diverging currents – cannot fail to move those who are interested in the problem of artistic life. [. . .] Two types of mind are there in essence; two poles of art are brought into the clearest apprehension, and the insoluble problem, whether it be better to strive for almost everything, or for almost nothing, stares the reader in the face; we see Zola attempting to grasp the universe, and Degas following the vein of gold, following it unerringly, preserving it scrupulously from running into slate. The whole of Degas' life is in the phrase spoken while showing his visitor the drawing in red chalk by Ingres. For no man's practice ever accorded more nearly with his theory than Degas'. He has shut himself up all his life to draw again and again, in a hundred different combinations, only slightly varied, those few aspects of life which his nature led him to consider artistically, and for which his genius alone holds the artistic formulae. [. . .]

In accordance with this philosophy, Degas thinks as little of Turkey carpets and Japanese screens as of newspaper applause, and is unconcerned to paint his walls lemon yellow;[20] he puts his aestheticism upon his canvases, and leaves time to tint the fading whitewash with golden tints. They are naked of ornament, except a few *chefs-d' Oeuvre* which he will not part with, a few portraits, a few pictures painted in his youth. [. . .]

To pass through the world unobserved by those who cannot understand him – that is, by the crowd – and to create all the while an art so astonishingly new and so personal that it will defy imitator, competitor, or rival, seems to be his ambition, if so gross a term can be used without falsifying the conception of his character. For Degas seems without desire of present or future notoriety. If he could create his future as he has created his present, his future would be found to be no more than a continuation of his present. As he has in life resolutely separated himself from all possibility of praise, except from those who understand him, he would probably, if he could, defend himself against all those noisy and posthumous honours which came to the share of J. F. Millet;[21] and there can be but little doubt that he desires not at all to be sold by picture-dealers for fabulous prices, but rather to have a quiet nook in a public gallery where the few would come to study. However this may be, it is certain that to-day his one wish is to escape the attention of the crowd. [. . .] To this end he has for many years consistently refused to exhibit in the Salon; now he declines altogether to show his pictures publicly. [. . .]

Artists will understand the almost superhuman genius it requires to take subject-matter that has never received artistic treatment before, and bring it at once within the sacred pale.[22] Baudelaire was the only poet who ever did this; Degas is the only painter. Of all impossible things in this world to treat artistically, the ballet-girl seemed the most impossible, but Degas accomplished that feat. [. . .] The philosophy of this art is in Degas' own words. "La danseuse n'est qu'un prétexte pour le dessin." Dancers fly out of the picture, a single leg crosses the foreground. The première danseuse stands on tiptoe, supported by the coryphées, or she rests on one knee, the light upon her bosom, her arms leaned back, the curtain all the while falling. As he has done with the ballet, so he has done with the race-course. A race-horse walks past a white post which cuts his head in twain. [. . .]

But perhaps the most astonishing of all Degas' innovations are his studies of the nude. The nude has become well-nigh incapable of artistic treatment. Even the more naïve are beginning to see that the well-known nymph exhibiting her beauty by the borders of a stream can be endured no longer. Let the artist strive as he will, he will not escape the conventional; he is running an impossible race. Broad harmonies of colour are hardly to be thought of; the gracious mystery of human emotion is out of all question – he must rely on whatever measure of elegant drawing he can include in his delineation of arms, neck, and thigh; and who in sheer beauty has a new word to say? Since Gainsborough and Ingres, all have failed to infuse new life into the worn-out theme. But cynicism was the great means of eloquence of the Middle Ages; and with cynicism Degas has again rendered the nude an artistic possibility. Three coarse women, middle-aged and deformed by toil, are perhaps the most wonderful. One sponges herself in a tin bath; another passes a rough night-dress over her lumpy shoulders, and the touching ugliness of this poor human creature goes straight to the heart. Then follows a long series conceived in the same spirit. A woman who has stepped out of a bath examines her arm. Degas says, "La bête humaine qui s'occupe d'elle-même; une chatte qui se lèche."[23] Yes, it is the portrayal of the animal-life of the human being, the animal conscious of nothing but itself. 'Hitherto,' Degas says, as he shows his visitor three large peasant women plunging into a river, not to bathe, but to wash or cool themselves (one drags a dog in after her), "the nude has always been represented in poses which presuppose an audience, but these women of mine are honest, simple folk, unconcerned by any other interests than those involved in their physical condition. Here is another; she is washing her feet. It is as if you looked through a key-hole."

The Failure of the Nineteenth Century[24]

Has the nineteenth century brought any new intention into art which did not exist before in England, Holland, or Italy? Yes, the nineteenth century has brought a new intention into art, and I think that it is this very new intention that has caused the failure of the nineteenth century. To explain myself, I will have to go back to first principles.

In the beginning the beauty of man was the artist's single theme. Science had not then relegated man to his exact place in creation: he reigned triumphant, Nature appearing, if at all, only as a kind of aureole. The Egyptian, the Greek, and the Roman artists saw nothing, and cared for nothing, except man; the representation of his beauty, his power, and his grandeur was their whole desire, whether they carved or painted their intention, [. . .] Michael Angelo's artistic outlook was the same as Phidias'. One chose the "Last Judgment" and the other "Olympus," but both subjects were looked at from the same point of view. In each instance the question asked was – what opportunity do they afford for the display of marvellous human form? And when Michael Angelo carved the "Moses" and painted the "St. Jerome" he was as deaf and blind as any Greek to all other consideration save the opulence and the magic of drapery, the vehemence and the splendour of muscle. Nearly two thousand years had gone by and the artistic outlook had not changed at all; three hundred years have passed since Michael Angelo, and in those three hundred years what revolution has not been effected? How different our aestheticism, our aims, our objects, our desires, our aspiration, and how different our art! [. . .] It was not until the end of the eighteenth century that the subject really began to make itself felt, and, like the potato blight or phyloxera, it soon became clear that it had come to stay. I think Greuze was the first to conceive a picture after the fashion of a scene in a play – I mean those domestic dramas which he invented, and in which the interest of the subject so clearly predominates.[25] [. . .]. And ever since the subject has taken first place in the art of France, England, and Germany, and in like measure as the subject made itself felt, so did art decline.

For the last hundred years painters seem to have lived in libraries rather than in studios. All literatures and all the sciences have been pressed into the service of painting, and an Academy catalogue is in itself a liberal education. In it you can read choice extracts from the Bible, from Shakespeare, from Goethe, from Dante. You can dip into Greek and Latin literature, history – ancient and modern – you can learn something of all mythologies – Pagan, Christian, and Hindoo; if your taste lies in the direction of Icelandic legends, you will not be disappointed in your sixpennyworth. For the last hundred years the painter seems to have neglected nothing except to learn how to paint.

For more than a hundred years painting has been in service. She has acted as a sort of handmaiden to literature, her mission being to make clear to the casual and the unlettered what the lettered had already understood and enjoyed in a more subtle and more erudite form. [. . .]

When Mr. Holman Hunt conceived the idea of a picture of Christ earning His livelihood by the sweat of His brow, it seemed to him to be quite necessary to go to Jerusalem. There he copied a carpenter's shop from nature, and he filled it with Arab tools and implements, feeling sure that, the manners and customs having changed but little in the East, it was to be surmised that such tools and implements must be nearly identical with those used eighteen centuries ago. To dress the Virgin in sumptuous flowing robes, as Raphael did, was clearly incorrect; the Virgin was a poor woman, and could not have worn more than a single garment, and the garment she wore probably resembled the dress of the Arab women of the present day, and so on and so on. Through the window we see the very landscape that Christ looked upon. From the point of view of the art critic of the *Daily Telegraph* nothing could be better; the various sites and prospects are explained and commented upon, and the heart of middle-class England beats in sympathetic response. But the real picture-lover sees nothing save two geometrically drawn figures placed in the canvas like diagrams in a book of Euclid. And the picture being barren of artistic interest, his attention is caught by the Virgin's costume, and the catalogue informs him that Mr. Hunt's model was an Arab woman in Jerusalem, whose dress in all probability resembled the dress the Virgin wore two thousand years ago. The carpenter's shop he is assured is most probably an exact counterpart of the carpenter's shop in which Christ worked. How very curious! how very curious!

Whistler[26]

In the Nocturnes Mr. Whistler stands alone, without a rival. In portraits he is at his best when they are near to his Nocturnes in intention, when the theme lends itself to an imaginative and decorative treatment; for instance, as in the mother or Miss Alexander. Mr. Whistler is at his worst when he is frankly realistic. [. . .]

The portrait of the mother is, as every one knows, in the Luxemburg[27] [. . .]; and after much hesitation and arguing with myself I feel sure that on the whole this picture is the painter's greatest work in portraiture. We forget relations, friends, perhaps even our parents; but that picture we never forget; it is for ever with us, in sickness and in health; and in moments of extreme despair, when life seems hopeless, the strange magic of that picture springs into consciousness, and we wonder by what strange wizard craft was accomplished the marvellous pattern on the black curtain that drops past the engraving on the wall. We muse on the extraordinary beauty of that grey wall, on the black silhouette sitting so tranquilly, on the large feet on a foot-stool, on the hands crossed, on the long black dress that fills the picture with such solemn harmony. Then mark the transition from grey to white, and how *le ton local* is carried through the entire picture, from the highest light to the deepest shadow. Note the tenderness of that white cap, the white lace cuffs, the certainty, the choice, and think of anything if you can, even in the best Japanese work, more beautiful, more delicate, subtle, illusive, certain in its handicraft; [. . .] And when we study the faint, subtle outline of the mother's face, we seem to feel that there the painter has told the story of his soul more fully than elsewhere. That soul, strangely alive to all that is delicate and illusive in Nature, found perhaps its fullest expression in that grave old Puritan lady looking through the quiet refinement of her grey room, sitting in solemn profile in all the quiet habit of her long life. [. . .] Still, for my own personal pleasure, to satisfy the innermost cravings of my own soul, I would choose to live with the portrait of Miss Alexander.[28] Truly, this picture seems to me the most beautiful in the world. I know very well that it has not the profound beauty of the Infantes by Velasquez in the Louvre; but for pure magic of inspiration, is it not more delightful? Just as Shelley's "Sensitive Plant" thrills the innermost sense like no other poem in the language, the portrait of Miss Alexander enchants with the harmony of colour, with the melody of composition.

Strangely original, a rare and unique thing, is this picture, yet we know whence it came, and may easily appreciate the influences that brought it into being. Exquisite and happy combination of the art of an entire nation and the genius of one man – the soul of Japan incarnate in the body of the immortal Spaniard. It was Japan that counselled the strange grace of the silhouette, and it was that country, too, that inspired in a dim, far-off way those subtly sweet and magical passages from grey to green, from green again to changing evanescent grey. But a higher intelligence massed and impelled those chords of green and grey than ever manifested itself in Japanese fan or screen; the means are simpler, the effect is greater, and by the side of this picture the best Japanese work seems only facile superficial improvisation. In the picture itself there is really little of Japan. The painter merely understood all that Japan might teach. He went to the very root, appropriating only the innermost essence of its art. We Westerns had thought it sufficient to copy Nature, but the Japanese know it was better to observe Nature. The whole art of Japan is selection, and Japan taught Mr. Whistler, or impressed upon Mr. Whistler, the imperative necessity of selection. No Western artist of the present or of past time – no, not Velasquez himself – ever selected from the model so tenderly as Mr. Whistler; Japan taught him to consider Nature as a storehouse whence the artist may pick and choose, combining the fragments of his choice into an exquisite whole.[29] Sir John Millais' art is the opposite; there we find no selection; the model is copied – and sometimes only with sufficient technical skill.

But this picture is throughout a selection from the model; nowhere has anything been copied brutally, yet the reality of the girl is not sacrificed. [. . .] But it was Velasquez that gave consistency and strength to what in Mr. Whistler might have run into an art of trivial but exquisite decoration. Velasquez, too, had a voice in the composition of the palette generally, so sober, so grave. The palette of Velasquez is the opposite of the palette of Rubens; the fantasy of Rubens' palette created the art of Watteau, Turner, Gainsborough; [. . .]. Chardin was the one exception. Alone amid the eighteenth-century painters he chose the palette of Velasquez in preference to that of Rubens, and in the nineteenth century Whistler too has chosen it.[30] It was Velasquez who taught Mr. Whistler that flowing, limpid execution. In the painting of that blonde hair there is something more than a souvenir of the blonde hair of the infante in the *sale carrée* in the Louvre. There is also something of Velasquez in the black notes of the shoes. Those blacks – are they not perfectly observed? How light and dry the colour is! How heavy and shiny it would have become in other hands! Notice, too, that in the frock nowhere is there a single touch of pure white, and yet it is all white – a rich, luminous white that makes every other white in the gallery seem either chalky or dirty. What an enchantment and a delight the handling is! How flowing, how supple, infinitely and beautifully sure, the music of perfect accomplishment! In the portrait of the mother the execution seems slower, hardly so spontaneous. For this, no doubt, the subject is accountable. But this little girl is the very finest flower, and the culminating point of Mr. Whistler's art. The eye travels over the canvas seeking a fault. In vain; nothing has been omitted that might have been included, nothing has been included that might have been omitted. There is much in Velasquez that is stronger, but nothing in this world ever seemed to me so perfect as this picture. [. . .]

I have spoken of his assimilation and combination of the art of Velasquez, and the entire art of Japan, but a still more striking instance of the power of assimilation, which, strange as it may seem, only the most original natures possess, is to hand in the early but extremely beautiful picture, *La femme en blanc*.[31] In the Chelsea period of his life Mr. Whistler saw a great deal of that singular man, Dante Gabriel Rossetti. Intensely Italian, though he had never seen Italy; and though writing no language but ours, still writing it with a strange hybrid grace, bringing into it the rich and voluptuous colour and fragrance of the south, expressing in picture and poem nothing but an uneasy haunting sense of Italy – opulence of women, not of the south, nor yet of the north, Italian celebration, mystic altar linen, and pomp of gold vestment and legendary pane. Of such hauntings Rossetti's life and art were made.

His hold on poetic form was surer than his hold on pictorial form, wherein his art is hardly more than poetic reminiscence of Italian missal and window pane. Yet even as a painter his attractiveness cannot be denied, nor yet the influence he has exercised on English art. Though he took nothing from his contemporaries, all took from him, poets and painters alike. Not even Mr. Whistler could refrain, and in *La femme en blanc* he took from Rossetti his manner of feeling and seeing. The type of woman is the same – beauty of dreaming eyes and abundant hair. And in this picture we find a poetic interest, a moral sense, if I may so phrase it, nowhere else to be detected, though you search Mr. Whistler's work from end to end. The woman stands idly dreaming by her mirror. She is what is her image in the glass, an appearance that has come, and that will go leaving no more trace than her reflection on the glass when she herself has moved away. She sees in her dream the world like passing shadows thrown on an illuminated cloth. She thinks of her soft, white, and opulent beauty which fills her white dress; her chin is lifted, and above her face shines the golden tumult of her hair.[. . .]

It was with the night that Mr. Whistler set his seal and sign-manual upon art; above all others he is surely the interpreter of the night. Until he came the night of the painter was as ugly and insignificant as any pitch barrel; it was he who first transferred to canvas the blue transparent darkness which folds the world from sunset to sunrise. The purple hollow, and all the illusive distances of the gas-lit river, are Mr. Whistler's own. It was not the unhabited night of lonely plain and desolate tarn that he chose to interpret, but the difficult populous city night – the night of tall bridges and vast water rained through with lights red and grey, the shores lined with the lamps of the watching city. Mr. Whistler's night is the vast blue and golden caravanry, where the jaded and the hungry and the heavy-hearted lay down their burdens, and the contemplative freed from the deceptive reality of the day understand humbly and pathetically the casualness of our habitation, and the limitless reality of a plan, the intention of which we shall never know. Mr. Whistler's nights are the blue transparent darknesses which are half of the world's life. [. . .] More than any other painter, Mr. Whistler's influence has made itself felt on English art. More than any other man, Mr. Whistler has helped to purge art of the vice of subject and belief that the mission of the artist is to copy nature. Mr. Whistler's method is more learned, more co-ordinate than that of any other painter of our time; all is preconceived from the first touch to the last, nor has there ever been much change in the method, the painting has grown looser, but the method was always the same; to have seen him paint at once is to have seen him paint at every moment of his life. Never did a man seem more admirably destined to found a school which should worthily carry on the tradition inherited from the old masters and represented only by him. All the younger generation has accepted him as master, and that my generation has not profited more than it has, leads me to think, however elegant, refined, emotional, educated it may be, and anxious to achieve, that it is lacking in creative force, that it is, in a word, slightly too slight.

OSCAR WILDE (1854–1900)

Oscar Fingal O'Flahertie Wills Wilde, the son of an eminent Dublin surgeon and a famous literary hostess, seemed destined for renown from an early age. A precocious interest in Greek literature in his teens enabled him to progress rapidly to Trinity College, Dublin, where he excelled in Classics, and from there he went to Magdalen College, Oxford, and even greater success. In 1878 he not only achieved first class Honours, but also won the Newdigate Prize for his poem 'Ravenna', containing a most unscholarly eulogy of Byron. His passion for the Hellenic world affected Wilde's thought throughout his life, but at Oxford he discovered other attractions in the then nascent phenomenon of Aestheticism. He attended Ruskin's Slade lectures, and for a time became an enthusiastic disciple of social service, joining the motley band of undergraduates who mended the Hinksey Road under Ruskin's direction. It was, however, to the contrary charm of Walter Pater that the young Wilde succumbed most fully. He called *The Renaissance* 'the most perfect book of modern times', and ever afterwards his work was larded with references to, echoes of, and unacknowledged borrowings from the hieratic don of Brasenose. He left Oxford in 1878, confident of his developing powers and ready to launch himself in the fashionable world of literary London.

Wilde has long been the figure most clearly associated with the Aesthetic Movement in England, and this is primarily due to his success in establishing himself in that glittering London world. His succession of brilliant stage comedies, with their sparkling blend of epigram and repartee, captivated audiences then as now. Within a few years he was in great demand for reviews and had become editor of a popular magazine. Yet the true source of his notoriety was not literary; to an even greater degree than Whistler, Wilde possessed a gift for self-advertisement and display. Indeed, it has often been remarked that whereas he put his talent into his work, his genius went into his life. Yeats said that he had never heard a man speak in such perfect sentences, as if he had written them out and corrected them the night before. Certainly his abilities as a *raconteur* and table wit were assiduously cultivated, with the effect that he was soon the most desired guest for smart London hostesses. He increased his reputation in this regard by several successful appearances as a lecturer. Perhaps more significantly his elaborate dress, varying between the severely correct and the outlandish, seemed to make him the final realization of Baudelaire's dandy. One of Wilde's own aphorisms sums up his intentions: 'One should either be a work of art or wear a work of art.' For much of his life, Wilde's energies were devoted to making himself just such an aesthetic object, a dazzling creation of language and style which could not help but be noticed.

In this effort of self-promotion Wilde drew together many of the artistic and critical ideas which had long formed the muted cultural undercurrent of England, and proceeded to give them clear and vivid form. He became, to adapt Pater's image, a sort of living glass which gathered the scattered rays of aesthetic thought and fused them into a burning focus. The more one looks through the glare, however, the more one finds a curious amalgam of other people's ideas as paradoxically linked as any of his epigrams. The earliest coherent statement of his position occurs in a lecture composed for his highly successful American tour in 1882. 'The English Renaissance of Art' (q.v.) is made up largely of plagiarisms from Ruskin, Morris and Pater – yet Wilde brought to the ideas of his predecessors an original stamp of clarity. He expressly identifies the new 'Renaissance' in England with the Pre-Raphaelites, and more importantly, he articulates clearly the Romantic context of the development. Here for the first time Keats is elevated to the head of the Pantheon, as Wilde stresses the importance of formal values as ends in themselves. This perception is further accompanied by the deliberate turn away from the high romantic faith in a transcendent realm of Eternity or Being – a faith which had supported Ruskin, the P.R.B., even Baudelaire. As a consequence Pater's implicit tendency to regard art as the ultimate value in life, a religion in its own right, is now brought forward and articulated with great boldness. Finally, Wilde acutely perceives the immense self-consciousness of this later phase of thought, and his emphasis on the importance of conscious crafting in verse and prose, on experiments to improve form and technique, at several points foreshadows the modernist doctrines of our own century.

Significantly, in this early lecture Wilde quotes William Blake to support a contention that the greatest art is delineated by a clear, firm outline. This concept was in keeping with his devotion to Hellenic lightness and clarity, but it ran counter to the powerful aesthetic of Baudelaire and Whistler, which elevated the more indistinct and affective medium of colour. From this hint it might have been expected that his relations with the American painter would come to grief. For a time Wilde attached himself to Whistler in a relation that was perfectly harmonious – so long as Whistler felt himself to be the master. But Wilde was not a man to remain subservient to anyone for long, and the friendship soured after Wilde's teasingly critical reviews of the 'Ten O'clock Lecture'. Besides this rivalry over who would command the Aesthetic Movement in England, there were fundamental disagreements between the two men. In contrast to Whistler's sacrifices to his work, Wilde ultimately believed that Art should serve as the inspiration to Life – a view which places an aesthetically arranged life above the work of art, as he argued at length in 'The Relation of Dress to Art' (q.v.). Elsewhere he expressed the matter succinctly: 'the young dandy sought to be somebody rather than to do something. He recognized that life itself is an art, and has its modes of style no less than the arts that seek to express it.' It was this kind of success that Wilde aspired to. For him life was an art, an infinitely flexible thing to be modelled according to one's own desires, one's own sense of fitness. His whole brilliant performance in the early eighties – the endless monologues, the epigrams, the business of living by his wits and making up a career as he went along – is an illustration of this principle.

Wilde's ideas become more paradoxical still, for while dissociating art from a transcendent aspiration, he imagined Beauty as an ideal, self-enclosed realm, aloof from contemporary reality. A dandy himself, he affected to loathe the modern habit of dress, and denounced the growing tendency to treat 'modern' subjects, the urban and industrial landscape, in art. This strain of thought hearkens back to Rossetti and the Pre-Raphaelites, and Wilde made his feelings clear in a striking review of a biography of Rossetti (q.v.). Here he warmly celebrates the inspiration of Rossetti's art and personality and distinguishes the obscuring accidents of a man's life from its spiritual essence – a lesson the current biographers of Wilde have found hard to learn. It was in his reviews of Pater's work (qq.v.) however, that Wilde expressed his deepest allegiances. His appreciation of Pater's mastery of prose is everywhere coupled to a deep sense of the deliberate creation of an artificial world which Pater undertook. It was this world of pure formal values and self-conscious style which formed the starting point of Wilde's own creative endeavour, and the extended quotation from Pater's essay on Wordsworth which closed his review of *Appreciations*, a paean to being rather than doing, is in effect a homage to his origins.

It is finally in this wholly artificial world, linked to but not dependent upon contemporary reality, that Wilde is most at home. He is at his best in expounding the paradoxes of artifice, both in his plays and in the sparkling imaginary dialogue, 'The Decay of Lying' (q.v.), which is perhaps the most elaborate and entertaining statement of Wilde's critical position. The dialogue can be read as one sustained attack upon the original Ruskinian idea of 'truth to Nature'. In contrast, Wilde asserts, 'Art never expresses anything but itself'; it is a hermetic, self-referring, self-sustaining world of formal concerns and artificial beauty. Thus the dialogue incorporates his strongest attacks on 'modern' subject matter (implicating, but not mentioning Whistler), as well as on the ethical calculus of the Philistine world. Similar beliefs are distilled in the two series of aphorisms which close this selection, perhaps best summed up in the opening epigram of 'Phrases and Philosophies for the Young': 'One's first duty in life is to be as artificial as possible.'

Ultimately Wilde extended – some would say, vulgarized – Pater's disciplined, hieratic beliefs in the saving power of art. If the keynote for Pater had been restraint, that of Wilde was relaxation – indeed in his review of *Imaginary Portraits* he complained of the master's too severe control. He pursued this doctrine of relaxation earnestly in both his life and his art, never fully channelling his imaginative energies and carelessly exposing his incautious homosexual affairs. The latter brought about the notorious series of trials and the prison sentence which capped his fall and made him, in the end, an even greater martyr to an ideal of style than Pater had been. Nevertheless, in the course of his life Wilde crystallized the stream of aesthetic ideas more dramatically and effectively than anyone before him had done, and in that effort helped to make them part of an enduring legacy to the modern world.

The English Renaissance of Art[1]

Among the many debts which we owe to that supreme aesthetic faculty of Goethe is that he was the first to teach us to define beauty in terms the most concrete possible, to realise it, I mean, always in its special manifestations. So, in the lecture which I have the honour to deliver before you, I will not try to give you any abstract definition of beauty [. . .] but rather to point out to you the general ideas which characterise the great English Renaissance of Art in this century, to discover their source, as far as that is possible, and to estimate their future as far as that is possible.

I call it our English Renaissance because it is indeed a sort of new birth of the spirit of man, like the great Italian Renaissance of the fifteenth century, in its desire for a more gracious and comely way of life, its passion for physical beauty, its exclusive attention to form, its seeking for new subjects for poetry, new forms of art, new intellectual and imaginative enjoyments: and I call it our romantic movement because it is our most recent expression of beauty.[2] [. . .] We must always remember that art has only one sentence to utter: there is for her only one high law, the law of form or harmony – yet between the classical and romantic spirit we may say that there lies this difference at least, that the one deals with the type and the other with the exception. In the work produced under the modern romantic spirit it is no longer the permanent, the essential truths of life that are treated of; it is the momentary situation of the one, the momentary aspect of the other that art seeks to render. [. . .]

Alien then from any wild, political passion, or from the harsh voice of a rude people in revolt, as our English Renaissance must seem, in its passionate cult of pure beauty, its flawless devotion to form, its exclusive and sensitive nature, it is to the French Revolution that we must look for the most primary factor of its production, the first condition of its birth: that great Revolution of which we are all the children, though the voices of some of us be often loud against it; that Revolution to which at a time when even such spirits as Coleridge and Wordsworth lost heart in England, noble messages of love blown across seas came from your young Republic. [. . .]

Yet in the womb of the Revolution itself, and in the storm and terror of that wild time, tendencies were hidden away that the artistic Renaissance bent to her own service when the time came – a scientific tendency first, which has borne in our own day a brood of somewhat noisy Titans, yet in the sphere of poetry has not been unproductive of good. I do not mean merely in its adding to enthusiasm that intellectual basis which is its strength, or that more obvious influence about which Wordsworth was thinking when he said very nobly that poetry was merely the impassioned expression in the face of science, and that when science would put on a form of flesh and blood the poet would lend his divine spirit to aid the transfiguration. Nor do I dwell much on the great cosmical emotion and deep pantheism of science to which Shelley has given its first and Swinburne its latest glory of song, but rather on its influence on the artistic spirit in preserving that close observation and the sense of limitation as well as of clearness of vision which are the characteristics of the real artist.[3]

The great and golden rule of art as well as of life, wrote William Blake, is that the more distinct, sharp and defined the boundary line, the more perfect is the work of art; and the less keen and sharp the greater is the evidence of weak imitation, plagiarism and bungling. 'Great inventors in all ages knew this – Michael Angelo and Albert Dürer are known by this and by this alone'; and another time he wrote, with all the simple directness of nineteenth-century prose, 'to generalise is to be an idiot.'[4]

And this love of definite conception, this clearness of vision, this artistic sense of limit, is the characteristic of all great work and poetry; of the vision of Homer as of the vision of Dante, of Keats and William Morris as of Chaucer and Theocritus. It lies at the base of all noble, realistic and romantic work as opposed to colourless and empty abstractions of our own eighteenth-century poets and of the classical dramatists of France, or of the vague spiritualities of the German sentimental school: opposed, too, to that spirit of transcendentalism which also was root and flower itself of the great Revolution, underlying the impassioned contemplation of Wordsworth and giving wings and fire to the eagle-like flight of Shelley, and which in the sphere of philosophy, though displaced by the materialism and positiveness of our day, bequeathed two great schools of thought, the school of Newman to Oxford, the school of Emerson to America. Yet is this spirit of transcendentalism alien to the spirit of art. For the artist can accept no sphere of life in exchange for life itself. For him there is no escape from the bondage of the earth: there is not even the desire of escape.[5]

He is indeed the only true realist: symbolism, which is the essence of the transcendental spirit, is alien to him. The metaphysical mind of Asia will create for itself the monstrous, many-breasted idol of Ephesus, but to the Greek, pure artist, that work is most instinct with spiritual life which conforms most clearly to the perfect facts of physical life. [. . .]

And soon that desire for perfection, which lay at the base of the Revolution, found in a young English poet its most complete and flawless realisation.

Phidias and the achievements of Greek art are foreshadowed in Homer: Dante prefigures for us the passion and colour and intensity of Italian painting: the modern love of landscape dates from Rousseau, and it is in Keats that one discerns the beginning of the artistic renaissance of England.

Byron was a rebel and Shelley a dreamer; but in the calmness and clearness of his vision, his perfect self-control, his unerring sense of beauty and his recognition of a separate realm for the imagination, Keats was the pure and serene artist, the forerunner of the Pre-Raphaelite school, and so of the great romantic movement of which I am to speak.

Blake had indeed, before him, claimed for art a lofty, spiritual mission, and had striven to raise design to the ideal level of poetry and music, but the remoteness of his vision both in painting and poetry and the incompleteness of his technical powers had been adverse to any real influence. It is in Keats that the artistic spirit of this century first found its absolute incarnation.

And these Pre-Raphaelites, what were they? If you ask nine-tenths of the British public what is the meaning of the word aesthetics, they will tell you it is the French for affectation or the German for a dado; and if you inquire about the pre-Raphaelites you will hear something about an eccentric lot of young men to whom a sort of divine crookedness and holy awkwardness in drawing were the chief objects of art. To know nothing about their great men is one of the necessary elements of English education. [. . .]

As regards the ideas these young men brought to the regeneration of English art, we may see at the base of their artistic creations a desire for a deeper spiritual value to be given to art as well as a more decorative value.

Pre-Raphaelites they called themselves; not that they imitated the early Italian masters at all, but that in their work, as opposed to the facile abstractions of Raphael, they found a stronger realism of imagination, a more careful realism of technique, a vision at once more fervent and more vivid, an individuality more intimate and more intense.

For it is not enough that a work of art should conform to the aesthetic demands of its age: there must be also about it, if it is to affect us with any permanent delight, the impress of a distinct individuality, an individuality remote from that of ordinary men, and coming near to us only by virtue of a certain newness and wonder in the work, and through channels whose very strangeness makes us more ready to give them welcome.

La personnalité, said one of the greatest of modern French critics, *voilà ce qui nous sauvera.*[6] [. . .]

But the revolution accomplished by this clique of young men, with Ruskin's faultless and fervent eloquence to help them, was not one of ideas merely but of execution, not one of conceptions but of creations.

For the great eras in the history of the development of all the arts have been eras not of increased feeling or enthusiasm in feeling for art, but of new technical improvements primarily and specially.[7] [. . .]

And so it is in poetry also: all this love of curious French metres like the Ballade, the Villanelle, the Rondel; all this increased value laid on elaborate alliterations, and on curious words and refrains, such as you will find in Dante Rossetti and Swinburne, is merely the attempt to perfect flute and viol and trumpet through which the spirit of the age and the lips of the poet may blow the music of their many messages.

And so it has been with this romantic movement of ours: it is a reaction against the empty conventional workmanship, the lax execution of previous poetry and painting, showing itself in the work of such men as Rossetti and Burne-Jones by a far greater splendour of colour, a far more intricate wonder of design than English imaginative art has shown before. In Rossetti's poetry and the poetry of Morris, Swinburne and Tennyson a perfect precision and choice of language, a style flawless and fearless, a seeking for all sweet and precious melodies and a sustaining consciousness of the musical value of each word are opposed to that value which is merely intellectual. In this respect they are one with the romantic movement of France of which not the least characteristic note was struck by Théophile Gautier's advice to the young poet to read his dictionary every day, as being the only book worth a poet's reading.

While, then, the material of workmanship is being thus elaborated and discovered to have in itself incommunicable and eternal qualities of its own, qualities entirely satisfying to the poetic sense and not needing for their aesthetic effect any lofty intellectual vision, any deep criticism of life or even any passionate human emotion at all, the spirit and the method of the poet's working – what people call his inspiration – have not escaped the controlling influence of the artistic spirit. Not that the imagination has lost its wings, but we have accustomed ourselves to count their innumerable pulsations, to estimate their limitless strength, to govern their ungovernable freedom.

To the Greeks this problem of the conditions of poetic production, and the places occupied by either spontaneity or self-consciousness in any artistic work, had a peculiar fascination. We find it in the mysticism of Plato and in the rationalism of Aristotle. We find it later in the Italian Renaissance agitating the minds of such men as Leonardo da Vinci. Schiller tried to adjust the balance between form and feeling, and Goethe to estimate the position of self-consciousness in art. Wordsworth's definition of poetry as 'emotion remembered in tranquillity' may be taken as an analysis of one of the stages through which all imaginative work has to pass; and in Keats's longing to be 'able to compose without this fever' (I quote from one of his letters), his desire to substitute for poetic ardour 'a more thoughtful and quiet power,' we may discern the most important moment in the evolution of that artistic life. The question made an early and strange appearance in your literature too; and I need not remind you how deeply the young poets of the French romantic movement were excited and stirred by Edgar Allan Poe's analysis of the workings of his own imagination in the creating of that supreme imaginative work which we know by the name of *The Raven*.

In the last century, when the intellectual and didactic element had intruded to such an extent into the kingdom which belongs to poetry, it was against the claims of the understanding that an artist like Goethe had to protest. 'The more incomprehensible to the understanding a poem is the better for it,' he said once, asserting the complete supremacy of the imagination in poetry as of reason in prose. But in this century it is rather against the claims of the emotional faculties, the claims of mere sentiment and feeling, that the artist must react. The simple utterance of joy is not poetry any more than a mere personal cry of pain, and the real experiences of the artist are always those which do not find their direct expression but are gathered up and absorbed into some artistic form which seems, from such real experiences, to be the farthest removed and the most alien.

'The heart contains passion but the imagination alone contains poetry,' says Charles Baudelaire. This too was the lesson that Théophile Gautier, most subtle of all modern critics, most fascinating of all modern poets, was never tired of teaching – 'Everybody is affected by a sunrise or a sunset.' The absolute distinction of the artist is not his capacity to feel nature so much as his power of rendering it. The entire subordination of all intellectual and emotional faculties to the vital and informing poetic principle is the surest sign of the strength of our Renaissance.

We have seen the artistic spirit working, first in the delightful and technical sphere of language, the sphere of expression as opposed to subject, then controlling the imagination of the poet in dealing with his subject. And now I would point out to you its operation in the choice of subject. The recognition of a separate realm for the artist, a consciousness of the absolute difference between the world of art and the world of real fact, between classic grace and absolute reality, forms not merely the essential element of any aesthetic charm but is the characteristic of all great imaginative work and of all great eras of artistic creation – of the age of Phidias as of the age of Michael Angelo, of the age of Sophocles as of the age of Goethe.

Art never harms itself by keeping aloof from the social problems of the day: rather, by so doing, it more completely realises for us that which we desire. For to most of us the real life is the life we do not lead, and thus, remaining more true to the essence of its own perfection, more jealous of its own unattainable beauty, is less likely to forget form in feeling or to accept the passion of creation as any substitute for the beauty of the created thing.[8] [. . .]

There is indeed a poetical attitude to be adopted towards all things, but all things are not fit subjects for poetry. Into the secure and sacred house of Beauty the true artist will admit nothing that is harsh or disturbing, nothing that gives pain, nothing that is debatable, nothing about which men argue. He can steep himself, if he wishes, in the discussion of all the social problems of his day, poor-laws and local taxation, free trade and bimetallic currency, and the like; but when he writes on these subjects it will be, as Milton nobly expressed it, with his left hand, in prose and not in verse, in a pamphlet and not in a lyric. This exquisite spirit of artistic choice was not in Byron: Wordsworth had it not. In the work of both these men there is much that we have to reject, much that does not give us that sense of calm and perfect repose which should be the effect of all fine, imaginative work. But in Keats it seemed to have been incarnate, and in his lovely *Ode on a Grecian Urn* it found its most secure and fautless expression; in the pageant of *The Earthly Paradise* and the knights and ladies of Burne-Jones it is the one dominant note. [. . .]

And so in our own day, also, the two most vital tendencies of the nineteenth century – the democratic and pantheistic tendency and the tendency to value life for the sake of art – found their most complete and perfect utterance in the poetry of Shelley and Keats who, to the blind eyes of their own time, seemed to be as wanderers in the wilderness, preachers of vague or unreal things. And I remember once, in talking to Mr. Burne-Jones about modern science, his saying to me, 'the more materialistic science becomes, the more angels shall I paint: their wings are my protest in favour of the immortality of the soul.' [. . .]

But this restless modern intellectual spirit of ours is not receptive enough of the sensuous element of art; and so the real influence of the arts is hidden from many of us: only a few, escaping from the tyranny of the soul, have learned the secret of those high hours when thought is not.

And this indeed is the reason of the influence which Eastern art is having on us in Europe, and of the fascination of all Japanese work. While the Western world has been laying on art the intolerable burden of its own intellectual doubts and the spiritual tragedy of its own sorrows, the East has always kept true to art's primary and pictorial conditions.

In judging of a beautiful statue the aesthetic faculty is absolutely and completely gratified by the splendid curves of those marble lips that are dumb to our complaint, the noble modelling of those limbs that are powerless to help us. In its primary aspect a painting has no more spiritual message or meaning than an exquisite fragment of Venetian glass or a blue tile from the wall of Damascus: it is a beautifully coloured surface, nothing more.[9] The channels by which all noble imaginative work in painting should touch, and do touch the soul, are not those of the truths of life, nor metaphysical truths. But that pictorial charm which does not depend on any literary reminiscence for its effect on the one hand, nor is yet a mere result of communicable technical skill on the other, comes of a certain inventive and creative handling of colour. Nearly always in Dutch painting and often in the works of Giorgione or Titian, it is entirely independent of anything definitely poetical in the subject, a kind of form and choice in workmanship which is itself entirely satisfying, and is (as the Greeks would say) an end in itself.

And so in poetry too, the real poetical quality, the joy of poetry, comes never from the subject but from an inventive handling of rhythmical language, from what Keats called the 'sensuous life of verse.' The element of song in the singing accompanied by the profound joy of motion, is so sweet that, while the incomplete lives of ordinary men bring no healing power with them, the thorn-crown of the poet will blossom into roses for our pleasure; for our delight his despair will gild its own thorns, and his pain, like Adonis, be beautiful in its agony; and when the poet's heart breaks it will break in music.

And health in art – what is that? It has nothing to do with a sane criticism of life. There is more health in Baudelaire than there is in [Kingsley]. Health is the artist's recognition of the limitations of the form in which he works. It is the honour and the homage which he gives to the material he uses – whether it be language with its glories, or marble or pigment with their glories – knowing that the true brotherhood of the arts consists

1. Walter Pater in 1872 (reproduced by permission of the BBC Hulton Picture Library)

2. Whistler, caricature of Oscar Wilde (reproduced by permission of the Hunterian Art Gallery, Glasgow)

3. Degas, *Rehearsal on the Stage* (reproduced by permission of the Metropolitan Museum of Art, New York)

4. Degas, *The Tub* (reproduced by permission of the Hill-Stead Museum, Farmington, Connecticut)

5. Monticelli, *Sunset* (reproduced by permission of The National Gallery, London)

6. Monticelli, *Meeting in a Park* (reproduced by permission of the The National Gallery, London)

not in their borrowing one another's method, but in their producing, each of them by its own individual means, each of them by keeping its objective limits, the same unique artistic delight. The delight is like that given to us by music – for music is the art in which form and matter are always one, the art whose subject cannot be separated from the method of its expression, the art which most completely realises the artistic ideal, and is the condition to which all the other arts are constantly aspiring.

And criticism – what place is that to have in our culture? [. . .] The true critic addresses not the artist ever but the public only. His work lies with them. Art can never have any other claim but her own perfection: it is for the critic to create for art the social aim, too, by teaching the people the spirit in which they are to approach all artistic work, the love they are to give it, the lesson they are to draw from it.

All these appeals to art to set herself more in harmony with modern progress and civilisation, and to make herself the mouthpiece for the voice of humanity, these appeals to art 'to have a mission,' are appeals which should be made to the public. The art which has fulfilled the conditions of beauty has fulfilled all conditions: it is for the critic to teach the people how to find in the calm of such art the highest expression of their own most stormy passions. 'I have no reverence,' said Keats, 'for the public, nor for anything in existence but the Eternal Being, the memory of great men and the principle of Beauty.'[10]

Such then is the principle which I believe to be guiding and underlying our English Renaissance, a Renaissance many-sided and wonderful, productive of strong ambitions and lofty personalities, yet for all its splendid achievements in poetry and in the decorative arts and in painting, for all the increased comeliness and grace of dress, and the furniture of houses and the like, not complete. For there can be no great sculpture without a beautiful national life, and the commercial spirit of England has killed that; no great drama without a noble national life, and the commercial spirit of England has killed that too. [. . .]

Love art for its own sake, and then all things that you need will be added to you.

This devotion to beauty and to the creation of beautiful things is the test of all great civilised nations. Philosophy may teach us to bear with equanimity the misfortunes of our neighbours, and science resolve the moral sense into a secretion of sugar, but art is what makes the life of each citizen a sacrament and not a speculation, art is what makes the life of the whole race immortal.

For beauty is the only thing that time cannot harm. Philosophies fall away like sand, and creeds follow one another like the withered leaves of autumn; but what is beautiful is a joy for all seasons and a possession for all eternity. [. . .]

We spend our days, each one of us, in looking for the secret of life. Well, the secret of life is in art.

The Relation of Dress to Art
A note in black and white on Mr. Whistler's lecture[11]

'How can you possibly paint these ugly three-cornered hats?' asked a reckless art critic once of Sir Joshua Reynolds. 'I see light and shade in them,' answered the artist. '*Les grands coloristes*,' says Baudelaire, in a charming article on the artistic value of frock coats, '*les grands coloristes savent faire de la couleur avec un habit noir, une cravate blanche, et un fond gris.*'[12]

'Art seeks and finds the beautiful in all times, as did her high priest Rembrandt, when he saw the picturesque grandeur of the Jews' quarter of Amsterdam, and lamented not that its inhabitants were not Greeks,' were the fine and simple words used by Mr. Whistler in one of the most valuable passages of his lecture. The most valuable, that is, to the painter: for there is nothing of which the ordinary English painter needs more to be reminded than that the true artist does not wait for life to be made picturesque for him, but sees life under picturesque conditions always – under conditions, that is to say, which are at once new and delightful. But between the attitude of the painter towards the public and the attitude of a people towards art, there is a wide difference. That, under certain conditions of light and shade, what is ugly in fact may in its effect become beautiful, is true; and this, indeed, is the real *modernité* of art: but these conditions are exactly what we cannot be always sure of, as we stroll down Piccadilly in the glaring vulgarity of the noonday, or lounge in the park with a foolish sunset as a background. Were we able to carry our *chiaroscuro* about with us, as we do our umbrellas, all would be well; but this being impossible, I hardly think that pretty and delightful people will continue to wear a style of dress as ugly as it is useless and as meaningless as it is monstrous, even on the chance of such a master as Mr. Whistler spiritualising them into a symphony or refining them into a mist. For the arts are made for life, and not life for the arts.

Nor do I feel quite sure that Mr. Whistler has been himself always true to the dogma he seems to lay down, that a painter should paint only the dress of his age and of his actual surroundings: far be it from me to burden a butterfly with the heavy responsibility of its past: I have always been of opinion that consistency is the last refuge of the unimaginative: but have we not all seen, and most of us admired, a picture from his hand of exquisite English girls strolling by an opal sea in the fantastic dresses of Japan? Has not Tite Street been thrilled with the tidings that the models of Chelsea were posing to the master, in peplums, for pastels?

Whatever comes from Mr. Whistler's brush is far too perfect in its loveliness to stand or fall by any intellectual dogmas on art, even by his own: for Beauty is justifed of all her children, and cares nothing for explanations: but it is impossible to look through any collection of modern pictures in London, from Burlington House to the Grosvenor Gallery, without feeling that the professional model is ruining painting and reducing it to a condition of mere pose and *pastiche*. [. . .]

For all costumes are caricatures. The basis of Art is not the Fancy Ball. Where there is loveliness of dress, there is no dressing up. And so, were our national attire delightful in colour, and in construction simple and sincere; were dress the expression of the loveliness that it shields and of the swiftness and motion that it does not impede; did its lines break from the shoulder instead of bulging from the waist; did the inverted wineglass cease to be the ideal of form; were these things brought about, as brought about they will be, then would painting be no longer an artificial reaction against the ugliness of life, but become, as it should be, the natural expression of life's beauty. Nor would painting merely, but all the other arts also, be the gainers by a change such as that which I propose; the gainers, I mean, through the increased atmosphere of Beauty by which the artists would be surrounded and in which they would grow up. For Art is not to be taught in Academies. It is what one looks at, not what one listens to, that makes the artist. The real schools should be the streets. There is not, for instance, a single delicate line, or delightful proportion, in the dress of the Greeks, which is not echoed exquisitely in their architecture. A nation arrayed in stove-pipe hats and dress-improvers might have built the Pantechnichon possibly, but the Parthenon never. And finally, there is this to be said: Art, it is true, can never have any other claim but her own perfection, and it may be that the artist, desiring merely to contemplate and to create, is wise in not busying himself about change in others: yet wisdom is not the level of common-sense; and from the passionate folly of those – and there are many – who desire that Beauty shall be confined no longer to the *bric-à-brac* of the collector and the dust of the museum, but shall be, as it should be, the natural and national inheritance of all, – from this noble unwisdom, I say, who knows what new loveliness shall be given to life, and, under these more exquisite conditions, what perfect artist born? *Le milieu se renouvelant, l'art se renouvelle.*

Speaking, however, from his own passionless pedestal, Mr. Whistler, in pointing out that the power of the painter is to be found in his power of vision, not in his cleverness of hand, has expressed a truth which needed expression, and which, coming from the lord of form and colour, cannot fail to have its influence. His lecture, the Apocrypha though it be for the people, yet remains from this time as the Bible for the painter, the masterpiece of masterpieces, the song of songs. It is true he has pronounced the panegyric of the Philistine, but I fancy Ariel praising Caliban for a jest: and, in that he has read the Commination Service over the critics, let all men thank him, the critics themselves, indeed, most of all, for he has now relieved them from the necessity of a tedious existence. Considered, again, merely as an orator, Mr. Whistler seems to me to stand almost alone. Indeed, among all our public speakers I know but few who can combine so felicitously as he does the mirth and malice of Puck with the style of the minor prophets.

A Cheap Edition of a Great Man[13]

Formerly we used to canonise our great men; nowadays we vulgarise them. The vulgarisation of Rossetti has been going on for some time past with really remarkable success, and there seems no probability at present of the process being discontinued. The grass was hardly green upon the quiet grave in Birchington churchyard when Mr. Hall Caine and Mr. William Sharp rushed into print with their Memoirs and Recollections.[14] Then came the usual mob of magazine-hacks with their various views and attitudes, and now Mr. Joseph Knight has produced for the edification of the British public a popular biography of the poet of the Blessed Damozel, the painter of Dante's Dream.

It is only fair to state that Mr. Knight's work is much better than that of his predecessors in the same field. His book is, on the whole, modestly and simply written; whatever its other faults may be, it is at least free from affectation of any kind; and it makes no serious pretence at being either exhaustive or definitive. Yet the best we can say of it is that it is just the sort of biography Guildenstern might have written of Hamlet. Nor does its unsatisfactory character come merely from the ludicrous inadequacy of the materials at Mr. Knight's disposal; it is the whole scheme and method of the book that is radically wrong. Rossetti's was a great personality, and personalities such as his do not easily survive shilling primers. Sooner or later they have inevitably to come down to the level of their biographers, and in the present instance nothing could be more absolutely commonplace than the picture Mr. Knight gives us of the wonderful seer and singer whose life he has so recklessly essayed to write.

No doubt there are many people who will be deeply interested to know that Rossetti was once chased round his garden by an infuriated zebu he was tying to exhibit to Mr. Whistler, or that he had a great affection for a dog called 'Dizzy,' or that 'sloshy' was one of his favourite words of contempt, or that Mr. Gosse thought him very like Chaucer in appearance, or that he had 'an absolute disqualification' for whist-playing, or that he was very fond of quoting the *Bab Ballads*, or that he once said that if he could live by writing poetry he would see painting d—d![15] For our part, however, we cannot help expressing our regret that such a shallow and superficial biography as this should ever have been published. It is but a sorry task to rip the twisted ravel from the worn garment of life and to turn the grout in a drained cup. Better, after all, that we knew a painter only through his vision and a poet through his song, than that the image of a great man should be marred and made mean for us by the clumsy geniality of good intentions. A true artist, and such Rossetti undoubtedly was, reveals himself so perfectly in his work, that unless a biographer has something more valuable to give us than idle anecdotes and unmeaning tales, his labour is misspent and his industry misdirected. [. . .]

We sincerely hope that there will soon be an end to all biographies of this kind. They rob life of much of its dignity and its wonder, add to death itself a new terror, and make one wish that all art were anonymous. Nor could there have been any more unfortunate choice of a subject for popular treatment than that to which we owe the memoir that now lies before us. A pillar of fire to the few who knew him, and of cloud to the few who knew him not, Dante Gabriel Rossetti lived apart from the gossip and tittle-tattle of a shallow age. He never trafficked with the merchants for his soul, nor brought his wares into the market-place for the idle to gape at. Passionate and romantic though he was, yet there was in his nature something of high austerity. He loved seclusion, and hated notoriety, and would have shuddered at the idea that within a few years after his death he was to make his appearance in a series of popular biographies, sandwiched between the author of *Pickwick* and the Great Lexicographer. One man alone, the friend his verse won for him, did he desire should write his life, and it is to Mr. Theodore Watts that we, too, must look to give us the real Rossetti. It may be admitted at once that Mr. Watt's subject has for the moment been a little spoiled for him. Rude hands have touched it, and unmusical voices have made it sound almost common in our ears. Yet none the less is it for him to tell us of the marvel of this man whose art he has analysed with such exquisite insight, whose life he knows as no one else can know it, whom he so loyally loved and tended, and by whom he was so loyally beloved in turn. As for the others, the scribblers and nibblers of literature, if they indeed reverence Rossetti's memory, let them pay him the one homage he would most have valued, the gracious homage of silence. 'Though you can fret me, yet you cannot play upon me,' says Hamlet to his false friend, and even so might Rossetti speak to those well-intentioned mediocrities who would seem to know his stops and would sound him to the top of his compass. True, they cannot fret him now, for he has passed beyond the possibility of pain; yet they cannot play upon him either; it is not for them to pluck out the heart of his mystery.

Mr. Pater's *Imaginary Portraits*[16]

To convey ideas through the medium of images has always been the aim of those who are artists as well as thinkers in literature, and it is to a desire to give a sensuous environment to intellectual concepts that we owe Mr. Pater's last volume. For these Imaginary or, as we should prefer to call them, Imaginative Portraits of his, form a series of philosophic studies in which the philosophy is tempered by personality, and the thought shown under varying conditions of mood and manner, the very permanence of each principle gaining something through the change and colour of the life through which it finds expression. The most fascinating of all these pictures is undoubtedly that of Sebastian Van Storck. The account of Watteau is perhaps a little too fanciful, and the description of him as one who was 'always a seeker after something in the world, that is there in no satisfying measure, or not at all,' seems to us more applicable to him who saw Mona Lisa sitting among the rocks than to the gay and debonair *peintre des fêtes galantes*. But Sebastian, the grave young Dutch philosopher, is charmingly drawn. [. . .]

On the whole, [. . .] this is a singularly attractive book. Mr. Pater is an intellectual impressionist. He does not weary us with any definite doctrine or seek to suit life to any formal creed. He is always looking for exquisite moments and, when he has found them, he analyses them with delicate and delightful art and then passes on, often to the opposite pole of thought or feeling, knowing that every mood has its own quality and charm and is justified by its mere existence. He has taken the sensationalism of Greek philosophy and made it a new method of art criticism. As for his style, it is curiously ascetic. Now and then, we come across phrases with a strange sensuousness of expression, as when he tells us how Denys l'Auxerrois, on his return from a long journey, 'ate flesh for the first time, tearing the hot, red morsels with his delicate fingers in a kind of wild greed,' but such passages are rare. Asceticism is the keynote of Mr. Pater's prose; at times it is almost too severe in its self-control and makes us long for a little more freedom. For indeed, the danger of such prose as his is that it is apt to become somewhat laborious. Here and there, one is tempted to say of Mr. Pater that he is 'a seeker after something in language, that is there in no satisfying measure, or not at all.' The continual preoccupation with phrase and epithet has its drawbacks as well as its virtues. And yet, when all is said, what wonderful prose it is, with its subtle preferences, its fastidious purity, its rejection of what is common or ordinary! Mr. Pater has the true spirit of selection, the true tact of omission. If he be not among the greatest prose writers of our literature he is, at least, our greatest artist in prose; and though it may be admitted that the best style is that which seems an unconscious result rather than a conscious aim, still in these latter days when violent rhetoric does duty for eloquence and vulgarity usurps the name of nature, we should be grateful for a style that deliberately aims at perfection of form, that seeks to produce its effect by artistic means and sets before itself an ideal of grave and chastened beauty.

Mr. Pater's Last Volume[17]

When I first had the privilege – and I count it a very high one – of meeting Mr. Walter Pater, he said to me, smiling, 'Why do you always write poetry? Why do you not write prose? Prose is so much more difficult.' [. . .]

I may frankly confess now that at the time I did not quite

comprehend what Mr. Pater really meant; and it was not till I had carefully studied his beautiful and suggestive essays on the Renaissance that I fully realised what a wonderful self-conscious art the art of English prose-writing really is, or may be made to be. Carlyle's stormy rhetoric, Ruskin's winged and passionate eloquence, had seemed to me to spring from enthusiasm rather than from art. I do not think I knew then that even prophets correct their proofs. As for Jacobean prose, I thought it too exuberant; and Queen Anne prose appeared to me terribly bald, and irritatingly rational. But Mr. Pater's essays became to me 'the golden book of spirit and sense, the holy writ of beauty.'[18] They are still this to me. It is possible, of course, that I may exaggerate about them. I certainly hope that I do; for where there is no exaggeration there is no love, and where there is no love there is no understanding. It is only about things that do not interest one, that one can give a really unbiassed opinion; and this is no doubt the reason why an unbiassed opinion is always valueless.[19] [. . .]

Appreciations, in the fine Latin sense of the word, is the title given by Mr. Pater to his book, which is an exquisite collection of exquisite essays, of delicately wrought works of art – some of them being almost Greek in their purity of outline and perfection of form, others medieval in their strangeness of colour and passionate suggestion, and all of them absolutely modern, in the true meaning of the term modernity. For he to whom the present is the only thing that is present, knows nothing of the age in which he lives. To realise the nineteenth century one must realise every century that has preceded it, and that has contributed to its making. To know anything about oneself, one must know all about others. There must be no mood with which one cannot sympathise, no dead mode of life that one cannot make alive. The legacies of heredity may make us alter our views of moral responsibility, but they cannot but intensify our sense of the value of Criticism; for the true critic is he who bears within himself the dreams and ideas and feelings of myriad generations, and to whom no form of thought is alien, no emotional impulse obscure.

Perhaps the most interesting, and certainly the least successful, of the essays contained in the present volume is that on

Style. It is the most interesting because it is the work of one who speaks with the high authority that comes from the noble realisation of things nobly conceived. It is the least successful, because the subject is too abstract. A true artist like Mr. Pater is most felicitous when he deals with the concrete, whose very limitations give him finer freedom, while they necessitate more intense vision. And yet what a high ideal is contained in these few pages! How good it is for us, in these days of popular education and facile journalism, to be reminded of the real scholarship that is essential to the perfect writer, who, 'being a true lover of words for their own sake, a minute and constant observer of their physiognomy,' will avoid what is mere rhetoric, or ostentatious ornament, or negligent misuse of terms, or ineffective surplusage, and will be known by his tact of omission, by his skilful economy of means, by his selection and self-restraint, and perhaps above all by that conscious artistic structure which is the expression of mind in style. I think I have been wrong in saying that the subject is too abstract. In Mr. Pater's hands it becomes very real to us indeed, and he shows us how, behind the perfection of a man's style, must lie the passion of a man's soul.

As one passes to the rest of the volume, one finds essays on Wordsworth and on Coleridge, on Charles Lamb and on Sir Thomas Browne, on some of Shakespeare's plays and on the English kings that Shakespeare fashioned, on Dante Rossetti, and on William Morris. As that on Wordsworth seems to be Mr. Pater's last work, so that on the singer of the *Defence of Guenevere* is certainly his earliest, or almost his earliest, and it is interesting to mark the change that has taken place in his style. This change is, perhaps, at first sight not very apparent. In 1868 we find Mr. Pater writing with the same exquisite care for words, with the same studied music, with the same temper, and something of the same mode of treatment. But, as he goes on, the architecture of the style becomes richer and more complex, the epithet more precise and intellectual. Occasionally one may be inclined to think that there is, here and there, a sentence which is somewhat long, and possibly, if one may venture to say so, a little heavy and cumbersome in movement. But if this be so, it comes from those side-issues suddenly suggested by the idea in its progress, and really revealing the idea more perfectly; or from those felicitous after-thoughts that give a fuller completeness to the central scheme, and yet convey something of the charm of chance; or from a desire to suggest the secondary shades of meaning with all their accumulating effect, and to avoid, it may be, the violence and harshness of too definite and exclusive an opinion. For in matters of art, at any rate, thought is inevitably coloured by emotion, and so is fluid rather than fixed, and, recognising its dependence upon moods and upon the passion of fine moments, will not accept the rigidity of a scientific formula or a theological dogma. The critical pleasure, too, that we receive from tracing, through what may seem the intricacies of a sentence, the working of the constructive intelligence, must not be overlooked. As soon as we have realised the design, everything appears clear and simple. After a time, these long sentences of Mr. Pater's come to have the charm of an elaborate piece of music, and the unity of such music also.

I have suggested that the essay on Wordsworth is probably the most recent bit of work contained in this volume. If one might choose between so much that is good, I should be inclined to say it is the finest also. [. . .] It appeals, not to the ordinary Wordsworthian with his uncritical temper, and his gross confusion of ethical and aesthetical problems, but rather to those who desire to separate the gold from the dross, and to reach at the true Wordsworth through the mass of tedious and prosaic work that bears his name, and that serves often to conceal him from us. The presence of an alien element in Wordsworth's art is, of course, recognised by Mr. Pater, but he touches on it merely from the psychological point of view, pointing out how this quality of higher and lower moods gives the effect in his poetry 'so that the old fancy which made the poet's art an enthusiasm, a form of divine possession, seems almost true of him.' Mr. Pater's earlier essays had their *purpurei panni*,* so eminently suitable for quotation, such as the famous passage on *Mona Lisa*, and that other in which Botticelli's strange conception of the Virgin is so strangely set forth. From the present volume it is difficult

* purple patches

to select any one passage in preference to another as specially characteristic of Mr. Pater's treatment. This, however, is worth quoting at length. It contains a truth eminently suitable for our age:

That the end of life is not action but contemplation – *being* as distinct from *doing* – a certain disposition of the mind: is, in some shape or other, the principle of all the higher morality. In poetry, in art, if you enter into their true spirit at all, you touch this principle in a measure; these, by their sterility, are a type of beholding for the mere joy of beholding. To treat life in the spirit of art is to make life a thing in which means and ends are identified; to encourage such treatment, the true moral significance of art and poetry. Wordsworth, and other poets who have been like him in ancient or more recent times, are the masters, the experts, in this art of impassioned contemplation. Their work is not to teach lessons, or enforce rules, or even to stimulate us to noble ends, but to withdraw the thoughts for a while from the mere machinery of life, to fix them, with appropriate emotions, on the spectacle of those great facts in man's existence which no machinery affects, 'on the great and universal passions of men, the most general and interesting of their occupations, and the entire world of nature' – on 'the operations of the elements and the appearances of the visible universe, on storm and sunshine, on the revolutions of the seasons, on cold and heat, on loss of friends and kindred, on injuries and resentments, on gratitude and hope, on fear and sorrow.' To witness this spectacle with appropriate emotions is the aim of all culture; and of these emotions poetry like Wordsworth's is a great nourisher and stimulant. He sees nature full of sentiment and excitement; he sees men and women as parts of nature, passionate, excited, in strange grouping and connection with the grandeur and beauty of the natural world: – images, in his own words, 'of men suffering, amid awful forms and powers.'

Certainly the real secret of Wordsworth has never been better expressed. After having read and re-read Mr. Pater's essay – for it requires re-reading – one returns to the poet's work with a new sense of joy and wonder, and with something of eager and impassioned expectation. And perhaps this might be roughly taken as the test or touchstone of the finest criticism.

Finally, one cannot help noticing the delicate instinct that has gone to fashion the brief epilogue that ends this delightful volume. The difference between the classical and romantic spirits in art has often, and with much over-emphasis, been discussed. But with what a light sure touch does Mr. Pater write of it! How subtle and certain are his distinctions! If imaginative prose be really the special art of this century, Mr. Pater must rank amongst our century's most characteristic artists. In certain things he stands almost alone. The age has produced wonderful prose styles, turbid with individualism, and violent with excess of rhetoric. But in Mr. Pater, as in Cardinal Newman, we find the union of personality with perfection. He has no rival in his own sphere, and he has escaped disciples. And this, not because he has not been imitated, but because in art so fine as his there is something that, in its essence, is inimitable.

The Decay of Lying[20]

A DIALOGUE. *Persons: Cyril and Vivian. Scene: the library of a country house in Nottinghamshire.*

CYRIL

(*coming in through the open window from the terrace*)

My dear Vivian, don't coop yourself up all day in the library. It is a perfectly lovely afternoon. The air is exquisite. There is a mist upon the woods like the purple bloom upon a plum. Let us go and lie on the grass, and smoke cigarettes, and enjoy Nature.

VIVIAN

Enjoy Nature! I am glad to say that I have entirely lost that faculty. People tell us that Art makes us love Nature more than we loved her before; that it reveals her secrets to us; and that after a careful study of Corot and Constable we see things in her that had escaped our observation. My own experience is that the more we study Art, the less we care for Nature. What Art really reveals to us is Nature's lack of design, her curious crudities, her extraordinary monotony, her absolutely unfinished condition. Nature has good intentions, of course, but, as Aristotle once said, she cannot carry them out. When I look at a landscape I cannot help seeing all its defects. It is fortunate for us, however, that Nature is so imperfect, as otherwise we should have had no art at all. Art is our spirited protest, our gallant attempt to teach Nature her proper place. As for the infinite variety of Nature, that is a pure myth. It is not to be found in Nature herself. It resides in the imagination, or fancy, or cultivated blindness of the man who looks at her.

CYRIL

Well, you need not look at the landscape. You can lie on the grass and smoke and talk.

VIVIAN

But Nature is so uncomfortable. Grass is hard and lumpy and damp, and full of dreadful black insects. Why, even Morris' poorest workman could make you a more comfortable seat than the whole of Nature can. [. . .] If Nature had been comfortable, mankind would never have invented architecture, and I prefer houses to the open air. In a house we all feel of the proper proportions. Everything is subordinated to us, fashioned for our use and our pleasure. Egotism itself, which is so necessary to a proper sense of human dignity, is entirely the result of indoor life. Out of doors one becomes abstract and impersonal. One's individuality absolutely leaves one. [. . .] Nothing is more evident than that Nature hates Mind. Thinking is the most unhealthy thing in the world, and people die of it just as they die of any other disease. Fortunately, in England at any rate, thought is not catching. Our splendid physique as a people is entirely due to our national stupidity. I only hope we shall be able to keep this great historic bulwark of our happiness for many years to come; [. . .] In the meantime, you had better go back to your wearisome uncomfortable Nature, and leave me to correct my proofs.

CYRIL

Writing an article! That is not very consistent after what you have just said.

VIVIAN

Who wants to be consistent? The dullard and the doctrinaire, the tedious people who carry out their principles to the bitter end of action, to the *reductio ad absurdum* of practice. Not I. Like Emerson, I write over the door of my library the word "Whim." Besides, my article is really a most salutary and valuable warning. If it is attended to, there may be a new Renaissance of Art. [. . .]

CYRIL

Do you object to modernity of form, then?

VIVIAN

Yes. It is a huge price to pay for a very poor result. Pure modernity of form is always somewhat vulgarizing. It cannot help being so. The public imagine that, because they are interested in their immediate surroundings, Art should be interested in them also, and should take them as her subject-matter. But the mere fact that they are interested in these things makes them unsuitable subjects for Art. The only beautiful things, as somebody once said, are the things that do not concern us. As long as a thing is useful or necessary to us, or affects us in any way, either for pain or for pleasure, or appeals strongly to our sympathies, or is a vital part of the environment in which we live, it is outside the proper sphere of art. To art's subject-matter we should be more or less indifferent. [. . .] Believe me, my dear Cyril, modernity of form and modernity of subject-matter are entirely and absolutely wrong. We have mistaken the common livery of the age for the vesture of the Muses, and spend our days in the sordid streets and hideous suburbs of our vile cities when we should be out on the hillside with Apollo.[21] Certainly we are a degraded race, and have sold our birthright for a mess of facts. [. . .]

CYRIL

What do you mean by saying that Nature is always behind the age?

VIVIAN

Well, perhaps that is rather cryptic. What I mean is this. If we take Nature to mean natural simple instinct as opposed to self-conscious culture, the work produced under this influence is always old-fashioned, antiquated, and out of date. One touch of Nature may make the whole world kin, but two touches of Nature will destroy any work of Art. If, on the other hand, we regard Nature as the collection of phenomena external to man, people only discover in her what they bring to her. She has no suggestions of her own. Wordsworth went to the lakes, but he was never a lake poet. He found in stones the sermons he had already hidden there. He went moralizing about the district, but his good work was produced when he returned, not to Nature but to poetry. Poetry gave him *Laodamia*, and the fine sonnets, and the great Ode, such as it is. Nature gave him *Martha Ray* and Peter Bell, and the address to Mr. Wilkinson's spade.[22] [. . .]

(*reading*)

"Art begins with abstract decoration, with purely imaginative and pleasurable work dealing with what is unreal and non-existent. This is the first stage. Then Life becomes fascinated with this new wonder, and asks to be admitted into the charmed circle. Art takes life as part of her rough material, recreates it, and refashions it in fresh forms, is absolutely indifferent to fact, invents, imagines, dreams, and keeps between herself and reality the impenetrable barrier of beautiful style, of decorative or ideal treatment. The third stage is when Life gets the upper hand, and drives Art out into the wilderness. This is the true decadence, and it is from this that we are now suffering.

"Art finds her own perfection within, and not outside of, herself. She is not to be judged by any external standard of resemblance. She is a veil, rather than a mirror. She has flowers that no forests know of, birds that no woodland possesses. She makes and unmakes many worlds, and can draw the moon from heaven with a scarlet thread. Hers are the 'forms more real than living man,' and hers the great archetypes of which things that have existence are but unfinished copies. Nature has, in her eyes, no laws, no uniformity. [. . .]"

CYRIL

I like that. I can see it. Is that the end?

VIVIAN

No. There is one more passage, but it is purely practical. It simply suggests some methods by which we could revive this lost art of Lying.

CYRIL

Well, before you read it to me, I should like to ask you a question. What do you mean by saying that Life, 'poor, probable, uninteresting human life,' will try to reproduce the marvels of Art? I can quite understand your objection to Art being treated as a mirror. You think it would reduce genius to the position of a cracked looking-glass. But you don't mean to say that you seriously believe that Life imitates Art, that Life in fact is the mirror, and Art the reality?

VIVIAN

Certainly I do. Paradox though it may seem – and paradoxes are always dangerous things – it is none the less true that Life imitates Art far more than Art imitates Life. We have all seen in our own day in England how a certain curious and fascinating type of beauty, invented and emphasized by two imaginative painters, has so influenced Life that when ever one goes to a private view or to an artistic salon one sees, here the mystic eyes of Rossetti's dream, the long ivory throat, the strange square-cut jaw, the loosened shadowy hair that he so ardently loved, there the sweet maidenhood of "The Golden Stair," the blossom-like mouth and weary loveliness of the "Laus Amoris," the passion-pale face of Andromeda, the thin hands and lithe beauty of the Vivien in "Merlin's Dream."[23] And it has always been so. A great artist invents a type, and Life tries to copy it, to reproduce it in a popular form like an enterprising publisher. Neither Holbein nor Vandyck found in England what they have given us. They brought their types with them, and Life with her keen imitative faculty set herself to supply the master with models. The Greeks, with their quick artistic instinct, understood this, and set in the bride's chamber the statue of Hermes or of Apollo, that she might bear children as lovely as the works of art that she looked at in her rapture or her pain. They knew that Life gains from Art not merely spirituality, depth of thought and feeling, soul-turmoil or soul-peace, but that she can form herself on the very lines and colours of Art, and can reproduce the dignity of Pheidias as well as the grace of Praxiteles. Hence came their objection to realism. They disliked it on purely social grounds. They felt that it inevitably makes people ugly, and they were perfectly right. We try to improve the conditions of the race by means of good air, free sunlight, wholesome water, and hideous bare buildings for the better housing of the lower orders. But these things merely produce health, they do not produce beauty. For this, Art is required, and the true disciples of the great artist are not his studio-imitators, but those who become like his works of art, be they plastic as in Greek days, or pictorial as in modern times; in a word, Life is Art's best, Art's only pupil. [. . .]

CYRIL

The theory is certainly a very curious one, but to make it complete you must show that Nature, no less than Life, is an imitation of Art. Are you prepared to prove that?

VIVIAN

My dear fellow, I am prepared to prove anything.

CYRIL

Nature follows the landscape painter then, and takes her effects from him?

VIVIAN

Certainly. Where, if not from the Impressionists, do we get those wonderful brown fogs that come creeping down our streets, blurring the gas-lamps and changing the houses into monstrous shadows? To whom, if not to them and their master, do we owe the lovely silver mists that brood over our river, and turn to faint forms of fading grace curved bridge and swaying barge? The extraordinary change that has taken place in the climate of London during the last ten years is entirely due to this particular school of Art. You smile. Consider the matter from a scientific or metaphysical point of view, and you will find that I am right. For what is Nature? Nature is no great mother who has borne us. She is our creation. It is in our brain that she quickens to life. Things are because we see them, and what we see, and how we see it, depends on the Arts that have influenced us. To look at a thing is very different from seeing a thing. One does not see anything until one sees its beauty. Then, and then only, does it come into existence. At present, people see fogs, not because there are fogs, but because poets and painters have taught them the mysterious loveliness of such effects. There may have been fogs for centuries in London. I dare say there were. But no one saw them, and so we do not know anything about them. They did not exist till Art had invented them. [. . .] That white quivering sunlight that one sees now in France, with its strange blotches of mauve, and its restless violet shadows, is her latest fancy, and, on the whole, Nature reproduces it quite admirably. Where she used to give us Corots and Daubignys, she gives us now exquisite Monets and entrancing Pissaros. Indeed there are moments, rare, it is true, but still to be observed from time to time, when Nature becomes absolutely modern. Of course she is not always to be relied upon. The fact is that she is in this unfortunate position. Art creates an incomparable and unique effect, and, having done so, passes on to other things. Nature, upon the other hand, forgetting that imitation can be made the sincerest form of insult, keeps on repeating this effect until we all become absolutely wearied of it. Nobody of any real culture, for instance, ever talks nowadays about the beauty of a sunset. Sunsets are quite old-fashioned. They belong to the time when Turner was the last note in art. To admire them is a distinct sign of provincialism of temperament. [. . .] but then, when Art is more varied, Nature will, no doubt, be more varied also. That she imitates Art, I don't think even her worst enemy would deny now. It is the one thing that keeps her in touch with civilized man. But have I proved my theory to your satisfaction?

CYRIL

You have proved it to my dissatisfaction, which is better. But even admitting this strange imitative instinct in Life and Nature, surely you would acknowledge that Art expresses the temper of its age, the spirit of its time, the moral and social conditions that surround it, and under whose influence it is produced.

VIVIAN

Certainly not! Art never expresses anything but itself. This is the principle of my new aesthetics; and it is this, more than that vital connection between form and substance, on which Mr. Pater dwells, that makes music the type of all the arts. Of course, nations and individuals, with that healthy natural vanity which is the secret of existence, are always under the impression that it is of them that the Muses are talking, always trying to find in the calm dignity of imaginative art some mirror of their own turbid passions, always forgetting that the singer of life is not Apollo, but Marsyas. Remote from reality, and with her eyes turned away from the shadows of the cave, Art reveals her own perfection, and the wondering crowd that watches the opening of the marvellous, many-petalled rose fancies that it is its own history that is being told to it, its own spirit that is finding expression in a new form. But it is not so. The highest art rejects the burden of the human spirit, and gains more from a new medium or a fresh material than she does from any enthusiasm for Art, or from any lofty passion, or from any great awakening of the human consciousness. She develops purely on her own lines. She is not symbolic of any age. It is the ages that are her symbols. [. . .] The sibyls and prophets of the Sistine may indeed serve to interpret for some that new birth of the emancipated spirit that we call the Renaissance; but what do the drunken boors and brawling peasants of Dutch art tell us about the great soul of Holland? The more abstract, the more ideal an art is, the more it reveals to us the temper of its age. If we wish to understand a nation by means of its art, let us look at its architecture or its music.

CYRIL

I quite agree with you there. The spirit of an age may be best expressed in the abstract ideal arts, for the spirit itself is abstract and ideal. Upon the other hand, for the visible aspect of an age, for its look, as the phrase goes, we must of course go to the arts of imitation.

VIVIAN

I don't think so. After all, what the imitative arts really give us are merely the various styles of particular artists, or of certain schools of artists. [. . .] No great artist ever sees things as they really are. If he did, he would cease to be an artist. Take an example from our own day. I know that you are fond of Japanese things. Now, do you really imagine that the Japanese people, as they are presented to us in Art, have any existence? If you do, you have never understood Japanese art at all. The Japanese people are the deliberate self-conscious creation of certain individual artists. If you set a picture by Hokusai, or Hokkei, or any of the great native painters, beside a real Japanese gentleman or lady, you will see that there is not the slightest resemblance between them. The actual people who live in Japan are not unlike the general run of English people; that is to say, they are extremely commonplace, and have nothing curious or extraordinary about them. In fact the whole of Japan is a pure invention. There is no such country, there are no such people. [. . .] Or, to return again to the past, take as another instance the ancient Greeks. Do you think that Greek art ever tells us what the Greek people were like? Do you believe that the Athenian women were like the stately dignified figures of the Parthenon frieze, or like those marvellous goddesses who sat in the triangular pediments of the same building? If you judge from the art, they certainly were so. But read an authority, like Aristophanes for instance. You will find that the Athenian ladies laced tightly, wore high-heeled shoes, dyed their hair yellow, painted and rouged their faces, and were exactly like any silly fashionable or fallen creature of our own day. The fact is that we look back on the ages entirely through the medium of Art, and Art, very fortunately, has never once told us the truth.

CYRIL

Then we must certainly cultivate it at once. But in order to avoid making any error I want you to tell me briefly the doctrines of the new aesthetics.

VIVIAN

Briefly, then, they are these. Art never expresses anything but itself. It has an independent life, just as Thought has, and develops purely on its own lines. It is not necessarily realistic in an age of realism, nor spiritual in an age of faith. So far from being the creation of its time, it is usually in direct opposition to it, and the only history that it preserves for us is the history of its own progress. Sometimes it returns upon its footsteps, and revives some antique form, as happened in the archaistic movement of late Greek Art, and in the Pre-Raphaelite movement of our own day. At other times it entirely anticipates its age, and produces in one century work that it takes another century to understand, to appreciate, and to enjoy. In no case does it reproduce its age. To pass from the art of a time to the time itself is the great mistake that all historians commit.

The second doctrine is this. All bad art comes from returning to Life and Nature, and elevating them into ideals. Life and Nature may sometimes be used as part of Art's rough material, but before they are of any real service to Art they must be translated into artistic conventions. The moment Art surrenders its imaginative medium it surrenders everything. As a method Realism is a complete failure, and the two things that every artist should avoid are modernity of form and modernity of subject-matter. To us, who live in the nineteenth century, any century is a suitable subject for Art except our own. The only beautiful things are the things that do not concern us. It is, to have the pleasure of quoting myself, exactly because Hecuba is nothing to us that her sorrows are so suitable a motive for a tragedy. Besides, it is only the modern that ever becomes old-fashioned. M. Zola sits down to give us a picture of the Second Empire. Who cares for the Second Empire now? It is out of date. Life goes faster than Realism, but Romanticism is always in front of Life.

The third doctrine is that Life imitates Art far more than Art imitates Life. This results not merely from Life's imitative instinct, but from the fact that the self-conscious aim of Life is to find expression, and that Art offers it certain beautiful forms through which it may realize that energy. It is a theory that has never been put forward before, but it is extremely fruitful, and throws an entirely new light upon the history of Art.

It follows, as a corollary from this, that external Nature also imitates Art. The only effects that she can show us are effects that we have already seen through poetry, or in paintings. This is the secret of Nature's charm, as well as the explanation of Nature's weakness.

The final revelation is that Lying, the telling of beautiful untrue things, is the proper aim of Art.

Preface to *The Picture of Dorian Gray*[24]

The artist is the creator of beautiful things.

To reveal art and conceal the artist is art's aim.

The critic is he who can translate into another manner or a new material his impression of beautiful things.

The highest, as the lowest, form of criticism is a mode of autobiography.

Those who find ugly meanings in beautiful things are corrupt without being charming. This is a fault.

Those who find beautiful meanings in beautiful things are the cultivated. For these there is hope.

They are the elect to whom beautiful things mean only Beauty.

There is no such thing as a moral or an immoral book. Books are well written, or badly written. That is all.

The nineteenth century dislike of Realism is the rage of Caliban seeing his own face in a glass.

The nineteenth century dislike of Romanticism is the rage of Caliban not seeing his own face in a glass.

The moral life of man forms part of the subject-matter of the artist, but the morality of art consists in the perfect use of an imperfect medium. Not artist desires to prove anything. Even things that are true can be proved.

No artist has ethical sympathies. An ethical sympathy in an artist is an unpardonable mannerism of style.

No artist is ever morbid. The artist can express everything.

Thought and language are to the artist instruments of an art.

Vice and virtue are to the artist materials for an art.

From the point of view of form, the type of all the arts is the art of the musician. From the point of view of feeling, the actor's craft is the type.

All art is at once surface and symbol.

Those who go beneath the surface do so at their peril.

Those who read the symbol do so at their peril.

It is the spectator, and not life, that art really mirrors.

Diversity of opinion about a work of art shows that the work is new, complex, and vital.

When critics disagree the artist is in accord with himself.

We can forgive a man for making a useful thing as long as he does not admire it. The only excuse for making a useless thing is that one admires it intensely.

All art is quite useless.

Phrases and Philosophies for the Use of the Young[25]

The first duty in life is to be as artificial as possible. What the second duty is no one has as yet discovered.

Wickedness is a myth invented by good people to account for the curious attractiveness of others.

If the poor only had profiles there would be no difficulty in solving the problem of poverty.

Those who see any difference between soul and body have neither.

A really well-made buttonhole is the only link between Art and Nature.

Religions die when they are proved to be true. Science is the record of dead religions.

The well-bred contradict other people. The wise contradict themselves.

Nothing that actually occurs is of the smallest importance.

Dulness is the coming of age of seriousness.

In all unimportant matters, style, not sincerity, is the essential. In all important matters, style, not sincerity, is the essential.

If one tells the truth one is sure, sooner or later, to be found out.

Pleasure is the only thing one should live for. Nothing ages like happiness.

It is only by not paying one's bills that one can hope to live in the memory of the commercial classes.

No crime is vulgar, but all vulgarity is crime. Vulgarity is the conduct of others.

Only the shallow know themselves.

Time is waste of money.

One should always be a little improbable.

There is a fatality about all good resolutions. They are invariably made too soon.

The only way to atone for being occasionally a little overdressed is by being always absolutely over-educated.

To be premature is to be perfect.

Any preoccupation with ideas of what is right or wrong in conduct shows an arrested intellectual development.

Ambition is the last refuge of the failure.

A truth ceases to be true when more than one person believes in it.

In examinations the foolish ask questions that the wise cannot answer.

Greek dress was in its essence inartistic. Nothing should reveal the body but the body.

One should either be a work of art, or wear a work of art.

It is only the superficial qualities that last. Man's deeper nature is soon found out.

Industry is the root of all ugliness.

The ages live in history through their anachronisms.

It is only the gods who taste of death. Apollo has passed away, but Hyacinth, whom men say he slew, lives on. Nero and Narcissus are always with us.

The old believe everything: the middle-aged suspect everything: the young know everything.

The condition of perfection is idleness: the aim of perfection is youth.

Only the great masters of style ever succeed in being obscure.

There is something tragic about the enormous number of young men there are in England at the present moment who start life with perfect profiles, and end by adopting some useful profession.

To love oneself is the beginning of a life-long romance.

WILLIAM BUTLER YEATS (1865–1939)

It is just over forty years since the death of Yeats, and his dominance in the poetry of this century is still undisputed. Poets since his time have chosen other paths, and some have actively turned away from his influence, but he is still felt to be a larger figure, bestriding a wider span of history and experience than any of his successors. It is partly a matter of chronology: born when Queen Victoria's reign had still thirty-five years to run, he survived until the eve of the Second World War. His formation therefore was entirely within the nineteenth century. But by a startling act of self-renewal, some time between 1910 and 1914, he cast off many of the honoured and well-established beauties of his earlier verse, rejected all the period mannerisms, seductive as they were, and turned himself into a far more powerful poet of a distinctively modern cast. This development, so rich and so idiosyncratic, has been described and celebrated many times, and it is not our subject here. There is another side of Yeats's writing that has never been noticed enough, or has been noticed only as an appendix to his own poetry. Yeats is the one major poetic figure who starts his career among the late Pre-Raphaelites and ends by casting a slightly sceptical glance over the modernists of the period between the wars. Much of this progress, especially the earlier parts of it, he has recorded in prose, some of it straightforwardly autobiographical, some of it critical and reflective; and though the wisdom and charm of these essays and reminiscences are a perpetual delight to their readers, their value as cultural history has never been fully recognized. No one else lived through the experience of the *fin-de-siècle* and came out as triumphantly on the other side as Yeats, and his testimony to the spirit of the age, as witness, participant and creator, remains without rival.

Yeats's prose writings are extensive, and some of them remain still uncollected. Our selections come from *Ideas of Good and Evil* (1896–1903), *The Cutting of an Agate* (1903–15) and *The Trembling of the Veil* (1922). In addition there is a reminiscent broadcast given in 1936, near the end of his life. It shows that his interpretation of the state of literature in his formative years changed very little, although he had added to it the experience of new kinds of poetry widely divergent from his own. All this material is to be found now in the two volumes *Autobiographies* and *Essays and Introductions*.

The autobiographical passages dealing with the Rhymers' Club and Yeats's circle in the Nineties paint a picture of a group of young poets already distancing themselves from the literary attitudes of the Victorians, already seeing themselves as outsiders, alien to the society around them. In this they are of course simply developing more openly that antithetical culture within Victorian England itself that we have already seen growing among the Pre-Raphaelites and in the work of Pater. This becomes evident first in their life-style. Where Tennyson and Browning had become culture-heroes to the bourgeois world, whose values they implicitly celebrated and idealized, the Rhymers regarded the whole socio-economic apparatus with indifference or contempt. Since Britain was Protestant they turned Catholic; while the life of the typical Victorian sage was long, sober and continent, the life of the typical Rhymer was short, drunken and dissolute. The career of Oscar Wilde (though he was never a Rhymer), ending in spectacular downfall in 1895, became the English exemplar of the already established French type, the *poète maudit*. The aesthetic justification for these shattered lives was the imperative demand of art – art increasingly seen not as an expression or continuation of the life of the common world, but as something set over against it, a counterweight or a flight into loneliness. From this time on the artists who are most acutely aware of their creativity and of breaking new ground come to feel more and more isolated from their public. The painters feel this as much as the poets: 'The people are not with us', as Paul Klee put it.

Yeats writes with sympathy and loyalty of his old companions, and speculates without reaching a conclusion on what brought about so many tragic fates. If we ask what enabled him, alone of the group, to live unscathed through this 'decadent' interlude and come out of it with renewed strength, we can find the answer in his prose reflections. It was the intellectual and spiritual energy that left him unsatisfied by the Rhymers' languid disdain and drove him to find a true foundation for his poetic faith. He found it in the great international movement of Symbolism, but in his case it was not a matter of following a French fashion, or of being carried away by a cultural wave. He owed much to French influences, mediated by Pater and Arthur Symons, but in his hands they were transformed. The symbols of poetry for him were not techniques or literary devices, they were fundamental elements of human experience, lying too deep for expression in abstract concepts and rational argument. Emblems, images, sounds, colours and rhythms were the only possible embodiments of these profound emotions and moods; and now that the conventionally established religions were losing their power it was only through the arts that they could be realized. Here Yeats was, as it were, ignoring the High Victorian compromise and returning to an earlier Romantic faith in the imagination and in its spiritual reality. It was this above all that attracted him to Shelley and to Blake. But in the course of the nineteenth century the arts had gone far towards refusing their true function; poetry had become mere rumination, fiction a passionless recording of the common scene. The time for renewal was at hand. And it was because truly living art was recapturing something lost to the general culture that the artists were isolated, alone on a quest that was little understood.

Yeats was never satisfied with this situation. He was always torn between two visions of himself – one as the hieratic devotee of Symbolism, in lofty isolation from the world; the other as a prophet and leader, speaking to Humanity, or at least to a nation. This links him to the more generous and human aspirations of earlier romanticism. 'Did that song of mine send out/Certain men the English shot?' Very unlikely; but in some moods Yeats was apt to think it should have done. Unlike the Baudelairean dandy, he passionately desired a poetry that should be truly of the people. In a little poem of 1908 he wishes that the poet might be cheered like the rider at a race-meeting, and by the same crowd. Here Yeats's position was peculiar. As an Irishman he belonged to a small country where an individual voice could be heard above the chatter of publicity and the tramping of the big battalions. As a Nationalist Irishman he was intensely aware of his part in creating a culture for his own people. The story of this effort by Yeats and his friends – the story of its defeat, as he later came to see it – cannot detain us here; but it is the background to Yeats's concern with popular poetry. He is anxious to distinguish the true poetry of the people – folk-songs, ballads and lays, usually ancient – from the merely popularized versions of middle-class literary tradition, Longfellow, Campbell, Mrs Hemans, Macaulay's *Lays*, that have had the widest printed circulation. He even contrives to persuade himself that the true popular poetry is of the same kind as that written by himself and his allies, with the same qualities of simplicity and poignancy, abruptness, resistance to easy interpretation, working through images rather than concepts. This is hardly more than a piece of brilliant casuistry, but it is important, because this same mirage of an alliance between the *avant-garde* of the arts and a popular audience has haunted the imagination of the twentieth century.

Since the Ireland of Yeats's day had not yet been overtaken by commercial-industrial barbarization, his task seemed easier, and he continued to be haunted by it, in one way or another, throughout his life. But he was always aware that any social solution to the problems of the arts was precarious and untrustworthy. He was always anxious to find a foundation for his aesthetic creed beyond the vicissitudes of politics and history. And indeed the tenets of literary symbolism remain incomplete unless it is also believed that the symbols of poetry are more than local and individual, that they rise from some great all-encompassing sea of thought and emotion, which is a source of power, from which all human thoughts and emotions are derived. Yeats sometimes calls this the Great Memory, sometimes, following the Neo-Platonists, the Anima Mundi or soul of the world. This world-soul could be evoked by symbols, and to do so was the way to knowledge and strength. Yeats called it magic, and abruptly announced his belief in the practice and philosophy of magic in an essay of 1901. Then and for long afterwards this belief was generally regarded as an eccentricity and treated with varying degrees of rejection or patronizing tolerance. But the Great Memory of Yeats, though different in expression, is no different in essence from the collective unconscious of Jungian psychology – a supposition from which even the great positivist Freud did not dissent in later years. In another guise it had appeared as *Geist*, the self-realizing world-spirit of Hegel, already by Pater's day established in English thought. Almost unnoticed, ideas of this kind have penetrated the imagination of the twentieth century, and the arts of our time have been haunted by the ambition to lay their hands on the sources of power. In Yeats's case this led to a fusion of the aesthetic and the religious impulse, and ultimately to the elaboration of a huge symbolic-philosophical system in his prose treatise *A Vision*. Its leading ideas were communicated to him through the automatic writings of his wife; and what the unknown communicators said was 'We come to bring you metaphors for poetry.'

Besides his importance as the most complete and articulate exponent of the Symbolist aesthetic in England, Yeats was a fine critic in the more conventional sense, and he often develops his own thought by a commentary on other poets. For long Blake was his master, and he devoted years to the exposition of Blake's work, in which he found an anticipation of the poetic beliefs of his own time. In the superb essay on Shelley he not only identifies Shelley's ruling symbols and their significance, but distinguishes between those poems that, however beautiful, are the product of arbitrary fancy, and those that spring from the deep archetypal level characteristic of Shelley's greatest work. It is in such essays as these that Yeats charts the link between the advancing energies of Symbolism and its High Romantic origins, and it is here that he establishes himself as the most resonant and sympathetic mediator between the two.

The Legacy of the Pre-Raphaelites[1]

[. . .] Yet I was in all things Pre-Raphaelite. When I was fifteen or sixteen my father had told me about Rossetti and Blake and given me their poetry to read; and once at Liverpool on my way to Sligo I had seen *Dante's Dream* in the gallery there, a picture painted when Rossetti had lost his dramatic power and to-day not very pleasing to me, and its colour, its people, its romantic architecture had blotted all other pictures away. It was a perpetual bewilderment that when my father, moved perhaps by some memory of his youth, chose some theme from poetic tradition, he would soon weary and leave it unfinished. I had seen the change coming bit by bit and its defence elaborated by young men fresh from the Paris art schools. 'We must paint what is in front of us', or 'A man must be of his own time', they would say, and if I spoke of Blake or Rossetti they would point out his bad drawing and tell me to admire Carolus Duran and Bastien-Lepage.[2] Then, too, they were very ignorant men; they read nothing, for nothing mattered but 'knowing how to paint', being in reaction against a generation that seemed to have wasted its time upon so many things. I thought myself alone in hating these young men, their contempt for the past, their monopoly of the future, but in a few months I was to discover others of my own age who thought as I did, for it is not true that youth looks before it with the mechanical gaze of a well-drilled soldier. Its quarrel is not with the past, but with the present, where its elders are so obviously powerful and no cause seems lost if it seem to threaten that power. Does cultivated youth ever really love the future, where the eye can discover no persecuted Royalty hidden among oak leaves, though from it certainly does come so much proletarian rhetoric?

I was unlike others of my generation in one thing only. I am very religious, and deprived by Huxley and Tyndall,[3] whom I detested, of the simple-minded religion of my childhood, I had made a new religion, almost an infallible Church of poetic tradition, of a fardel of stories, and of personages, and of emotions, inseparable from their first expression, passed on from generation to generation by poets and painters with some help from philosophers and theologians. I wished for a world where I could discover this tradition perpetually, and not in pictures and in poems only, but in tiles round the chimney-piece and in the hangings that kept out the draught. I had even created a dogma: 'Because those imaginary people are created out of the deepest instinct of man, to be his measure and his norm, whatever I can imagine those mouths speaking may be the nearest I can go to truth'. When I listened they seemed always to speak of one thing only: they, their loves, every incident of their lives, were steeped in the supernatural. Could even Titian's *Ariosto* that I loved beyond other portraits have its grave look, as if waiting for some perfect final event, if the painters before Titian had not learned portraiture while painting into the corner of compositions full of saints and Madonnas their kneeling patrons? At seventeen years old I was already an old-fashioned brass cannon full of shot, and nothing had kept me from going off but a doubt as to my capacity to shoot straight.

Modern Poetry: A Broadcast[4]

The period from the death of Tennyson until the present moment has, it seems, more good lyric poets than any similar period since the seventeenth century – no great overpowering figures, but many poets who have written some three or four lyrics apiece which may be permanent in our literature. It did not always seem so; even two years ago I should have said the opposite; I should have named three or four poets and said there was nobody else who mattered. Then I gave all my time to the study of that poetry. There was a club of poets – you may know its name, 'The Rhymers' Club'[5] – which first met, I think, a few months before the death of Tennyson and lasted seven or eight years. It met in a Fleet Street tavern called 'The Cheshire Cheese.' Two members of the Club are vivid in my memory: Ernest Dowson, timid, silent, a little melancholy, lax in body, vague in attitude; Lionel Johnson, determined, erect, his few words dogmatic, almost a dwarf but beautifully made, his features cut in ivory. His thought dominated the scene and gave the Club its character. Nothing of importance could be discovered, he would say, science must be confined to the kitchen or the workshop; only philosophy and religion could solve the great secret, and they said all their say years ago; a gentleman was a man who understood Greek. I was full of crude speculation that made me ashamed. I remember praying that I might get my imagination fixed upon life itself, like the imagination of Chaucer. In those days I was a convinced ascetic, yet I envied Dowson his dissipated life. I thought it must be easy to think like Chaucer when you lived among those morbid, elegant, tragic women suggested by Dowson's poetry, painted and drawn by his friends Conder and Beardsley.[6] You must all know those famous lines that are in so many anthologies: –

> Unto us they belong,
> Us the bitter and gay,
> Wine and woman and song.

When I repeated those beautiful lines it never occurred to me to wonder why the Dowson I knew seemed neither gay nor bitter. A provincial, conscious of clumsiness and lack of self-possession, I still more envied Lionel Johnson, who had met, as I believed, everybody of importance. If one spoke of some famous ecclesiastic or statesman he would say: 'I know him intimately,' and quote some conversation that laid bare that man's soul. He was never a satirist, being too courteous, too just, for that distortion. One felt that these conversations had happened exactly as he said. Years were to pass before I discovered that Dowson's life, except when he came to the Rhymers' or called upon some friend selected for an extreme respectability, was a sordid round of drink and cheap harlots; that Lionel Johnson had never met those famous men, that he never met anybody, because he got up at nightfall, got drunk at a public-house or worked half the night, sat the other half, a glass of whisky at his elbow, staring at the brown corduroy curtains that protected from dust the books that lined his walls, imagining the puppets that were the true companions of his mind. He met Dowson, but then Dowson was nobody and he was convinced that he did Dowson good. He had no interest in women, and on that subject was perhaps eloquent. Some friends of mine saw them one moonlight night returning from the 'Crown' public-house which had just closed, their zig-zagging feet requiring the whole width of Oxford Street, Lionel Johnson talking. My friend stood still eavesdropping; Lionel Johnson was expounding a Father of the Church. Their piety, in Dowson a penitential sadness, in Lionel Johnson more often a noble ecstasy, was, as I think, illuminated and intensified by their contrasting puppet-shows, those elegant, tragic penitents, those great men in their triumph. You may know Lionel Johnson's poem on the statue of King Charles, or that characteristic poem that begins: 'Ah, see the fair chivalry come, the Companions of Christ.' In my present mood, remembering his scholarship, remembering that his religious sense was never divided from his sense of the past, I recall most vividly his 'Church of a Dream': –

Sadly the dead leaves rustle in the whistling wind,
Around the weather-worn, grey church, low down the vale:
The Saints in golden vesture shake before the gale;
The glorious windows shake, where still they dwell enshrined;
Old Saints by long-dead, shrivelled hands, long since designed:
There still, although the world autumnal be, and pale,
Still in their golden vesture the old Saints prevail;
Alone with Christ, desolate else, left by mankind.

Only one ancient priest offers the Sacrifice,
Murmuring holy Latin immemorial:
Swaying with tremulous hands the old censer full of spice,
In grey, sweet incense clouds; blue, sweet clouds mystical:
To him, in place of men, for he is old, suffice
Melancholy remembrances and vesperal.

There were other poets, generally a few years younger, who having escaped that first wave of excitement lived tame and orderly lives. But they, too, were in reaction against everything Victorian.

A church in the style of Inigo Jones opens on to a grass lawn a few hundred yards from the Marble Arch. It was designed by a member of the Rhymers' Club, whose architecture, like his poetry, seemed to exist less for his own sake than to illustrate his genius as a connoisseur. I have sometimes thought that masterpiece, perhaps the smallest church in London, the most appropriate symbol of all that was most characteristic in the art of my friends. Their poems seemed to say: 'You will remember us the longer because we are very small, very unambitious.' Yet my friends were most ambitious men; they wished to express life at its intense moments, those moments that are brief because of their intensity, and at those moments alone.[7] In the Victorian era the most famous poetry was often a passage in a poem of some length, perhaps of great length, a poem full of thoughts that might have been expressed in prose. A short lyric seemed an accident, an interruption amid more serious work. Somebody has quoted Browning as saying that he could have written many lyrics had he thought them worth the trouble. The aim of my friends, my own aim, if it sometimes made us prefer the acorn to the oak, the small to the great, freed us from many things that we thought an impurity. Swinburne, Tennyson, Arnold, Browning, had admitted so much psychology, science, moral fervour. Had not Verlaine[8] said of *In Memoriam*, 'When he should have been broken-hearted he had many reminiscences'? We tried to write like the poets of the Greek Anthology, or like Catullus, or like the Jacobean lyrists, men who wrote while poetry was still pure. We did not look forward or look outward, we left that to the prose writers; we looked back. We thought it was in the very nature of poetry to look back, to resemble those Swedenborgian angels who are described as moving for ever towards the dayspring of their youth. In this we were all, orderly and disorderly alike, in full agreement.

1936.

The Tragic Generation[9]

The Rhymers had begun to break up in tragedy, though we did not know that till the play had finished. I have never found a full explanation of that tragedy; sometimes I have remembered that, unlike the Victorian poets, almost all were poor men, and had made it a matter of conscience to turn from every kind of money-making that prevented good writing, and that poverty meant strain, and, for the most part, a refusal of domestic life. Then I have remembered that Johnson had private means, and that others who came to tragic ends had wives and families. Another day I think that perhaps our form of lyric, our insistence upon emotion which has no relation to any public interest, gathered together overwrought, unstable men; and remember, the moment after, that the first to go out of his mind had no lyrical gift, and that we valued him mainly because he seemed a witty man of the world; and that a little later another who seemed, alike as man and writer, dull and formless, went out of his mind, first burning poems which I cannot believe would have proved him, as the one man who saw them claims, a man of genius. The meetings were always decorous and often dull; some one would read out a poem and we would comment, too politely for the criticism to have great value; and yet that we read out our poems, and thought that they could be so tested, was a definition of our aims. *Love's Nocturne*[10] is one of the most beautiful poems in the world, but no one can find out its beauty, so intricate its thought and metaphor, till he has read it over several times, or stopped several times to re-read a passage; and the *Faustine* of Swinburne, where much is powerful and musical, could not, were it read out, be understood with pleasure, however clearly it were read, because it has no more logical structure than a bag of shot. I shall, however, remember all my life that evening when Lionel Johnson read or spoke aloud in his musical monotone, where meaning and cadence found the most precise elocution, his poem suggested 'by the Statue of King Charles at Charing Cross'. It was as though I listened to a great speech. Nor will that poem be to me again what it was that first night. For long I only knew Dowson's *O Mors*, to quote but the first words of its long title, and his *Villanelle of Sunset* from his reading, and it was because of the desire to hold them in my hand that I suggested the first *Book of The Rhymers' Club*. They were not speech but perfect song, though song for the speaking voice. It was perhaps our delight in poetry that was, before all else, speech or song, and could hold the attention of a fitting audience like a good play or good conversation, that made Francis Thompson,[11] whom we admired so much – before the publication of his first poem I had brought to the Cheshire

Cheese the proof-sheets of his *Ode to the Setting Sun*, his first published poem – come but once and refuse to contribute to our book. Preoccupied with his elaborate verse, he may have seen only that which we renounced, and thought what seemed to us simplicity, mere emptiness. To some members this simplicity, was perhaps created by their tumultuous lives, they praised a desired woman and hoped that she would find amid their praise her very self, or at worst their very passion; and knew that she, ignoramus that she was, would have slept in the middle of *Love's Nocturne*, lofty and tender though it be. Woman herself was still in our eyes, for all that, romantic and mysterious, still the priestess of her shrine, our emotions remembering the *Lilith* and the *Sibylla Palmifera*[12] of Rossetti; for as yet that sense of comedy which was soon to mould the very fashion-plates, and, in the eyes of men of my generation, to destroy at last the sense of beauty itself, had scarce begun to show here and there, in slight subordinate touches, among the designs of great painters and craftsmen. It could not be otherwise, for Johnson's favourite phrase, that life is ritual, expressed something that was in some degree in all our thoughts, and how could life be ritual if woman had not her symbolical place?

If Rossetti was a subconscious influence, and perhaps the most powerful of all, we looked consciously to Pater for our philosophy.[13] Three or four years ago I re-read *Marius the Epicurean*, expecting to find I cared for it no longer, but it still seemed to me, as I think it seemed to us all, the only great prose in modern English, and yet I began to wonder if it, or the attitude of mind of which it was the noblest expression, had not caused the disaster of my friends. It taught us to walk upon a rope tightly stretched through serene air, and we were left to keep our feet upon a swaying rope in a storm. Pater had made us learned; and, whatever we might be elsewhere, ceremonious and polite, and distant in our relations to one another, and I think none knew as yet that Dowson, who seemed to drink so little and had so much dignity and reserve, was breaking his heart for the daughter of the keeper of an Italian eating-house, in dissipation and drink; and that he might that very night sleep upon a sixpenny bed in a doss-house. It seems to me that even yet, and I am speaking of 1894 and 1895, we knew nothing of one another but the poems that we read and criticized; perhaps I have forgotten or was too much in Ireland for knowledge, but of this I am certain, we shared nothing but the artistic life. Sometimes Johnson and Symons would visit our sage at Oxford, and I remember Johnson, whose reports, however, were not always to be trusted, returning with a sentence that long ran in my head. He had noticed books on political economy among Pater's books, and Pater had said, 'Everything that has occupied man, for any length of time, is worthy of our study'. Perhaps it was because of Pater's influence that we, with an affectation of learning, claimed the whole past of literature for our authority, instead of finding it, like the young men in the age of comedy that followed us, in some new, and so still unrefuted authority; that we preferred what seemed still uncrumbled rock to the still unspotted foam; that we were traditional alike in our dress, in our manner, in our opinions, and in our style.

Why should men who spoke their opinions in low voices, as though they feared to disturb the readers in some ancient library, and timidly as though they knew that all subjects had long since been explored, all questions long since decided in books whereon the dust settled, live lives of such disorder and seek to rediscover in verse the syntax of impulsive common life? Was it that we lived in what is called 'an age of transition' and so lacked coherence, or did we but pursue antithesis?[14]

Art and Ideas[15]

I.

Two days ago I was at the Tate Gallery to see the early Millais's, and before his *Ophelia*, as before the *Mary Magdalene* and *Mary of Galilee* of Rossetti that hung near, I recovered an old emotion. I saw these pictures as I had seen pictures in my childhood. I forgot the art criticism of friends and saw wonderful, sad, happy people, moving through the scenery of my dreams. The painting of the hair, the way it was smoothed from its central parting, something in the oval of the peaceful faces, called up memories of sketches of my father's on the margins of the first Shelley I had read, while the strong colours made me half remember studio conversations, words of Wilson, or of

Potter[16] perhaps, praise of the primary colours, heard, it may be, as I sat over my toys or a child's story-book. One picture looked familiar, and suddenly I remembered it had hung in our house for years. It was Potter's *Field Mouse.* I had learned to think in the midst of the last phase of Pre-Raphaelitism and now I had come to Pre-Raphaelitism again and rediscovered my earliest thought. I murmured to myself, 'The only painting of modern England that could give pleasure to a child, the only painting that would seem as moving as *The Pilgrim's Progress* or Hans Andersen.' 'Am I growing old,' I thought, 'like the woman in Balzac, the rich bourgeois' ambitious wife, who could not keep, when old age came upon her, from repeating the jokes of the concierge's lodge where she had been born and bred; or is it because of some change in the weather that I find beauty everywhere, even in Burne-Jones's *King Cophetua*, one of his later pictures, and find it without shame?' I have had like admiration many times in the last twenty years, for I have always loved those pictures where I meet persons associated with the poems or the religious ideas that have most moved me; but never since my boyhood have I had it without shame, without the certainty that I would hear the cock crow presently. I remembered that as a young man I had read in Schopenhauer that no man – so unworthy a thing is life seen with unbesotted eyes – would live another's life, and had thought I would be content to paint, like Burne-Jones and Morris under Rossetti's rule, the Union at Oxford, to set up there the traditional images most moving to young men while the adventure of uncommitted life can still change all to romance, even though I should know that what I painted must fade from the walls.

II.

Thereon I ask myself if my conception of my own art is altering, if there, too, I praise what I once derided. When I began to write I avowed for my principles those of Arthur Hallam in his essay upon Tennyson.[17] Tennyson, who had written but his early poems when Hallam wrote, was an example of the school of Keats and Shelley, and Keats and Shelley, unlike Wordsworth, intermixed into their poetry no elements from the general thought, but wrote out of the impression made by the world upon their delicate senses. They were of the aesthetic school – was he the inventor of the name? – and could not be popular because their readers could not understand them without attaining to a like delicacy of sensation and so must needs turn from them to Wordsworth or another, who condescended to moral maxims, or some received philosophy, a multitude of things that even common sense could understand. Wordsworth had not less genius than the others – even Hallam allowed his genius; we are not told that Mary of Galilee was more beautiful than the more popular Mary; but certainly we might consider Wordsworth a little disreputable.

I developed these principles to the rejection of all detailed description, that I might not steal the painter's business, and indeed I was always discovering some art or science that I might be rid of: and I found encouragement by noticing all round me painters who were ridding their pictures, and indeed their minds, of literature. Yet those delighted senses, when I had got from them all that I could, left me discontented. Impressions that needed so elaborate a record did not seem like the handiwork of those careless old writers one imagines squabbling over a mistress, or riding on a journey, or drinking round a tavern fire, brisk and active men. Crashaw could hymn Saint Teresa in the most impersonal of ecstasies and seem no sedentary man out of reach of common sympathy, no disembodied mind, and yet in his day the life that appeared most rich and stirring was already half forgotten with Villon and Dante.

This difficulty was often in my mind, but I put it aside, for the new formula was a good switch while the roads were beset with geese; it set us free from politics, theology, science, all that zeal and eloquence Swinburne and Tennyson found so intoxicating after the passion of their youth had sunk, free from the conventional nobility borne hither from ancient Rome in the galley that carried academic form to vex the painters. Among the little group of poets that met at the Cheshire Cheese I alone loved criticism of Arthur Hallam's sort, with a shamefaced love – criticism founded upon general ideas was itself an impurity – and perhaps I alone knew Hallam's essay, but all silently obeyed a canon that had become powerful for all the arts since Whistler, in the confidence of his American *naïveté*, had told everybody that Japanese painting had no literary ideas. Yet all the while envious of the centuries before the Renaissance, before the coming of our intellectual class with its separate interests, I filled my imagination with the popular beliefs of Ireland, gathering them up among forgotten novelists in the British Museum or in Sligo cottages. I sought some symbolic language reaching far into the past and associated with familiar names and conspicuous hills that I might not be alone amid the obscure impressions of the senses, and I wrote essays recommending my friends to paint on chapel walls the Mother of God flying with Saint Joseph into Egypt along some Connacht road, a Connemara shawl about her head, or mourned the richness or reality lost to Shelley's *Prometheus Unbound* because he had not discovered in England or in Ireland his Caucasus.

I notice like contradictions among my friends who are still convinced that art should not be 'complicated by ideas' while picturing Saint Brandan in stained glass for a Connemara chapel, and even among those exuberant young men who make designs for a Phallic Temple, but consider Augustus John lost amid literature.

III.

But, after all, could we clear the matter up we might save some hours from sterile discussion. The arts are very conservative and have a great respect for those wanderers who still stitch into their carpets among the Mongolian plains religious symbols so old they have not even a meaning. It cannot be they would lessen an association with one another and with religion that gave them authority among ancient peoples. They are not radicals, and if they deny themselves to any it can only be to the *nouveau riche*, and if they have grown rebellious it can only be against something that is modern, something that is not simple.

I think that before the religious change that followed on the Renaissance men were greatly preoccupied with their sins, and that to-day they are troubled by other men's sins, and that this trouble has created a moral enthusiasm so full of illusion that art, knowing itself for sanctity's scapegrace brother, cannot be of the party. We have but held to our ancient Church, where there is an altar and no pulpit, and founded, the guide-book tells us, upon the ruins of the temple of Jupiter Ammon, and turned away from the too great vigour of those who, living for mutual improvement, have a pulpit and no altar. We fear that a novel enthusiasm might make us forget the little round of poetical duties and imitations – humble genuflexions and circumambulations as it were – that does not unseat the mind's natural impulse, and seems always but half-conscious, almost bodily.

Painting had to free itself from a classicalism that denied the senses, a domesticity that denied the passions, and poetry from a demagogic system of morals which destroyed the humility, the daily dying of the imagination in the presence of beauty. A soul shaken by the spectacle of its sins, or discovered by the Divine Vision in tragic delight, must offer to the love that cannot love but to infinity, a goal unique and unshared; while a soul busied with others' sins is soon melted to some shape of vulgar pride. What can I offer to God but the ghost that must return undisfeatured to the hands that have not made the same thing twice, but what would I have of others but that they do some expected thing, reverence my plans, be in some way demure and reliable? The turning of Rossetti to religious themes, his dislike of Wordsworth, were but the one impulse, for he more than any other was in reaction against the period of philanthropy and reform that created the pedantic composure of Wordsworth, the rhetoric of Swinburne, the passionless sentiment of Tennyson. The saint does not claim to be a good example, hardly even to tell men what to do, for is he not the chief of sinners, and of how little can he be certain whether in the night of the soul or lost in the sweetness coming after? Nor can that composure of the moralists be dear to one who has heard the commandment, that is for the saint and his brother the poet alike, 'Make excess ever more abundantly excessive', even were it possible to one shaken and trembling from his daily struggle.

IV.

We knew that system of popular instruction was incompatible with our hopes, but we did not know how to refute it and so turned away from all ideas. We would not even permit ideas, so greatly had we come to distrust them, to leave their impressions upon our senses. Yet works of art are always begotten by previous works of art, and every masterpiece becomes the Abraham of a chosen people. When we delight in a spring day there mixes, perhaps, with our personal emotion an emotion Chaucer found in Guillaume de Lorris, who had it from the poetry of Provence;[18] we celebrate our draughty May with an enthusiasm made ripe by more meridian suns; and all our art has its image in the Mass that would lack authority were it not descended from savage ceremonies taught amid what perils and by what spirits to naked savages. The old images, the old emotions, awakened again to overwhelming life, like the gods Heine tells of,[19] by the belief and passion of some new soul, are the only masterpieces. The resolution to stand alone, to owe nothing to the past, when it is not mere sense of property, the greed and pride of the counting-house, is the result of that individualism of the Renaissance which had done its work when it gave us personal freedom. The soul which may not obscure or change its form can yet receive those passions and symbols of antiquity, certain they are too old to be bullies, too well-mannered not to respect the rights of others.

Nor had we better warrant to separate one art from another, for there has been no age before our own wherein the arts have been other than a single authority, a Holy Church of Romance, the might of all lying behind all, a circle of cliffs, a wilderness where every cry has its echoes. Why should a man cease to be a scholar, a believer, a ritualist before he begin to paint or rhyme or to compose music, or why if he have a strong head should he put away any means of power?

V.

Yet it is plain that the casting out of ideas was the more natural, misunderstanding though it was, because it had come to matter very little. The manner of painting had changed, and we were interested in the fall of drapery and the play of light without concerning ourselves with the meaning, the emotion of the figure itself. How many successful portrait-painters gave their sitters the same attention, the same interest they might have given to a ginger-beer bottle and an apple? and in our poems an absorption in fragmentary sensuous beauty or detachable ideas had deprived us of the power to mould vast material into a single image. What long modern poem equals the old poems in architectural unity, in symbolic importance? *The Revolt of Islam*, *The Excursion*, *Gebir*, *Idylls of the King*, even perhaps *The Ring and the Book*, which fills me with so much admiring astonishment that my judgment sleeps, are remembered for some occasional passage, some moment which gains little from the context. Until very lately even the short poems which contained as clearly as an Elizabethan lyric the impression of a single idea seemed accidental, so much the rule were the 'Faustines' and 'Dolores' where the verses might be arranged in any order, like shot poured out of a bag. Arnold when he withdrew his *Empedocles on Etna*, though one had been sorry to lose so much lyrical beauty for ever, showed himself a great critic by his reasons, but his *Sohrab and Rustum* proves that the unity he imagined was a classical imitation and not an organic thing, not the flow of flesh under the impulse of passionate thought.

Those poets with whom I feel myself in sympathy have tried to give to little poems the spontaneity of a gesture or of some casual emotional phrase. Meanwhile it remains for some greater time, living once more in passionate reverie, to create a *King Lear*, a *Divine Comedy*, vast worlds moulded by their own weight like drops of water.

In the visual arts, indeed, 'the fall of man into his own circumference' seems at an end, and when I look at the photograph of a picture by Gauguin, which hangs over my breakfast-table, the spectacle of tranquil Polynesian girls crowned with lilies gives me, I do not know why, religious ideas. Our appreciations of the older schools are changing too, becoming simpler, and when we take pleasure in some Chinese painting of an old man meditating upon a mountain path, we share his meditation, without forgetting the beautiful intricate pattern of the lines like those we have seen under our eyelids as we fell asleep; nor do the Bride and Bridegroom of Rajput painting, sleeping upon a house-top, or wakening when out of the still water the swans fly upward at the dawn, seem the less well painted because they remind us of many poems. We are becoming interested in expression in its first phase of energy, when all the arts play like children about the one chimney, and turbulent innocence can yet amuse those brisk and active men who have paid us so little attention of recent years. Shall we be rid of the pride of intellect, of sedentary meditation, of emotion that leaves us when the book is closed or the picture seen no more; and live amid the thoughts that can go with us by steamboat and railway as once upon horseback, or camel-back, rediscovering, by our reintegration of the mind, our more profound Pre-Raphaelitism, the old abounding, nonchalant reverie?

1913.

What is 'Popular Poetry'?[20]

I think it was a Young Ireland Society that set my mind running on 'popular poetry.' We used to discuss everything that was known to us about Ireland, and especially Irish literature and Irish history. We had no Gaelic, but paid great honour to the Irish poets who wrote in English, and quoted them in our speeches. [. . .] I wanted to write 'popular poetry' like those Irish poets, for I believed that all good literatures were popular, and even cherished the fancy that the Adelphi melodrama, which I had never seen, might be good literature, and I hated what I called the coteries. I thought that one must write without care, for that was of the coteries, but with a gusty energy that would put all straight if it came out of the right heart. I had a conviction, which indeed I have still, that one's verses should hold, as in a mirror, the colours of one's own climate and scenery in their right proportion; and, when I found my verses too full of the reds and yellows Shelley gathered in Italy, I thought for two days of setting things right, not as I should now by making my rhythms faint and nervous and filling my images with a certain coldness, a certain wintry wildness, but by eating little and sleeping upon a board. I felt indignant with Matthew Arnold because he complained that somebody, who had translated Homer into a ballad measure, had tried to write epic to the tune of 'Yankee Doodle.' It seemed to me that it did not matter what tune one wrote to, so long as that gusty energy came often enough and strongly enough. And I delighted in Victor Hugo's book upon Shakespeare, because he abused critics and coteries and thought that Shakespeare wrote without care or premeditation and to please everybody. I would indeed have had every illusion had I believed in that straightforward logic, as of newspaper articles, which so tickles an ignorant ear; but I always knew that the line of Nature is crooked, that, though we dig the canal-beds as straight as we can, the rivers run hither and thither in their wildness.

From that day to this I have been busy among the verses and stories that the people make for themselves, but I had been busy a very little while before I knew that what we call 'popular poetry' never came from the people at all. Longfellow, and Campbell, and Mrs. Hemans, and Macaulay in his *Lays*, and Scott in his longer poems are the poets of a predominant portion of the middle class, of people who have unlearned the unwritten tradition which binds the unlettered, so long as they are masters of themselves, to the beginning of time and to the foundation of the world, and who have not learned the written tradition which has been established upon the unwritten. I became certain that Burns, whose greatness had been used to justify the littleness of others, was in part a poet of this portion of the middle class, because though the farmers he sprang from and lived among had been able to create a little tradition of their own, less a tradition of ideas than of speech, they had been divided by religious and political changes from the images and emotions which had once carried their memories backward thousands of years. Despite his expressive speech which sets him above all other popular poets, he has the triviality of emotion, the poverty of ideas, the imperfect sense of beauty of a poetry whose most typical expression is in Longfellow. Longfellow has his popularity, in the main, because he tells his story or his ideas so that one needs nothing but his verses to understand it. No words of his borrow their beauty from those that used them before, and one can get all that there is in story and idea without seeing them as if moving before a half-faded curtain embroidered with kings and queens, their loves and battles and their days out hunting, or else with holy letters and images of so great antiquity that nobody can tell the god or goddess they would commend to an unfading memory. Poetry that is not 'popular poetry' presupposes, indeed, more than it says, though we, who cannot know what it is to be disinherited, only understand how much more, when we read it in its most typical expressions, in the *Epipsychidion* of Shelley, or in Spenser's description of the gardens of Adonis,[21] or when we meet the misunderstandings of others. Go down into the street and read to your baker or your candlestick-maker any poem which is not 'popular poetry.' I have heard a baker, who was clever enough with his oven, deny that Tennyson could have known what he was writing when he wrote, 'Warming his five wits, the white owl in the belfry sits,' and once when I read out Omar Khayyám to one of the best of candlestick-makers, he said, 'What is the meaning of "I came like water and like wind I go"?' Or go down into the street with some thought whose bare meaning must be plain to everybody; take with you Ben Jonson's 'Beauty like sorrow dwelleth everywhere,' and find out how utterly its enchantment depends on an association of beauty with sorrow which written tradition has from the unwritten, which had it in its turn from ancient religion; or take with you these lines in whose bare meaning also there is nothing to stumble over, and find out what men lose who are not in love with Helen –

> Brightness falls from the air,
> Queens have died young and fair,
> Dust hath closed Helen's eye.[22]

I pick my examples at random, for I am writing where I have no books to turn the pages of, but one need not go east of the sun or west of the moon in so simple a matter.

On the other hand, when Walt Whitman writes in seeming defiance of tradition, he needs tradition for protection, for the butcher and the baker and the candlestick-maker grow merry over him when they meet his work by chance. Nature, being unable to endure emptiness, has made them gather conventions which cannot hide that they are low-born things though copies, as from far off, of the dress and manners of the well-bred and the well-born. The gatherers mock all expression that is wholly unlike their own, just as little boys in the street mock at strangely dressed people and at old men who talk to themselves.

There is only one kind of good poetry, for the poetry of the coteries, which presupposes the written tradition, does not differ in kind from the true poetry of the people, which presupposes the unwritten tradition. Both are alike strange and obscure, and unreal to all who have not understanding, and both, instead of that manifest logic, that clear rhetoric of the 'popular poetry,' glimmer with thoughts and images whose 'ancestors were stout and wise,' 'anigh to Paradise' 'ere yet men knew the gift of corn.' It may be that we know as little of their descent as men knew of 'the man born to be a king' when they found him in that cradle marked with the red lion crest, and yet we know somewhere in the heart that they have been sung in temples, in ladies' chambers, and quiver with a recognition our nerves have been shaped to by a thousand emotions. If men did not remember or half remember impossible things, and, it may be, if the worship of sun and moon had not left a faint reverence behind it, what Aran fisher-girl would sing: – [. . .]

'You have taken the east from me, you have taken the west from me, you have taken what is before me and what is behind me; you have taken the moon, you have taken the sun from me, and my fear is great you have taken God from me.' [. . .]

I soon learned to cast away one other illusion of 'popular poetry.' I learned from the people themselves, before I learned it from any book, that they cannot separate the idea of an art or a craft from the idea of a cult with ancient technicalities and mysteries. They can hardly separate mere learning from witchcraft, and are fond of words and verses that keep half their secret to themselves. Indeed, it is certain that before the counting-house had created a new class and a new art without breeding and without ancestry, and set this art and this class between the hut and the castle, and between the hut and the cloister, the art of the people was as closely mingled with the art of the coteries as was the speech of the people that delighted in rhythmical animation, in idiom, in images, in words full of far-off suggestion, with the unchanging speech of the poets.

1901.

The Symbolism of Poetry[23]

I.

Symbolism, as seen in the writers of our day, would have no value if it were not seen also, under one 'disguise or another, in every great imaginative writer,' writes Mr. Arthur Symons in *The Symbolist Movement in Literature*, a subtle book which I cannot praise as I would, because it has been dedicated to me; and he goes on to show how many profound writers have in the last few years sought for a philosophy of poetry in the doctrine of symbolism, and how even in countries where it is almost scandalous to seek for any philosophy of poetry, new writers are following them in their search. We do not know what the writers of ancient times talked of among themselves, and one bull is all that remains of Shakespeare's talk, who was on the edge of modern times; and the journalist is convinced, it seems, that they talked of wine and women and politics, but never about their art, or never quite seriously about their art. He is certain that no one who had a philosophy of his art, or a theory of how he should write, has ever made a work of art, that people have no imagination who do not write without forethought and afterthought as he writes his own articles. He says this with enthusiasm, because he has heard it at so many comfortable dinner-tables, where some one had mentioned through carelessness, or foolish zeal, a book whose difficulty had offended indolence, or a man who had not forgotten that beauty is an accusation. Those formulas and generalisations, in which a hidden sergeant has drilled the ideas of journalists and through them the ideas of all but all the modern world, have created in their turn a forgetfulness like that of soldiers in battle, so that journalists and their readers have forgotten, among many like events, that Wagner spent seven years arranging and explaining his ideas before he began his most characteristic music; that opera, and with it modern music, arose from certain talks at the house of one Giovanni Bardi of Florence; and that the Pléiade laid the foundations of modern French literature with a pamphlet.[24] Goethe has said, 'a poet needs all philosophy, but he must keep it out of his work,' though that is not always necessary; and almost certainly no great art, outside England, where journalists are more powerful and ideas less plentiful than elsewhere, has arisen without a great criticism, for its herald or its interpreter and protector, and it may be for this reason that great art, now that vulgarity has armed itself and multiplied itself, is perhaps dead in England.

All writers, all artists of any kind, in so far as they have had any philosophical or critical power, perhaps just in so far as they have been deliberate artists at all, have had some philosophy, some criticism of their art; and it has often been this philosophy, or this criticism, that has evoked their most startling inspiration, calling into outer life some portion of the divine life, or of the buried reality, which could alone extinguish in the emotions what their philosophy or their criticism would extinguish in the intellect. They have sought for no new thing, it may be, but only to understand and to copy the pure inspiration of early times, but because the divine life wars upon our outer life, and must needs change its weapons and its movements as we change ours, inspiration has come to them in beautiful startling shapes. The scientific movement brought with it a literature which was always tending to lose itself in externalities of all kinds, in opinion, in declamation, in picturesque writing, in word-painting, or in what Mr. Symons has called an attempt 'to build in brick and mortar inside the covers of a book'; and now writers have begun to dwell upon the element of evocation, of suggestion, upon what we call the symbolism in great writers.

II.

In 'Symbolism in Painting,' I tried to describe the element of symbolism that is in pictures and sculpture, and described a little the symbolism in poetry, but did not describe at all the continuous indefinable symbolism which is the substance of all style.

There are no lines with more melancholy beauty than these by Burns: –

> The white moon is setting behind the white wave,
> And Time is setting with me, O![25]

and these lines are perfectly symbolical. Take from them the whiteness of the moon and of the wave, whose relation to the setting of Time is too subtle for the intellect, and you take from them their beauty. But, when all are together, moon and wave and whiteness and setting Time and the last melancholy cry, they evoke an emotion which cannot be evoked by any other arrangement of colours and sounds and forms. We may call this metaphorical writing, but it is better to call it symbolical writing, because metaphors are not profound enough to be moving, when they are not symbols, and when they are symbols they are the most perfect of all, because the most subtle, outside of pure sound, and through them one can best find out what symbols are. If one begins the reverie with any beautiful lines that one can remember, one finds they are like those by Burns. Begin with this line by Blake: –

> The gay fishes on the wave when the moon sucks up the dew;

or these lines by Nash: –

> Brightness falls from the air,
> Queens have died young and fair,
> Dust hath closed Helen's eye;

or these lines by Shakespeare: –

> Timon hath made his everlasting mansion
> Upon the beached verge of the salt flood;
> Who once a day with his embossed froth
> The turbulent surge shall cover;[26]

or take some line that is quite simple, that gets its beauty from its place in a story, and see how it flickers with the light of the many symbols that have given the story its beauty, as a sword-blade may flicker with the light of burning towers.

All sounds, all colours, all forms, either because of their preordained energies or because of long association, evoke indefinable and yet precise emotions, or, as I prefer to think, call down among us certain disembodied powers, whose footsteps over our hearts we call emotions; and when sound, and colour, and form are in a musical relation, a beautiful relation to one another, they become, as it were, one sound, one colour, one form, and evoke an emotion that is made out of their distinct evocations and yet is one emotion. The same relation exists between all portions of every work of art, whether it be an epic or a song, and the more perfect it is, and the more various and numerous the elements that have flowed into its perfection, the more powerful will be the emotion, the power, the god it calls among us. Because an emotion does not exist, or does not become perceptible and active among us, till it has found its expression, in colour or in sound or in form, or in all of these, and because no two modulations or arrangements of these evoke the same emotion, poets and painters and musicians, and in a less degree because their effects are momentary, day and night and cloud and shadow, are continually making and unmaking mankind. It is indeed only those things which seem useless or very feeble that have any power, and all those things that seem useful or strong, armies, moving wheels, modes of architecture, modes of government, speculations of the reason, would have been a little different if some mind long ago had not given itself to some emotion, as a woman gives herself to her lover, and shaped sounds or colours or forms, or all of these, into a musical relation, that their emotion might live in other minds. A little lyric evokes an emotion, and this emotion gathers others about it and melts into their being in the making of some great epic; and at last, needing an always less delicate body, or symbol, as it grows more powerful, it flows out, with all it has gathered, among the blind instincts of daily life, where it moves a power within powers, as one sees ring within ring in the stem of an old tree. This is maybe what Arthur O'Shaughnessy meant when he made his poets say they had built Nineveh with their sighing;[27] and I am certainly never sure, when I hear of some war, or of some religious excitement, or of some new manufacture, or of anything else that fills the ear of the world, that it has not all happened because of something that a boy piped in Thessaly. I remember once telling a seeress to ask one among the gods who, as she believed, were standing about her in their symbolic bodies, what would come of a charming but seeming trivial labour of a friend, and the form answering, 'the devastation of peoples and the overwhelming of cities.' I doubt indeed if the crude circumstance of the world, which seems to create all our emotions, does more than reflect, as in multiplying mirrors, the emotions that have come to solitary men in moments of poetical contemplation; or that love itself would be more than an animal hunger but for the poet and his shadow the priest, for unless we believe that outer things are the reality, we must believe that the gross is the shadow of the subtle, that things are wise before they become foolish, and secret before they cry out in the market-place. Solitary men in moments of contemplation receive, as I think, the creative impulse from the lowest of the Nine Hierarchies, and so make and unmake mankind, and even the world itself, for does not 'the eye altering alter all'?[28]

> Our towns are copied fragments from our breast;
> And all man's Babylons strive but to impart
> The grandeurs of his Babylonian heart.

III.

The purpose of rhythm, it has always seemed to me, is to prolong the moment of contemplation, the moment when we are both asleep and awake, which is the one moment of creation, by hushing us with an alluring monotony, while it holds us waking by variety, to keep us in that state of perhaps real trance, in which the mind liberated from the pressure of the will is unfolded in symbols. If certain sensitive persons listen persistently to the ticking of a watch, or gaze persistently on the monotonous flashing of a light, they fall into the hypnotic trance; and rhythm is but the ticking of a watch made softer, that one must needs listen, and various, that one may not be swept beyond memory or grow weary of listening; while the patterns of the artist are but the monotonous flash woven to take the eyes in a subtler enchantment. I have heard in meditation voices that were forgotten the moment they had spoken; and I have been swept, when in more profound meditation, beyond all memory but of those things that came from beyond the threshold of waking life. I was writing once at a very symbolical and abstract poem, when my pen fell on the ground; and as I stooped to pick it up, I remembered some fantastic adventure that yet did not seem fantastic, and then another like adventure, and when I asked myself when these things had happened, I found that I was remembering my dreams for many nights. I tried to remember what I had done the day before, and then what I had done that morning; but all my waking life had perished from me, and it was only after a struggle that I came to remember it again, and as I did so that more powerful and startling life perished in its turn. Had my pen not fallen on the ground and so made me turn from the images that I was weaving into verse, I would never have known that meditation had become trance, for I would have been like one who does not know that he is passing through a wood because his eyes are on the pathway. So I think that in the making and understanding of a work of art, and the more easily if it is full of patterns and symbols and music, we are lured to the threshold of sleep, and it may be far beyond it, without knowing that we have ever set our feet upon the steps of horn or of ivory.

IV.

Besides emotional symbols, symbols that evoke emotions alone, – and in this sense all alluring or hateful things are symbols, although their relations with one another are too subtle to delight us fully, away from rhythm and pattern, – there are intellectual symbols, symbols that evoke ideas alone, or ideas mingled with emotions; and outside the very definite traditions of mysticism and the less definite criticism of certain modern poets, these alone are called symbols. Most things belong to one or another kind, according to the way we speak of them and the companions we give them, for symbols, associated with ideas that are more than fragments of the shadows thrown upon the intellect by the emotions they evoke, are the playthings of the allegorist or the pedant, and soon pass away. If I say 'white' or 'purple' in an ordinary line of poetry, they evoke emotions so exclusively that I cannot say why they move me; but if I bring them into the same sentence with such obvious intellectual symbols as a cross or a crown of thorns, I think of purity and sovereignty. Furthermore, innumerable meanings, which are held to 'white' or to 'purple' by bonds of subtle suggestion, and alike in the emotions and in the intellect, move visibly through my mind, and move invisibly beyond the threshold of sleep, casting lights and shadows of an indefinable wisdom on what had seemed before, it may be, but sterility and noisy violence. It is the intellect that decides where the reader shall ponder over the procession of the symbols, and if the symbols are merely emotional, he gazes from amid the accidents and destinies of the world; but if the symbols are intellectual too, he becomes himself a part of pure intellect, and he is himself mingled with the procession. If I watch a rushy pool in the moonlight, my emotion at its beauty is mixed with memories of the man that I have seen ploughing by its margin, or of the lovers I saw there a night ago; but if I look at the moon herself and remember any of her ancient names and meanings, I move among divine people, and things that have shaken off our mortality, the tower of ivory, the queen of waters, the shining stag among enchanted woods, the white hare sitting upon the hilltop, the fool of Faery with his shining cup full of dreams, and it may be 'make a friend of one of these images of wonder,' and 'meet the Lord in the air'. So, too, if one is moved by Shakespeare, who is content with emotional symbols that he may come the nearer to our sympathy, one is mixed with the whole spectacle of the world; while if one is moved by Dante, or by the myth of Demeter, one is mixed into the shadow of God or of a goddess. So, too, one is furthest from symbols when one is busy doing this or that, but the soul moves among symbols and unfolds in symbols when trance, or madness, or deep meditation has withdrawn it from every impulse but its own. 'I then saw,' wrote Gérard de Nerval of his madness, 'vaguely drifting into form, plastic images of antiquity, which outlined themselves, became definite, and seemed to represent symbols of which I only seized the idea with difficulty.' In an earlier time he would have been of that multitude whose souls austerity withdrew, even more perfectly than madness could withdraw his soul, from hope and memory, from desire and regret, that they might reveal those processions of symbols that men bow to before altars, and woo with incense and offerings. But being of our time, he has been like Maeterlinck, like Villiers de l'Isle-Adam in *Axël*, like all who are preoccupied with intellectual symbols in our time, a foreshadower of the new sacred book, of which all the arts, as somebody has said, are beginning to dream.[29] How can the arts overcome the slow dying of men's hearts that we call the progress of the world, and lay their hands upon men's heart-strings again, without becoming the garment of religion as in old times?

V.

If people were to accept the theory that poetry moves us because of its symbolism, what change should one look for in the manner of our poetry? A return to the way of our fathers, a casting out of descriptions of nature for the sake of nature, of the moral law for the sake of the moral law, a casting out of all anecdotes and of that brooding over scientific opinion that so often extinguished the central flame in Tennyson, and of that vehemence that would make us do or not do certain things; or, in other words, we should come to understand that the beryl stone was enchanted by our fathers that it might unfold the pictures of its heart, and not to mirror our own excited faces, or the boughs waving outside the window. With this change of substance, this return to imagination, this understanding that the laws of art, which are hidden laws of the world, can alone bind the imagination, would come a change of style, and we would cast out of serious poetry those energetic rhythms, as of a man running, which are the invention of the will with its eyes always on something to be done or undone; and we would seek out those wavering, meditative, organic rhythms, which are the embodiment of the imagination, that neither desires nor hates, because it has done with time, and only wishes to gaze upon some reality, some beauty; nor would it be any longer possible for anybody to deny the importance of form, in all its kinds, for although you can expound an opinion, or describe a thing, when your words are not quite well chosen, you cannot give a body to something that moves beyond the senses, unless your words are as subtle, as complex, as full of mysterious life, as the body of a flower or of a woman. The form of sincere poetry, unlike the form of the 'popular poetry,' may indeed be sometimes obscure, or ungrammatical as in some of the best of the *Songs of Innocence and Experience*, but it must have the perfections that escape analysis, the subtleties that have a new meaning every day, and it must have all this whether it be but a little song made out of a moment of dreamy indolence, or some great epic made out of the dreams of one poet and of a hundred generations whose hands were never weary of the sword.

1900.

Magic[30]

I.

I believe in the practice and philosophy of what we have agreed to call magic, in what I must call the evocation of spirits, though I do not know what they are, in the power of creating magical illusions, in the visions of truth in the depths of the mind when the eyes are closed; and I believe in three doctrines, which have, as I think, been handed down from early times, and been the foundations of nearly all magical practices. These doctrines are: –

(1) That the borders of our mind are ever shifting, and that many minds can flow into one another, as it were, and create or reveal a single mind, a single energy.
(2) That the borders of our memories are as shifting, and that our memories are a part of one great memory, the memory of Nature herself.
(3) That this great mind and great memory can be evoked by symbols.

I often think I would put this belief in magic from me if I could, for I have come to see or to imagine, in men and women, in houses, in handicrafts, in nearly all sights and sounds, a certain evil, a certain ugliness, that comes from the slow perishing through the centuries of a quality of mind that made this belief and its evidence common over the world. [. . .]

I once saw a young Irishwoman, fresh from a convent school, cast into a profound trance, though not by a method known to any hypnotist. In her waking state she thought the apple of Eve was the kind of apple you can buy at the greengrocer's, but in her trance she saw the Tree of Life with ever-sighing souls moving in its branches instead of sap, and among its leaves all the fowls of the air, and on its highest bough one white fowl wearing a crown. When I went home I took from the shelf a translation of *The Book of Concealed Mystery*, an old Jewish book, and cutting the pages came upon this passage, which I cannot think I had ever read: 'The Tree, . . . is the Tree of the Knowledge of Good and Evil . . . in its branches the birds lodge and build their nests, the souls and the angels have their place.'

I once saw a young Church of Ireland man, a bank-clerk in the West of Ireland, thrown in a like trance. I have no doubt that he, too, was quite certain that the apple of Eve was a greengrocer's apple, and yet he saw the tree and heard the souls sighing through its branches, and saw apples with human faces, and laying his ear to an apple heard a sound as of fighting hosts within. Presently he strayed from the tree and came to the edge of Eden, and there he found himself not by the wilderness he had learned of at the Sunday-school, but upon the summit of a great mountain, of a mountain 'two miles high.' The whole summit, in contradiction to all that would have seemed probable to his waking mind, was a great walled garden. Some years afterwards I found a mediaeval diagram, which pictured Eden as a walled garden upon a high mountain.

Where did these intricate symbols come from? Neither I nor the one or two people present nor the seers had ever seen, I am convinced, the description in *The Book of Concealed Mystery*, or the mediaeval diagram. Remember that the images appeared in a moment perfect in all their complexity. If one can imagine that the seers or that I myself or another had indeed read of these images and forgotten it, that the supernatural artist's knowledge of what was in our buried memories accounted for these visions, there are numberless other visions to account for. One cannot go on believing in improbable knowledge for ever. For instance, I find in my diary that on December 27, 1897, a seer, to whom I had given a certain old Irish symbol, saw Brigid, the goddess, holding out 'a glittering and wriggling serpent,' and yet I feel certain that neither I nor he knew anything of her association with the serpent until *Carmina Gadelica*[31] was published a few months ago. And an old Irishwoman who can neither read nor write has described to me a woman dressed like Dian, with helmet, and short skirt and sandals, and what seemed to be buskins. Why, too, among all the countless stories of visions that I have gathered in Ireland, or that a friend has gathered for me, are there none that mix the dress of different periods? The seers when they are but speaking from tradition will mix everything together, and speak of Finn mac Cumhal[32] going to the Assizes at Cork. Almost every one who has ever busied himself with such matters has come, in trance or dream, upon some new and strange symbol or event, which he has afterwards found in some work he had never read or heard of. Examples like this are as yet too little classified, too little analysed, to convince the stranger, but some of them are proof enough for those they have happened to, proof that there is a memory of Nature that reveals events and symbols of distant centuries. Mystics of many countries and many centuries have spoken of this memory.

William Blake and the Imagination[33]

There have been men who loved the future like a mistress, and the future mixed her breath into their breath and shook her hair about them, and hid them from the understanding of their times. William Blake was one of these men, and if he spoke confusedly and obscurely it was because he spoke of things for whose speaking he could find no models in the world he knew. He announced the religion of art, of which no man dreamed in the world he knew; and he understood it more perfectly than the thousands of subtle spirits who have received its baptism in the world we know, because in the beginning of important things – in the beginning of love, in the beginning of the day, in the beginning of any work – there is a moment when we understand more perfectly than we understand again until all is finished. In his time educated people believed that they amused themselves with books of imagination, but that they 'made their souls' by listening to sermons and by doing or by not doing certain things. When they had to explain why serious people like themselves honoured the great poets greatly they were hard put to it for lack of good reasons. In our time we are agreed that we 'make our souls' out of some one of the great poets of ancient times, or out of Shelley or Wordsworth, or Goethe or Balzac, or Flaubert, or Count Tolstoy, in the books he wrote before he became a prophet and fell into a lesser order, or out of Mr. Whistler's pictures, while we amuse ourselves, or, at best, make a poorer sort of soul, by listening to sermons or by doing or by not doing certain things. We write of great writers, even of writers whose beauty would once have seemed an unholy beauty, with rapt sentences like those our fathers kept for the beatitudes and mysteries of the Church; and no matter what we believe with our lips, we believe with our hearts that beautiful things, as Browning said in his one prose essay that was not in verse, have 'lain burningly on the Divine hand,' and that when time has begun to wither, the Divine hand will fall heavily on bad taste and vulgarity.[34] When no man believed these things William Blake believed them, and began that preaching against the Philistines which is as the preaching of the Middle Ages against the Saracen.

He had learned from Jacob Boehme[35] and from old alchemist writers that imagination was the first emanation of divinity, 'the body of God,' 'the Divine members,' and he drew the deduction, which they did not draw, that the imaginative arts were therefore the greatest of Divine revelations, and that the sympathy with all living things, sinful and righteous alike, which the imaginative arts awaken, is that forgiveness of sins commanded by Christ. The reason, and by the reason he meant deductions from the observations of the senses, binds us to mortality because it binds us to the senses, and divides us from each other by showing us our clashing interests; but imagination divides us from mortality by the immortality of beauty, and binds us to each other by opening the secret doors of all hearts. He cried again and again that everything that lives is holy, and that nothing is unholy except things that do not live – lethargies, and cruelties, and timidities, and that denial of imagination which is the root they grew from in old times. Passions, because most living, are most holy – and this was a scandalous paradox in his time – and man shall enter eternity borne upon their wings.

And he understood this so literally that certain drawings to *Vala*,[36] had he carried them beyond the first faint pencillings, the first faint washes of colour, would have been a pretty scandal to his time and to our time. The sensations of this 'foolish body,' this 'phantom of the earth and water,' were in themselves but half-living things, 'vegetative' things, but passion, that 'eternal glory,' made them a part of the body of God.

This philosophy kept him more simply a poet than any poet of his time, for it made him content to express every beautiful feeling that came into his head without troubling about its utility or chaining it to any utility. Sometimes one feels, even when one is reading poets of a better time – Tennyson or Wordsworth, let us say – that they have troubled the energy and simplicity of their imaginative passions by asking whether they were for the helping or for the hindrance of the world, instead of believing that all beautiful things have 'lain burningly on the Divine hand.' But when one reads Blake, it is as though the spray of an inexhaustible fountain of beauty was blown into our faces, and not merely when one reads the *Songs of Innocence*, or the lyrics he wished to call 'Ideas of Good and Evil,' but when one reads those 'Prophetic Books' in which he spoke confusedly and obscurely because he spoke of things for whose speaking he could find no models in the world about him. He was a symbolist who had to invent his symbols; and his counties of England, with their correspondence to tribes of Israel, and his mountains and rivers, with their correspondence to a man's body, are arbitrary as some of the symbolism in the *Axël* of the symbolist Villiers de l'Isle-Adam is arbitrary while they mix incongruous things as *Axël* does not. He was a man crying out for a mythology, and trying to make one because he could not find one to his hand. Had he been a Catholic of Dante's time he would have been well content with Mary and the angels; or had he been a scholar of our time he would have taken his symbols where Wagner took his, from Norse mythology; or have followed, with the help of Professor Rhys, that pathway into Welsh mythology which he found in *Jerusalem*; or have gone to Ireland and chosen for his symbols the sacred mountains, along whose sides the peasant still sees enchanted fires, and the divinities which have not faded from the belief, if they have faded from the prayers, of simple hearts; and have spoken without mixing incongruous things because he spoke of things that had been long steeped in emotion; and have been less obscure because a traditional mythology stood on the threshold of his meaning and on the margin of his sacred darkness. If Enitharmon had been named Freia, or Gwydeon, or Dana, and made live in Ancient Norway, or Ancient Wales, or Ancient Ireland, we would have forgotten that her maker was a mystic; and the hymn of her harping, that is in *Vala*, would but have reminded us of many ancient hymns.

1897.

The Philosophy of Shelley's Poetry[37]

I. HIS RULING IDEAS

When I was a boy in Dublin I was one of a group who rented a room in a mean street to discuss philosophy. My fellow-students got more and more interested in certain modern schools of mystical belief, and I never found anybody to share my one unshakable belief. I thought that whatever of philosophy has been made poetry is alone permanent, and that one should begin to arrange it in some regular order, rejecting nothing as the make-believe of the poets. I thought, so far as I can recollect my thoughts after so many years, that if a powerful and benevolent spirit has shaped the destiny of this world, we can better discover that destiny from the words that have gathered up the heart's desire of the world, than from historical records, or from speculation, wherein the heart withers. Since then I have observed dreams and visions very carefully, and am now certain that the imagination has some way of lighting on the truth that the reason has not, and that its commandments, delivered when the body is still and the reason silent, are the most binding we can ever know. I have re-read *Prometheus Unbound*, which I had hoped my fellow-students would have studied as a sacred book, and it seems to me to have an even more certain place than I had thought among the sacred books of the world. I remember going to a learned scholar to ask about its deep meanings, which I felt more than understood, and his telling me that it was Godwin's *Political Justice* put into rhyme, and that Shelley was a crude revolutionist, and believed that the overturning of kings and priests would regenerate mankind. I quoted the lines which tell how the halcyons ceased to prey on fish, and how poisonous leaves became good for food, to show that he foresaw more than any political regeneration, but was too timid to push the argument. I still believe that one cannot help believing him, as this scholar I know believes him, a vague thinker, who mixed occasional great poetry with a fantastic rhetoric, unless one compares such passages, and above all such passages as describe the liberty he praised, till one has discovered the system of belief that lay behind them. It should seem natural to find his thought full of subtlety, for Mrs. Shelley has told how he hesitated whether he should be a metaphysician or a poet, and has spoken of his 'huntings after the obscure' with regret, and said of that *Prometheus Unbound*, which so many for three generations have thought *Political Justice* put into rhyme, 'It requires a mind as subtle and penetrating as his own to understand the mystic meanings scattered throughout the poem. They elude the ordinary reader by their abstraction and delicacy of distinction, but they are far from vague. It was his design to write prose metaphysical essays on the nature of Man, which would have served to explain much of what is obscure in his poetry; a few scattered fragments of observations and remarks alone remain. He considered these philosophical views of Mind and Nature to be instinct with the intensest spirit of poetry.' From these scattered fragments and observations, and from many passages read in their light, one soon comes to understand that his liberty was so much more than the liberty of *Political Justice* that it was one with Intellectual Beauty, and that the regeneration he foresaw was so much more than the regeneration many political dreamers have foreseen, that it could not come in its perfection till the Hours bore 'Time to his tomb in eternity.' In *A Defence of Poetry*, he will have it that the poet and the lawgiver hold their station by the right of the same faculty, the one uttering in words and the other in the forms of society his vision of the divine order, the Intellectual Beauty. 'Poets, according to the circumstances of the age and nation in which they appeared, were called in the earliest epoch of the world legislators or prophets, and a poet essentially comprises and unites both these characters. For he not only beholds intensely the present as it is, and discovers those laws according to which present things are to be ordained, but he beholds the future in the present, and his thoughts are the germs of the flowers and the fruit of latest time.' 'Language, colour, form, and religious and civil habits of action are all the instruments and materials of poetry.' Poetry is 'the creation of actions according to the unchangeable process of human nature as existing in the mind of the creator, which is itself the image of all other minds.' 'Poets have been challenged to resign the civic crown to reasoners and merchants. . . . It is admitted that the exercise of the imagination is the most delightful, but it is alleged that that of reason is the more useful. . . . Whilst the mechanist abridges and the political economic combines labour, let them be sure that their speculations, for want of correspondence with those first principles which belong to the imagination, do not tend, as they have in modern England, to exasperate at once the extremes of luxury and want. . . . The rich have become richer, the poor have become poorer, . . . such are the effects which must ever flow from an unmitigated exercise of the calculating faculty.' The speaker of these things might almost be Blake, who held that the Reason not only created Ugliness, but all other evils. The books of all wisdom are hidden in the cave of the Witch of Atlas, who is one of his personifications of beauty, and when she moves over the enchanted river that is an image of all life, the priests cast aside their deceits, and the king crowns an ape to mock his own sovereignty, and the soldiers gather about the anvils to beat their swords to ploughshares, and lovers cast away their timidity, and friends are united; while the power which, in *Laon and Cythna*, awakens the mind of the reformer to contend, and itself contends, against the tyrannies of the world, is first seen as the star of love or beauty. And at the end of the *Ode to Naples*, he cries out to 'the spirit of beauty' to overturn the tyrannies of the world, or to fill them with its 'harmonising ardours.' He calls the spirit of beauty liberty, because despotism, and perhaps, as 'the man of virtuous soul commands not, nor obeys,' all authority, pluck virtue from her path towards beauty, and because it leads us by that love whose service is perfect freedom. It leads all things by love, for he cries again and again that love is the perception of beauty in thought and things, and it orders all things by love, for it is love that impels the soul to its expressions in thought and in action, by making us 'seek to awaken in all things that are, a community with what we experience within ourselves.' 'We are born into the world, and there is something within us which, from the instant that we live, more and more thirsts after its likeness.' We have 'a soul within our soul that describes a circle around its proper paradise which pain and sorrow and evil dare not overleap,' and we labour to see this soul in many mirrors, that we may possess it the more abundantly. He would hardly seek the progress of the world by any less gentle labour, and would hardly have us resist evil itself. He bids the reformers in the *Philosophical Review of Reform* receive 'the onset of the cavalry,' if it be sent to disperse their meetings, 'with folded arms,' and 'not because active resistance is not justifiable, but because temperance and courage would produce greater advantages than the most decisive victory'; and he gives them like advice in *The Masque of Anarchy*, for liberty, the poem cries, 'is love,' and can make the rich man kiss its feet, and, like those who followed Christ, give away his goods and follow it throughout the world.

He does not believe that the reformation of society can bring this beauty, this divine order, among men without the regeneration of the hearts of men. Even in *Queen Mab*, which was written before he had found his deepest thought, or rather perhaps before he had found words to utter it, for I do not think men change much in their deepest thought, he is less anxious to change men's beliefs, as I think, than to cry out against that serpent more subtle than any beast of the field, 'the cause and the effect of tyranny.' He affirms again and again that the virtuous, those who have 'pure desire and universal love,' are happy in the midst of tyranny, and he foresees a day when the 'Spirit of Nature,' the Spirit of Beauty of his later poems, who has her 'throne of power unappealable' in every human heart, shall have made men so virtuous that 'kingly glare will lose its power to dazzle,' and 'silently pass by,' and, as it seems, commerce, 'the venal interchange of all that human art of nature yield; which wealth should purchase not,' come as silently to an end.

He was always, indeed in chief, a witness for that 'power unappealable.' Maddalo, in *Julian and Maddalo*, says that the soul is powerless, and can only, like a 'dreary bell hung in a heaven-illumined tower, toll our thoughts and our desires to meet below round the rent heart and pray'; but Julian, who is Shelley himself, replies, as the makers of all religion have replied: –

> Where is the love, beauty, and truth we seek
> But in our mind? And if we were not weak,
> Should we be less in deed than in desire?

while *Mont Blanc* is an intricate analogy to affirm that the soul has its sources in 'the secret strength of things which governs thought, and to the infinite dome of heaven is as a law.' He even thought that men might be immortal were they sinless, and his Cythna bids the sailors be without remorse, for all that live are stained as they are. It is thus, she says, that time marks men and their thoughts for the tomb. And the 'Red Comet,' the image of evil in *Laon and Cythna*, when it began its war with the star of beauty, brought not only 'Fear, Hatred, Fraud and Tyranny,' but 'Death, Decay, Earthquake, and Blight and Madness pale.' [. . .]

II. HIS RULING SYMBOLS

At a comparatively early time Shelley made his imprisoned Cythna become wise in all human wisdom through the contemplation of her own mind, and write out this wisdom upon the sands in 'signs' that were 'clear elemental shapes, whose smallest change' made 'a subtler language within language,' and were 'the key of truths which once were dimly taught in old Crotona.' His early romances and much throughout his poetry show how strong a fascination the traditions of magic and of the magical philosophy had cast over his mind; and one can hardly suppose that he had not brooded over their doctrine of symbols or signatures, though I do not find anything to show that he gave it any deep study. One finds in his poetry, besides innumerable images that have not the definiteness of symbols, many images that are certainly symbols, and as the years went by he began to use these with a more and more deliberately symbolic purpose. I imagine that when he wrote his earlier poems he allowed the subconscious life to lay its hands so firmly upon the rudder of his imagination that he was little conscious of the abstract meaning of the images that rose in what seemed the idleness of his mind. Any one who has any experience of any mystical state of the soul knows how there float up in the mind profound symbols,[38] whose meaning, if indeed they do not delude one into the dream that they are meaningless, one does not perhaps understand for years. Nor I think has any one, who has known that experience with any constancy, failed to find some day, in some old book or on some old monument, a strange or intricate image that had floated up before him, and to grow perhaps dizzy with the sudden conviction that our little memories are but a part of some great Memory that renews the world and men's thoughts age after age, and that our thoughts are not, as we suppose, the deep, but a little foam upon the deep. Shelley understood this, as is proved by what he says of the eternity of beautiful things and of the influence of the dead, but whether he understood that the great Memory is also a dwelling-house of symbols, of images that are living souls, I cannot tell. He had certainly experience of all but the most profound of the mystical states, and had known that union with created things which assuredly must precede the soul's union with the uncreated spirit. He says, in his fragment of an essay 'On Life', mistaking a unique experience for the common experience of all: 'Let us recollect our sensations as children . . . we less habitually distinguished all that we saw and felt from ourselves. They seemed as it were to constitute one mass. There are some persons who in this respect are always children. Those who are subject to the state called reverie, feel as if their nature were resolved into the surrounding universe or as if the surrounding universe were resolved into their being,' and he must have expected to receive thoughts and images from beyond his own mind, just in so far as that mind transcended its preoccupation with particular time and place, for he believed inspiration a kind of death; and he could hardly have helped perceive that an image that has transcended particular time and place becomes a symbol, passes beyond death, as it were, and becomes a living soul.

When Shelley went to the Continent with Godwin's daughter in 1814 they sailed down certain great rivers in an open boat, and when he summed up in his preface to *Laon and Cythna* the things that helped to make him a poet, he spoke of these voyages: 'I have sailed down mighty rivers, and seen the sun rise and set, and the stars come forth, whilst I have sailed night and day down a rapid stream among mountains.'

He may have seen some cave that was the bed of a rivulet by some river-side, or have followed some mountain stream to its source in a cave, for from his return to England rivers and streams and wells, flowing through caves or rising in them, came into every poem of his that was of any length, and always with the precision of symbols. Alastor passed in his boat along a river in a cave; and when for the last time he felt the presence of the spirit he loved and followed, it was when he watched his image in a silent well; and when he died it was where a river fell into 'an abysmal chasm'; and the Witch of Atlas in her gladness, as he in his sadness, passed in her boat along a river in a cave, and it was where it bubbled out of a cave that she was born; and when Rousseau, the typical poet of *The Triumph of Life*, awoke to the vision that was life, it was where a rivulet bubbled out of a cave;[39] and the poet of *Epipsychidion* met the evil beauty 'by a well, under blue nightshade bowers'; and Cythna bore her child imprisoned in a great cave beside 'a fountain round and vast, in which the wave, imprisoned, boiled and leaped perpetually'; and her lover Laon was brought to his prison in a high column through a cave where there was 'a putrid pool,' and when he went to see the conquered city he dismounted beside a polluted fountain in the market-place, foreshadowing thereby that spirit who at the end of *Prometheus Unbound* gazes at a regenerated city from 'within a fountain in the public square'; and when Laon and Cythna are dead they awake beside a fountain and drift into Paradise along a river; and at the end of things Prometheus and Asia are to live amid a happy world in a cave where a fountain 'leaps with an awakening sound'; and it was by a fountain, the meeting-place of certain unhappy lovers, that Rosalind and Helen told their unhappiness to one another; and it was under a willow by a fountain that the enchantress and her lover began their unhappy love; while his lesser poems and his prose fragments use caves and rivers and wells and fountains continually as metaphors. It may be that his subconscious life seized upon some passing scene, and moulded it into an ancient symbol without help from anything but that great Memory; but so good a Platonist as Shelley could hardly have thought of any cave as a symbol, without thinking of Plato's cave that was the world;[40] and so good a scholar may well have had Porphyry on 'the Cave of the Nymphs' in his mind.[41] When I compare Porphyry's description of the cave where the Phaeacian boat left Odysseus, with Shelley's description of the cave of the Witch of Atlas, to name but one of many, I find it hard to think otherwise. I quote

Taylor's translation, only putting Mr. Lang's prose for Taylor's bad verse. 'What does Homer obscurely signify by the cave in Ithaca which he describes in the following verses? "Now at the harbour's head is a long-leaved olive-tree, and hard by is a pleasant cave and shadowy, sacred to the nymphs, that are called Naiads. And therein are mixing-bowls and jars of stone, and there moreover do bees hive. And there are great looms of stone, whereon the nymphs weave raiment of purple stain, a marvel to behold; and there are waters welling evermore. Two gates there are to the cave, the one set towards the North wind, whereby men may go down, but the portals towards the South pertain rather to the gods, whereby men may not enter: it is the way of the immortals."' He goes on to argue that the cave was a temple before Homer wrote, and that 'the ancients did not establish temples without fabulous symbols,' and then begins to interpret Homer's description in all its detail. The ancients, he says, 'consecrated a cave to the world' and held 'the flowing waters' and the 'obscurity of the cavern' 'apt symbols of what the world contains,' and he calls to witness Zoroaster's cave with fountains; and often caves are, he says, symbols of 'all invisible power; because as caves are obscure and dark, so the essence of all these powers is occult,' and quotes a lost hymn to Apollo to prove that nymphs living in caves fed men 'from intellectual fountains'; and he contends that fountains and rivers symbolise generation, and that the word nymph 'is commonly applied to all souls descending into generation,' and that the two gates of Homer's cave are the gates of generation and the gate of ascent through death to the gods, the gate of cold and moisture, and the gate of heat and fire. Cold, he says, causes life in the world, and heat causes life among the gods, and the constellation of the Cup is set in the heavens near the sign Cancer, because it is there that the souls descending from the Milky Way receive their draught of the intoxicating cold drink of generation. 'The mixing-bowls and jars of stone' are consecrated to the Naiads, and are also, as it seems, symbolical of Bacchus, and are of stone because of the rocky beds of the rivers. And 'the looms of stone' are the symbols of the 'souls that descend into generation.' 'For the formation of the flesh is on or about the bones, which in the bodies of animals resemble stones,' and also because 'the body is a garment' not only about the soul, but about all essences that become visible, for 'the heavens are called by the ancients a veil, in consequence of being as it were the vestments of the celestial gods.' The bees hive in the mixing-bowls and jars of stone, for so Porphyry understands the passage, because honey was the symbol adopted by the ancients for 'pleasure arising from generation.' The ancients, he says, called souls not only Naiads but bees, 'as the efficient cause of sweetness'; but not all souls 'proceeding into generation' are called bees, 'but those who will live in it justly and who after having performed such things as are acceptable to the gods will again return (to their kindred stars). For this insect loves to return to the place from whence it came and is eminently just and sober.' I find all these details in the cave of the Witch of Atlas, the most elaborately described of Shelley's caves, except the two gates, and these have a far-off echo in her summer journeys on her cavern river and in her winter sleep in 'an inextinguishable well of crimson fire.' We have for the mixing-bowls, and jars of stone full of honey, those delights of the senses, 'sounds of air' 'folded in cells of crystal silence,' 'liquors clear and sweet' 'in crystal vials,' and for the bees, visions 'each in its thin sheath like a chrysalis,' and for 'the looms of stone' and 'raiment of purple stain' the Witch's spinning and embroidering; and the Witch herself is a Naiad, and was born from one of the Atlantides, who lay in a 'chamber of grey rock' until she was changed by the sun's embrace into a cloud.

When one turns to Shelley for an explanation of the cave and fountain one finds how close his thought was to Porphyry's. He looked upon thought as a condition of life in generation and believed that the reality beyond was something other than thought. He wrote in his fragment *On Life*: 'That the basis of all things cannot be as the popular philosophy alleges, mind, is sufficiently evident. Mind, as far as we have any experience of its properties, and beyond that experience how vain is argument, cannot create, it can only perceive'; and in another passage he defines mind as existence. Water is his great symbol of existence, and he continually meditates over its mysterious source. In his prose he tells how 'thought can with difficulty visit the intricate and winding chambers which it inhabits. It is like a river, whose rapid and perpetual stream flows outward. . . . The caverns of the mind are obscure and shadowy; or pervaded with a lustre, beautiful and bright indeed, but shining not beyond their portals.' When the Witch has passed in her boat from the caverned river, that is doubtless her own destiny, she passes along the Nile 'by Moeris and the Mareotid lakes,' and sees all human life shadowed upon its waters in shadows that 'never are erased but tremble ever'; and in 'many a dark and subterranean street under the Nile – new caverns – and along the bank of the Nile; and as she bends over the unhappy, she compares unhappiness to the strife that 'stirs the liquid surface of man's life'; and because she can see the reality of things she is described as journeying 'in the calm depths' of 'the wide lake' we journey over unpiloted. Alastor calls the river that he follows an image of his mind, and thinks that it will be as hard to say where his thought will be when he is dead as where its waters will be in ocean or cloud in a little while. In *Mont Blanc*, a poem so overladen with descriptions in parentheses that one loses sight of its logic, Shelley compares the flowing through our mind of 'the universe of things,' which are, he has explained elsewhere, but thoughts, to the flowing of the Arve through the ravine, and compares the unknown sources of our thoughts, in some 'remoter world' whose 'gleams' 'visit the soul in sleep,' to Arve's sources among the glaciers on the mountain heights. Cythna, in the passage where she speaks of making signs 'a subtler language within language' on the sand by the 'fountain' of sea water in the cave where she is imprisoned, speaks of the 'cave' of her mind which gave its secrets to her, and of 'one mind, the type of all' which is a 'moveless wave' reflecting 'all moving things that are'; and then passing more completely under the power of the symbol, she speaks of growing wise through contemplation of the images that rise out of the fountain at the call of her will. Again and again one finds some passing allusion to the cave of man's mind, or to the caves of his youth, or to the cave of mysteries we enter at death, for to Shelley as to Porphyry it is more than an image of life in the world. It may mean any enclosed life, as when it is the dwelling-place of Asia and Prometheus, or when it is 'the still cave of poetry,' and it may have all meanings at once, or it may have as little meaning as some ancient religious symbol enwoven from the habit of centuries with the patterns of a carpet or a tapestry.

As Shelley sailed along those great rivers and saw or imagined the cave that associated itself with rivers in his mind, he saw half-ruined towers upon the hill-tops, and once at any rate a tower is used to symbolise a meaning that is the contrary to the meaning symbolised by caves. Cythna's lover is brought through the cave where there is a polluted fountain to a high tower, for being man's far-seeing mind, when the world has cast him out he must to the 'towers of thought's crowned powers'; nor is it possible for Shelley to have forgotten this first imprisonment when he made men imprison Lionel in a tower for a like offence; and because I know how hard it is to forget a symbolical meaning, once one has found it, I believe Shelley had more than a romantic scene in his mind when he made Prince Athanase follow his mysterious studies in a lighted tower above the sea, and when he made the old hermit watch over Laon in his sickness in a half-ruined tower, wherein the sea, here doubtless, as to Cythna, 'the one mind,' threw 'spangled sands' and 'rarest sea shells.' The tower, important in Maeterlinck, as in Shelley, is, like the sea, and rivers, and caves with fountains, a very ancient symbol, and would perhaps, as years went by, have grown more important in his poetry. The contrast between it and the cave in *Laon and Cythna* suggests a contrast between the mind looking outward upon men and things and the mind looking inward upon itself, which may or may not have been in Shelley's mind, but certainly helps, with one knows not how many other dim meanings, to give the poem mystery and a shadow. It is only by ancient symbols, by symbols that have numberless meanings besides the one or two the writer lays an emphasis upon, or the half-score he knows of, that any highly subjective art can escape from the barrenness and shallowness of a too conscious arrangement, into the abundance and depth of Nature. The poet of essences and pure ideas must seek in the half-lights that glimmer from symbol to symbol as if to the ends of the earth, all that the epic and dramatic poet finds of mystery and shadow in the accidental circumstances of life.

The most important, the most precise of all Shelley's symbols, the one he uses with the fullest knowledge of its meaning, is the

Morning and Evening Star. It rises and sets for ever over the towers and rivers, and is the throne of his genius. Personified as a woman it leads Rousseau, the typical poet of *The Triumph of Life*, under the power of the destroying hunger of life, under the power of the sun that we shall find presently as a symbol of life, and it is the Morning Star that wars against the principle of evil in *Laon and Cythna*, at first as a star with a red comet, here a symbol of all evil as it is of disorder in *Epipsychidion*, and then as a serpent with an eagle – symbols in Blake too and in the Alchemists; and it is the Morning Star that appears as a winged youth to a woman, who typifies humanity amid its sorrows, in the first canto of *Laon and Cythna*; and it is invoked by the wailing women of *Hellas*, who call it 'lamp of the free' and 'beacon of love' and would go where it hides flying from the deepening night among those 'kingless continents sinless as Eden,' and 'mountains and islands' 'prankt on the sapphire sea' that are but the opposing hemispheres to the senses, but, as I think, the ideal world, the world of the dead, to the imagination; and in the *Ode to Liberty*, Liberty is bid lead wisdom out of the inmost cave of man's mind as the Morning Star leads the sun out of the waves. We know too that had *Prince Athanase* been finished it would have described the finding of Pandemos, the Star's lower genius, and the growing weary of her, and the coming of its true genius Urania at the coming of death, as the day finds the Star at evening. There is hardly indeed a poem of any length in which one does not find it as a symbol of love, or liberty, or wisdom, or beauty, or of some other expression of that Intellectual Beauty which was to Shelley's mind the central power of the world; and to its faint and fleeting light he offers up all desires, that are as –

The desire of the moth for the star,
Of the night for the morrow,
The devotion to something afar
From the sphere of our sorrow.

When its genius comes to Rousseau, shedding dew with one hand, and treading out the stars with her feet, for she is also the genius of the dawn, she brings him a cup full of oblivion and love. He drinks and his mind becomes like sand 'on desert

Labrador' marked by the feet of deer and a wolf. And then the new vision, life, the cold light of day moves before him, and the first vision becomes an invisible presence. The same image was in his mind too when he wrote: –

> Hesperus flies from awakening night
> And pants in its beauty and speed with light,
> Fast fleeting, soft and bright.

Though I do not think that Shelley needed to go to Porphyry's account of the cold intoxicating cup, given to the souls in the constellation of the Cup near the constellation Cancer, for so obvious a symbol as the cup, or that he could not have found the wolf and the deer and the continual flight of his Star in his own mind, his poetry becomes the richer, the more emotional, and loses something of its appearance of idle fantasy when I remember that these are ancient symbols, and still come to visionaries in their dreams. Because the wolf is but a more violent symbol of longing and desire than the hound, his wolf and deer remind me of the hound and deer that Oisin saw in the Gaelic poem chasing one another on the water before he saw the young man following the woman with the golden apple; and of a Galway tale that tells how Niamh, whose name means brightness or beauty, came to Oisin as a deer; and of a vision that a friend of mine saw when gazing at a dark-blue curtain. I was with a number of Hermetists, and one of them said to another, 'Do you see something in the curtain?' The other gazed at the curtain for a while and saw presently a man led through a wood by a black hound, and then the hound lay dead at a place the seer knew was called, without knowing why, 'the Meeting of the Suns,' and the man followed a red hound, and then the red hound was pierced by a spear. A white fawn watched the man out of the wood, but he did not look at it, for a white hound came and he followed it trembling, but the seer knew that he would follow the fawn at last, and that it would lead him among the gods. The most learned of the Hermetists said, 'I cannot tell the meaning of the hounds or where the Meeting of the Suns is, but I think the fawn is the Morning and Evening Star.' I have little doubt that when the man saw the white fawn he was coming out of the darkness and passion of the world into some day of partial regeneration, and that it was the Morning Star and would be the Evening Star at its second coming. I have little doubt that it was but the story of Prince Athanase and what may have been the story of Rousseau in *The Triumph of Life*, thrown outward once again from that great Memory, which is still the mother of the Muses, though men no longer believe in it.

It may have been this memory, or it may have been some impulse of his nature too subtle for his mind to follow, that made Keats, with his love of embodied things, of precision of form and colouring, of emotions made sleepy by the flesh, see Intellectual Beauty in the Moon; and Blake, who lived in that energy he called eternal delight, see it in the Sun, where his personification of poetic genius labours at a furnace. I think there was certainly some reason why these men took so deep a pleasure in lights that Shelley thought of with weariness and trouble. The Moon is the most changeable of symbols, and not merely because it is the symbol of change. As mistress of the waters she governs the life of instinct and the generation of things, for, as Porphyry says, even 'the apparition of images' in the 'imagination' is through 'an excess of moisture'; and, as a cold and changeable fire set in the bare heavens, she governs alike chastity and the joyless idle drifting hither and thither of generated things. She may give God a body and have Gabriel to bear her messages, or she may come to men in their happy moments as she came to Endymion, or she may deny life and shoot her arrows; but because she only becomes beautiful in giving herself, and is no flying ideal, she is not loved by the children of desire.

Shelley could not help but see her with unfriendly eyes. He is believed to have described Mary Shelley at a time when she had come to seem cold in his eyes, in that passage of *Epipsychidion* which tells how a woman like the Moon led him to her cave and made 'frost' creep over the sea of his mind, and so bewitched Life and Death with 'her silver voice' that they ran from him crying, 'Away, he is not of our crew.' When he describes the Moon as part of some beautiful scene he can call her beautiful, but when he personifies, when his words come under the influence of that great Memory or of some mysterious tide in the depth of our being, he grows unfriendly or not truly friendly or at the most pitiful. The Moon's lips 'are pale and waning,' it is 'the cold Moon,' or 'the frozen and inconstant Moon,' or it is 'forgotten' and 'waning,' or it 'wanders' and is 'weary,' or it is 'pale and grey,' or it is 'pale for weariness,' and 'wandering companionless' and 'ever changing,' and finding 'no object worth' its 'constancy,' or it is like a 'dying lady' who 'totters' 'out of her chamber led by the insane and feeble wanderings of her fading brain,' and even when it is no more than a star, it casts an evil influence that makes the lips of lovers 'lurid' or pale. It only becomes a thing of delight when Time is being borne to his tomb in eternity, for then the spirit of the Earth, man's procreant mind, fills it with his own joyousness. He describes the spirit of the Earth and of the Moon, moving above the rivulet of their lives, in a passage which reads like a half-understood vision. Man has become 'one harmonious soul of many a soul' and 'all things flow to all' and 'familiar acts are beautiful through love,' and an 'animation of delight' at this change flows from spirit to spirit till the snow 'is loosened' from the Moon's 'lifeless mountains.'

Some old magical writer, I forget who, says if you wish to be melancholy hold in your left hand an image of the Moon made out of silver, and if you wish to be happy hold in your right hand an image of the Sun made out of gold.[42] The Sun is the symbol of sensitive life, and of belief and joy and pride and energy, of indeed the whole life of the will, and of that beauty which neither lures from far off, nor becomes beautiful in giving itself, but makes all glad because it is beauty. Taylor quotes Proclus as calling it 'the Demiurgos of everything sensible.' It was therefore natural that Blake, who was always praising energy, and all exalted overflowing of oneself, and who thought art an impassioned labour to keep men from doubt and despondency, and woman's love an evil, when it would trammel man's will, should see the poetic genius not in a woman star but in the Sun, and should rejoice throughout his poetry in 'the Sun in his strength.' Shelley, however, except when he uses it to describe the peculiar beauty of Emilia Viviani, who was like 'an incarnation of the Sun when light is changed to love,' saw it with less friendly eyes.[43] He seems to have seen it with perfect happiness only when veiled in mist, or glimmering upon water, or when faint enough to do not more than veil the brightness of his own Star; and in *The Triumph of Life*, the one poem in which it is part of the avowed symbolism, its power is the being and the source of all tyrannies. When the woman personifying the Morning Star has faded from before his eyes, Rousseau sees a 'new vision' in 'a cold bright car' with a rainbow hovering over her, and as she comes the shadow passes from 'leaf and stone' and the souls she has enslaved seem 'in that light, like atomies to dance within a sunbeam,' or they dance among the flowers that grow up newly in 'the grassy vesture of the desert,' unmindful of the misery that is to come upon them. These are 'the great, the unforgotten,' all who have worn 'mitres and helms and crowns, or wreaths of light,' and yet have not known themselves. Even 'great Plato' is there, because he knew joy and sorrow, because life that could not subdue him by gold or pain, by 'age, or sloth, or slavery.' subdued him by love. All who have ever lived are there except Christ and Socrates and the 'sacred few' who put away all life could give, being doubtless followers throughout their lives of the forms borne by the flying ideal, or who, 'as soon as they had touched the world with living flame, fled back like eagles to their native noon.'

In ancient times, it seems to me that Blake, who for all his protest was glad to be alive, and ever spoke of his gladness, would have worshipped in some chapel of the Sun, but that Shelley, who hated life because he sought 'more in life than any understood,' would have wandered, lost in a ceaseless reverie, in some chapel of the Star of infinite desire.

I think too that as he knelt before an altar where a thin flame burnt in a lamp made of green agate, a single vision would have come to him again and again, a vision of a boat drifting down a broad river between high hills where there were caves and towers, and following the light of one Star; and that voices would have told him how there is for every man some one scene, some one adventure, some one picture that is the image of his secret life, for wisdom first speaks in images, and that this one image, if he would but brood over it his life long, would lead his soul, disentangled from unmeaning circumstance and the ebb and flow of the world, into that far household where the undying gods await all whose souls have become simple as flame, whose bodies have become quiet as an agate lamp.

But he was born in a day when the old wisdom had vanished and was content merely to write verses, and often with little thought of more than verses.

1900.

ARTHUR SYMONS (1865–1945)

Arthur William Symons has long been one of the ghosts of literary history. For a time one of Yeat's closest friends, he was an admitted influence on the theory and practice of the Irishman's poetry; similar tributes issued from T. S. Eliot and Ezra Pound, who claimed that the knowledge of contemporary French literature Symons provided had changed their verse. Then, too, it was Symons who helped the young James Joyce find a publisher for his poems, just as he championed Conrad and Hardy at a time – in the early decades of this century – when few spoke up for either. Yet despite such accolades and accomplishments, Symons has virtually dropped from sight. In a sense this is the inevitable fate of midvives, who are rarely as considerable as the creations they help foster; and certainly it is the case that Symons's creative achievement is much inferior to his criticism. Moreover, he himself did much to obscure his unique contribution. Forced to live entirely by means of his pen, he wrote too much, too fast,scattering genuine perceptions amid pot-boilers in innumerable small magazines and journals. The same pressure prevented him from refining his insights into a cogent and unified body of criticism, as Pater and Baudelaire had done. Most important of all, these and other pressures brought on a complete mental breakdown in 1908, at the height of his powers. Thought he eventually regained his sanity and lived on for another thirty years, he never produced anything of comparable quality again. Thus, having helped bring aesthetic awareness to the threshold of its twentieth-century form, Symons lived out his life under the shadow of modernist achievement, an obscure, rarely glimpsed figure.

The injustice of this situation has continued to be felt, and it is one of the truisms of literary history that Symons deserves to be better known than he is. A powerful assertion of this view came in Frank Kermode's *Romantic Image* (1957), which included a long chapter on Symons's role in the evolution of a modern aesthetic. Since that time there has been a trickle of books and articles, all believing in Symons's importance to the phenomenon of 'modernism'. Such a faith also animates this selection from his critical work; for the fact is that Symons, whose early verse is full of Baudelairean echoes, remained all his life committed to a key idea of aesthetic artificiality, the more-than-natural paradise that the imagination alone could bring into being. A country lad who fell in love with the modern city, a pious child who transferred his devotion to art, Symons was continually engaged in seeking out an artistic transformation of reality. Through all the various phases of his career, Symons courts a sublime dependent on conscious crafting, on the hieratic pleasures of composed arrangement, even on wilful distortions which leave the heavy and imperfect world farther and farther behind. The energy, deliberation and zest with which he develops this aesthetic of Baudelaire and Pater, together with the paradoxical fashion in which he works back to the High Romantic origins of the movement, thus make Symons an appropriate figure with which to end these volumes.

The arrangement of Symons's work here falls into four main sections, the last three following stages in his own life. The first section, however, disregards strict chronology for a kind of backward glance, an overview of the period and figures dealt with in the course of this anthology. These gathered selections reveal Symons surveying the past and commenting upon a critical tradition in which he clearly placed himself. The introduction to this opening section, indeed the preface to Symons's work as a whole, is a homage to his first master, Walter Pater. Born to extremely religious parents (his father was a Methodist minister), Symons's youthful piety was soon displaced into the realm of art – the agency for this operation being *The Renaissance*. The focus on 'an imaginative sense of fact' was the first lesson he absorbed from Pater, and such ancillary aspects as an elaborate style, a concern with discriminating fine shades of 'sensation', a pursuit of high 'moments' of awareness under the press of death and a completely interiorized existence, remained part of his outlook for the rest of his life.

For this reason quotations from Pater's work recur throughout Symons's criticism, and the 'aesthetic' training he received from this source enabled him to undertake sensitive, probing studies of Morris, Rossetti, Swinburne, Gautier, Baudelaire, as well as the earlier Romantic poets, of which a few representative examples are included here. Moreover, Pater's example also induced Symons to consider parallel developments in the visual arts, an interest consummated in his long, reflective account of 'The Painting of the Nineteenth Century' (q.v.). This suggestive tracing of visual art since Turner reveals that Symons had the makings of a first-rate art critic, since he rightly puts the painter's paradoxical relation to nature at the centre of discussion. The essay is marred by some eccentric judgements and an unwillingness to follow his argument clearly; even so, it is startling to realize how close Symons comes to suggesting a complete emancipation from natural form, thus pointing to the beginnings of what we now recognize as modern art.

With the second section begins a more closely chronological survey of Symons's work. Most observers have divided his productive life into three more or less distinct phases; the first of these, culminating in about 1893, may be characterized as his 'impressionist' period. During this time Symons struggled to find his critical voice, praising all that was 'modern' in literature; by this term he appears to have meant all that was psychologically daring, vivid and contemporary, elements he first began to distinguish in the poetry of Meredith and Browning. His first book, *An Introduction to the Study of Browning* (q.v.), sees Browning through Paterian eyes, noting the poet's tendency to internalize the drama within a single, reflecting soul, as well as his uncanny ability to communicate a complex state of mind in one 'flashed instant'. This is not only an extension of the romantic 'moment of being', but also the beginnings of Imagism, and it is Symons's enthusiasm for the image, the concentrated representation of an 'impression', which noticeably increases through this period. This concept is more complex than it appears, however, for at the same time Symons seeks an art which suggests rather than states, whose nuances lead beyond the object itself. Such a composite art is what he discovers in the poetry of Verlaine, and when one realizes that the material for such a contradictory ideal was furnished by urban scenery it becomes impossible to avoid thinking of Whistler. Indeed the painter becomes something of a touchstone during this phase, as Symons's celebration of contemporary reality caps the turn away from the remote, medieval fantasies of the earlier century.

The climax of this first phase occurred in 1893 with the publication of a long article entitled 'The Decadent Movement in Literature' (q.v.). Early in 1889 Symons had gone to France for the first time and there managed to meet Verlaine, Mallarmé, Huysmans and several other representatives of contemporary French culture. Symons dedicated himself to experiencing the 'sensations' of the Continent, and, following the lead of George Moore, he decided to bring the new school to the attention of a wider English public. The result was 'The Decadent Movement', which made Symons the spokesman for contemporary French literature and set him on the path to bigger and better things. The article itself has its peculiarities: Symons splits the 'Decadent' movement into two wings, Impressionist and Symbolist, united by a common desire to reach *la vrai vérité*, its own version of 'the essence of things'. This elusive goal is neither accurately defined nor sufficiently described, and Symons shows himself to be bored with the Symbolists as well as frankly impatient with the excesses of 'decadent' behaviour. Despite these flaws, however, Symons does identify the reaction to Positivist philosophy at the heart of the movement, and sees that the turn from Naturalism in France is part of a larger struggle to find a new expression of the soul's reality in a reductive and materialist age.

Even as this article appeared, Symons was moving into a very different phase of his career, represented by the third section of extracts. In 1891 Symons took up a London residence in Fountain Court, off the Strand, and in the same year he joined the Rhymers' Club. Exactly when he met Yeats is not known, but within a few years the two men had become fast friends and Yeats had moved into adjoining rooms. There, as conversations about art continued late into the night, the direction of Symons's thought began to change. With the weight of his occult knowledge, his faith in the truth of imagination, and the great force of his personality, Yeats impressed on Symons a belief in the existence of a higher, esoteric realm of being to which art and literature were the key. The effects of this influence can be seen in the Preface to the second edition of *London Nights* (q.v.), which was written while on holiday with Yeats in Sligo. Here Symons's concern with the impressionistic image deepens to a pursuit of the more revelatory symbol, and poems which had been written as the delicate 'impressions' of a London literary man become charged with significance as passing 'moods' linked to the 'universal consciousness'.

Under this influence Symons began to see his French authors in a new light, regarding the *Symbolistes* of his previous study as the central strand incorporating all the important figures in a search for an esoteric reality. The result of this cross-fertilization was Symons's most renowned work, *The Symbolist Movement in Literature* (1899), dedicated to Yeats as 'the chief representative of that movement in our country'. The stimulus may have come from Yeats, but the book displays a grasp of the French literary tradition and evidence of scholarly research into the various strands of Neo-Platonic philosophy which are Symons's alone. This extra study was amply repaid, for the argument of the book is at every turn more thoughtful and profound than that of 'The Decadent Movement'. The 'Introduction' points to the fact that literature is regaining the religious impulse and imaginative devotion that marked the earlier Romantics, and the individual chapters chart the shift away from science, materialism and Positivist philosophy to a new realm of wonder. At the same time Symons does not avoid the corresponding late romantic turn to this development, and with varying degrees of criticism he charts the move from a populist to a hieratic ideal, observing the movement's determination to establish a new aristocracy of letters. Though Symons has been criticized for failing to reach a consistent, generalized definition of 'symbolism', this is paradoxically the book's strength. Displaying that ability 'to slip into the mind of another' for which Yeats admired him, Symons follows the tortuous and subtle twists of each individual author, refusing to sacrifice particulars for the sake of a larger, abstract theory, and sketching a complex of intention and achievement which at several points touches central elements of the modernist aesthetic.

Symons may or may not have shared Yeats's faith in the higher reality – indeed, several pieces written at the turn of the century (such as 'The Choice' (q.v.), whose language echoes the 'Conclusion' to *The Symbolist Movement*) balance a note of doubt with somewhat anxious assertion. Nevertheless, the contact with Yeats unquestionably lifted Symons to his greatest heights. Between the publication of *The Symbolist Movement* and his breakdown in 1908, Symons entered the third and arguably greatest phase of his career. Here the ideal of artifice, of a non-natural nature more significant and expressive for man, becomes dominant, and Symons becomes obsessed with puppets, make-up, pantomime – anything which moves away from the local and unique to the abstract and universal. The application to what was shortly to come in the arts – even to our own day – is patent, and here Symons shows himself most truly as a man in advance of his time.

For the same reasons Symons now attempts to be more of a conscious theorist, drawing together his scattered articles on various branches of the arts and shaping them into more coherent form through a series of books. The desire to achieve a unified theory of aesthetics is prompted by the hints of such a possibility in Pater's essay, 'The School of Giorgione' (q.v.). It was announced in the Preface to *Plays, Acting and Music* (q.v.), but the idea had occurred to Symons much earlier, one of its most brilliant expressions being in the exhilarated essay of 1898, 'The World As Ballet' (q.v.). Here with typically paradoxical romantic logic, a series of antitheses – stillness and motion, silence and song, art and nature – are harmonized and resolved. The image of the dancer, perhaps another Yeatsian borrowing, became the ideal aesthetic reflection of human life itself, representing a matchless harmony of conflicting forces and thus the key to the universal realm Symons was striving to find. Variations on these themes animate the rest of Symons's criticism, with their strikingly 'modern' reflections on theatre, stage-design, opera, and dance.

There remains to be counted one final gift from Yeats, which led to what many consider Symons's greatest work. This is the interest in Blake which resulted in a critical study of the poet published in 1907 (q.v.). Admittedly Symons had been familiar with Blake in early life, and again his book displays a thoroughness of scholarly research which Yeats never approached. But Yeats's passionate interest in the High Romantic poet during the Nineties must have fanned the flames of Symons's curiosity, and it is highly unlikely that the book would have been as subtle and penetrating as it is if Yeats had not deepened Symons's understanding of the Imagination's truth. In this respect the study is something of a triumph, putting both man and work in a clearer light than any previous commentator had done. The plunge into esoteric philosophy Symons had undertaken with regard to the French Symbolists provided the context for dealing with many of the complexities of Blake's thought, and Symons was thus able to see Blake as the unacknowledged ancestor of the literature he had been directly concerned with. The resulting book is a more satisfactory and searching account of the poet than any previous critic – Rossetti, Swinburne, even Yeats himself – could boast.

As the man who brought the diverse swarm of aesthetic ideas in the late nineteenth century closest to their modern formulation, Arthur Symons thus brings to a close the bridge between the centuries we have tried to trace in these volumes. It is true that his criticism suffers from haste and imprecision, from energy untempered by sufficient deliberation. It is also true, as these selections show, that Symons at his best possesses a remarkable sensitivity and penetration, and that he has a secure place in literary history as the man who helped bring the modern aesthetic into being.

I.

Walter Pater[1]

Walter Pater was a man in whom fineness and subtlety of emotion were united with an exact and profound scholarship; in whom a personality singularly unconventional, and singularly full of charm, found for its expression an absolutely personal and absolutely novel style, which was the most carefully and curiously beautiful of all English styles. The man and his style, to those who knew him, were identical; for, as his style was unlike that of other men, concentrated upon a kind of perfection which, for the most part, they could not even distinguish, so his inner life was peculiarly his own, centred within a circle beyond which he refused to wander; his mind, to quote some words of his own, "keeping as a solitary prisoner its own dream of a world."[2] [. . .] As a critic, he selected for analysis only those types of artistic character in which delicacy, an exquisite fineness, is the principal attraction; or if, as with Michelangelo, he was drawn towards some more rugged personality, some more massive, less finished art, it was not so much from sympathy with these more obvious qualities or ruggedness and strength, but because he had divined the sweetness lying at the heart of the strength: "ex forti dulcedo." Leonardo da Vinci, Joachim du Bellay, Coleridge, Botticelli: we find always something a little exotic, or subtle, or sought out, a certain rarity, which it requires an effort to disengage, and which appeals for its perfect appreciation to a public within the public; those fine students of what is fine in art, who take their artistic pleasures consciously, deliberately, critically, with the learned love of the amateur.

And not as a critic only, judging others, but in his own person as a writer, both of critical and of imaginative work, Pater showed his preoccupation with the "delicacies of fine literature."[3] His prose was from the first conscious, and it was from the first perfect. That earliest book of his, *Studies in the History of the Renaissance*, as it was then called, entirely individual, the revelation of a rare and special temperament, though it was, had many affinities with the poetic and pictorial art of Rossetti, Mr. Swinburne, and Burne-Jones, and seems, on its appearance in 1873, to have been taken as the manifesto of the so-called "aesthetic" school And, indeed, it may well be compared, as artistic prose, with the poetry of Rossetti; as fine, as careful, as new a thing as that, and with something of the same exotic odour about it: a savour in this case of French soil, a Watteau grace and delicacy.[4] Here was criticism as a fine art, written in prose which the reader lingered over as over poetry; modulated prose which made the splendour of Mr. Ruskin seem gaudy, the neatness of Matthew Arnold a mincing neatness, and the brass sound strident in the orchestra of Carlyle.

That book of *Studies in the Renaissance*, even with the rest of

Pater to choose from, seems to me sometimes to be the most beautiful book of prose in our literature. Nothing in it is left to inspiration: but it is all inspired. Here is a writer who, like Baudelaire, would better nature;[5] [. . .] An almost oppressive quiet, a quiet which seems to exhale an atmosphere heavy with the odour of tropical flowers, broods over these pages; a subdued light shadows them. The most felicitous touches come we know not whence. [. . .]

The merit which, more than any other, distinguishes Pater's prose, though it is not the merit most on the surface, is the attention to, the perfection of, the ensemble. Under the soft and musical phrases an inexorable logic hides itself, sometimes only too well. Link is added silently, but faultlessly, to link; the argument marches, carrying you with it, while you fancy you are only listening to the music with which it keeps step. Take an essay to pieces, and you will find that it is constructed with mathematical precision; every piece can be taken out and replaced in order.[6] [. . .] And here, in *Marius*, which is not a story, but the philosophy of a soul, this art of the ensemble is not less rigorously satisfied; though indeed *Marius* is but a sequence of scenes, woven around a sequence of moods.

In this book, and in the *Imaginary Portraits* of three years later, which seems to me to show his imaginative and artistic faculties at their point of most perfect fusion, Pater has not endeavoured to create characters, in whom the flesh and blood should seem to be that of life itself; he had not the energy of creation, and he was content with a more shadowy life than theirs for the children of his dreams. What he has done is to give a concrete form to abstract ideas; to represent certain types of character, to trace certain developments, in the picturesque form of narrative. [. . .] Each, with perhaps one exception, is the study of a soul, or rather of a consciousness; such a study as might be made by simply looking within, and projecting now this now that side of oneself on an exterior plane.[7] [. . .] the attitude of mind, the outlook, in the most general sense, is always limited and directed in a certain way, giving one always the picture of a delicate, subtle, aspiring, unsatisfied personality, open to all impressions, living chiefly by sensations, little anxious to reap any of the rich harvest of its intangible but keenly possessed gains; a personality withdrawn from action, which it despises or dreads, solitary with its ideals, in the circle of its "exquisite moments," in the Palace of Art, where it is never quite at rest. It is somewhat such a soul, I have thought, as that which Browning has traced in *Sordello*. [. . .]

I remember that when he once said to me that the *Imaginary Portraits* seemed to him the best written of his books, he qualified that very just appreciation by adding: "It seems to me the most *natural*." I think he was even then beginning to forget that it was not natural to him to be natural.[8] There are in the world many kinds of beauty, and of these what is called natural beauty is but one. Pater's temperament was at once shy and complex, languid and ascetic, sensuous and spiritual. He did not permit life to come to him without a certain ceremony; he was on his guard against the abrupt indiscretion of events; and if his whole life was a service of art, he arranged his life so that, as far as possible, it might be served by that very dedication.

Dante Gabriel Rossetti[9]

Like Baudelaire and like Mallarmé in France, Rossetti was not only a wholly original poet, but a new personal force in literature. That he stimulated the sense of beauty is true in a way it is not true of Tennyson, for instance, as it is true of Baudelaire in a way it is not true of Victor Hugo. In Rossetti's work, perhaps because it is not the greatest, there is an actually hypnotic quality which exerts itself on those who come within his circle at all; a quality like that of an unconscious medium, or like that of a woman against whose attraction one is without defence.[10] It is the sound of a voice, rather than anything said; and, when Rossetti speaks, no other voice, for the moment, seems worth listening to. Even after one has listened, not very much seems to have been said; but the world is not quite the same. He has stimulated a new sense, by which a new mood of beauty can be apprehended.

Dreams are precise; it is only when we awake, when we go outside, that they become vague. In a certain sense Rossetti, with all his keen practical intelligence, was never wholly awake, had never gone outside that house of dreams in which the only real things were the things of the imagination. In the poetry of most poets there is a double kind of existence, of which each half is generally quite distinct; a real world, and a world of the imagination. But the poetry of Rossetti knows but one world, and it inhabits a corner there, like a perfectly contented prisoner, or like a prisoner to whom the sense of imprisonment is a joy. The love of beauty, the love of love, because love is the supreme energy of beauty, suffices for an existence in which every moment is a crisis; for to him, as Pater has said, 'life is a crisis at every moment': life, that is to say, the inner life, the life of imagination, in which the senses are messengers from the outer world, from which they can but bring disquieting tidings.[11] [. . .]

Circumstances have very little to do with the making of a poet's temperament or vision, and it would be enough to point to Christina Rossetti, who was hardly more in the country than her brother, but to whom a blade of grass was enough to summon the whole country about her, and whose poetry is full of the sense of growing things. Rossetti instinctively saw faces, and only faces, and he would have seen them if he had lived in the loneliest countryside, and he would never have learned to distinguish between oats and barley if he had had fields of them about his door from childhood. It was in the beauty of women, and chiefly in the mysterious beauty of faces, that Rossetti found the supreme embodiment of beauty; and it was in the love of women, and not in any more abstract love, of God, of nature, or of ideas, that he found the supreme revelation of love.

With this narrowness, with this intensity, he has rendered in his painting as in his poetry one ideal, one obsession. He calls what is really the House of Love *The House of Life*, and this is because the house of love was literally to him the house of life. There is no mystic to whom love has not seemed to be the essence or ultimate expression of the soul. Rossetti's whole work is a parable of this belief, and it is a parable written with his life-blood. Of beauty he has said, 'I drew it in as simply as my breath,' but, as the desire of beauty possessed him, as he laboured to create it over again, with rebellious words or colours, always too vague for him when they were most precise, never the precise embodiment of a dream, the pursuit turned to a labour and the labour to a pain.[12] Part of what hypnotises us in this work is, no doubt, that sense of personal tragedy which comes to us out of its elaborate beauty: the eternal tragedy of those who have loved the absolute in beauty too well, and with too mortal a thirst.

1904.

Charles Baudelaire[13]

Baudelaire is little known and much misunderstood in England. Only one English writer has ever done him justice, or said anything adequate about him. As long ago as 1862 Swinburne introduced Baudelaire to English readers: in the columns of the *Spectator*, it is amusing to remember. In 1868 he added a few more words of just and subtle praise in his book on Blake, and in the same year wrote the magnificent elegy on his death, *Ave atque Vale*. There have been occasional outbreaks of irrelevant abuse or contempt, and the name of Baudelaire (generally misspelled) is the journalist's handiest brickbat for hurling at random in the name of respectability. Does all this mean that we are waking up, over here, to the consciousness of one of the great literary forces of the age, a force which has been felt in every other country but ours?

It would be a useful influence for us. Baudelaire desired perfection, and we have never realised that perfection is a thing to aim at. He only did what he could do supremely well, and he was in poverty all his life, not because he would not work, but because he would work only at certain things, the things which he could hope to do to his own satisfaction. Of the men of letters of our age he was the most scrupulous. He spent his whole life in writing one book of verse (out of which all French poetry has come since his time), one book of prose in which prose becomes a fine art, some criticism which is the sanest, subtlest, and surest which his generation produced, and translation which is better than a marvellous original. What would French poetry be to-day if Baudelaire had never existed? As different a thing from what it is as English poetry would be without Rossetti. Neither of them is quite among the greatest poets, but they are more fascinating than the greatest, they influence more minds. And Baudelaire was an equally great critic. He discovered Poe, Wagner, and Manet. Where even Sainte-Beuve, with his vast materials, his vast general talent for criticism, went wrong in contemporary judgments, Baudelaire was infallibly right.[14] He wrote neither verse nor prose with ease, but he would not permit himself to write either without inspiration. His work is without abundance, but it is without waste. It is made out of his whole intellect and all his nerves. Every poem is a train of thought and every essay is the record of sensation. This "romantic" had something classic in his moderation, a moderation which becomes at times as terrifying as Poe's logic. To "cultivate one's hysteria" so calmly, and to affront the reader (*Hypocrite lecteur, mon semblable, mon frère*) as a judge rather than as a penitent; to be a casuist in confession; to be so much a moralist, with so keen a sense of the ecstasy of evil: that has always bewildered the world, even in his own country, where the artist is allowed to live as experimentally as he writes. Baudelaire lived and died solitary, secret, a confessor of sins who has never told the whole truth, *le mauvais moine* of his own sonnet, an ascetic of passion, a hermit of the brothel.[15]

The Decay of Craftsmanship in England[16]

For fifteen years the Society of Arts and Crafts has done its best to foster and to reward the making of beautiful things for every-day use. It has had from time to time beautiful things in its exhibitions. But now, after fifteen years of a sort of propaganda, after this persistent search for the craftsman, the craftsman has exhausted himself by his few little successes, and we see him relapsing into a kind of manufacturer of 'art nouveau' under another name, [. . .] What is called the movement of Morris was literally Morris's vivid personal movement; it began, and all but ended, in himself; and in many ways was an interesting expression of an extraordinarily interesting temperament, rather than a thing purely admirable in itself, or at all safe as a model for others. [. . .]

No, it is certain that we have outlived the age of the craftsman, the age in which beauty was the natural attendant on use. If you pass from a Greek woman's toilet-table, or indeed to the pots and pans of her kitchen, you will be conscious of no such sudden change as in passing from a modern host's private picture-gallery into the bedroom where you are to sleep. The saucepan and the hair-pins belong to the same atmosphere as the statue, they were made with the same grave simplicity. It had not yet occurred to the civilised world that it was possible to do without beauty in the things which one handled every day. And that strict, natural union of use and beauty kept extravagance out of things made for a definite purpose. The appropriate fulfilling of the purpose was what the craftsman aimed at.

Now-a-days we have our Art and we have our Utility, and if ever we attempt to unite them it is in some such unnatural bondage as in many of these inconvenient articles now on exhibition. The beauty, if there is any, is stuck on to some corner of the thing, is not an outcome of the nature of the thing.[17] Our artists, accustomed to the painting of detachable pictures, to be fixed in a frame, and carried about from place to place, are unable to conceive of this adjustment of beauty to use, this forgotten relation to cause to effect. We see them bringing their minds to this false problem: how to escape from the limitations of the thing as it is, as its purpose requires it to be, how to bring some new element into it. They cannot bring their minds to the right focus, and so the shapes get twisted. [. . .]

I suppose that the craftsmen who design our lamp-posts, our fire-irons, the stripes of our pyjamas and the shape of our pianos, are humble persons not in a "higher way of business" than the craftsmen who made those "vase-shaped dishes" I was speaking of, or the engraved weights with which the butchers weighed their meat in ancient Rome or Greece. But the latest artist in iron-work to the County Council does not exhibit at the Arts and Crafts. A craftsman must be fairly in earnest to send his goods to be judged by a Committee seated at the New Gallery. All these trivial and fantastical things are not made merely to sell; they are made with the best intentions; only the artist has put the "finish" all over them; it is not only the last touch that sends them wrong.

And in how many cases is not the very form itself founded on a misconception! Take, for instance, the wall-papers, and put aside the question of their merit as designs. May it not be reasonably contended that any design whatever on a wall-paper is decoratively wrong? In the modern house a wall-paper is a background, on which pictures and other objects are to be set. It is made, however, as if it were a thing in itself, a tapestry, which is itself to form the decoration of the room. What harmony can there possibly be between the crowded lines and colours of the wall-paper and the various pictures which are to be hung upon it?[18] A carpet, on which nothing is set which can be considered in closer relation to it than that of the most general colour-scheme, need not be plain, though one may prefer to have it plain; a designed wall-paper, unless it is to be the only decoration of the walls, is itself an anomaly. [. . .]

Modern craftsmanship is the craftsmanship of the machine, not of the man; and after a generation or two of the machine, those deadly pistons and hammers have got into our very brains, and a serious artist who gives himself the time to think out a piece of work, and do it with his own hands, can no longer either think or do anything that is not mechanical. We pride ourselves on being a business nation: look at one part of the result. The Americans pride themselves on being an even more businesslike business nation; and has any beautiful thing come out of America since we colonised it? In so far as it has tried to oppose commercialism the Arts and Crafts Society has done the right thing; the lamentable part of it is that it tilts with so ineffectual a lance. It is useless to show us feeble work merely because it is hand-made. Virtue never was its own reward on such dubious conditions. Baudelaire, in one of his priceless moralisings, pointed out that the unconventional artist must first be able to outdo the Philistine on the ground of the Philistine, before he goes on to triumph on his own. Just so the man must show the machine that he can do all its own work better, before he sets out to do what the machine cannot do at all.[19]

The Painting of the Nineteenth Century[20]

I.

The modern criticism of painting in England has been for the most part somewhat accidental; we have had, since Ruskin, one or two good books and a number of good detached essays, but no body of really fine art criticism. The influence of Ruskin has undoubtedly been a good influence; beauty was to him, literally, as a Frenchman has called it, a religion;[21] and he preached the religion of beauty at a period almost as much absorbed in the pedantries of science and the ignominies of material success as the present period. Much of his force came from his narrowness; you cannot be a prophet and a disinterested analyst at the same time. Ruskin did more than any man of our century to interest Englishmen in beautiful things, and it matters little whether his choice among beautiful things was always really the choice of an artist. He could convince the stubborn and Philistine British public, or he could brow-beat that public into fancying that it ought to be convinced. William Morris, who made all kinds of beautiful things himself, and who also tried to argue on behalf of beauty as a Socialist orator, has had very much less influence on the bulk of the British public. Morris, however, was really continuing the work which Ruskin began.

Had Walter Pater devoted himself exclusively to art criticism, there is no doubt that, in a sense, he would have been a great art critic. There are essays scattered throughout his work, the essay on "The School of Giorgione," for instance, in which the essential principles of the art of painting are divined and interpreted with extraordinary subtlety. I remember hearing him say, that, as he grew older, books interested him less and less, pictures delighted him more and more. But with him art criticism was but one function of a close, delicate, unceasing criticism of life; and the ideas at the root of painting, as well as of every other form of the activity of the spirit, meant more to him, in spite of his striving after absolute justice, than the painting itself. [. . .] As it was, he corrected many of the generous and hasty errors of Ruskin, and helped to bring back criticism to a wiser and more tolerant attitude toward the arts.

Everything that Mr. Whistler has written about painting deserves to be taken seriously, and read with understanding. Written in French, and signed by Baudelaire, his truths, and paradoxes reflecting truths, would have been realised for what they are. Written in English, and obscurely supposed to conceal some dangerous form of humour, they are left for the most part unconsidered by the "serious" public of the annual picture galleries.

There is one book by another writer who has not always been fairly treated, Mr. George Moore's "Modern Painting," which stands out among the art criticism of our time. It is full of injustice, brutality, and ignorance; but it is full also of the most generous justice, the most discriminating sympathy, and the genuine knowledge of the painter. It is hastily thought out, hastily written; but there, in those vivid, direct, unscrupulously logical pages, you will find some of the secrets of the art of painting, let out, so to speak, by an intelligence all sensation, which has soaked them up without knowing it. [. . .]

II.

"What exactly," says Mr. MacColl, "was the special and final addition made to the instrument of painting in the nineteenth century? It may be expressed by saying that painting accepted at last the full contents of vision as material, all that is given in the coloured camera-reflection of the real world." So far so good, but is that all, or even the essential part, of what the painting of the century has tried to do? Is it not rather that modern painters have tried to do with the aid of nature what the old painters did without it to find the pattern and rhythm of their pictures in nature itself rather than in their own brains and on their own palettes? It is not merely a question of seeing things as they are, and "accepting the full contents of vision as material"; it is the deeper and more difficult question of getting nature, seen frankly, into the pattern, instead of coming to nature with one's pattern ready-made. [. . .]

The sentiment of nature, as it enters into the painting of the nineteenth century, is a new thing in art. Try to imagine Millet in any other century! To the old painters nature did not exist as nature, only as decoration, or as the interest of locality. It was a matter for backgrounds, a device for "stationing," in Keats' phrase, their figures or their drama. When nature "put them out," it could be altered at will; when nature pleased them, it could be copied separately, with a separate focussing on each square inch of stones or grass. There was the play-building of topography, in clear Italian backgrounds, little walled cities on a hill, with their paved roads and chequer-work of streets and gardens; and there was the painter's delight in separate natural effects, in flowers or colours. But the interest has no guardian feeling of fidelity or sense of honour towards nature.[22] Even Giorgione is occupied in making the world a place of rest or enchantment for the men and women who enjoy its leisure. No one has realised that nature can be treated on terms of equality.

To the painters of the nineteenth century, nature is life, religion, responsibility, or seduction. There is the devout sincerity of the eye to things seen; there is the mind's acceptance of the principle of life in visible things. From the conjunction of this thought and sight we get the special character of modern painting. Impressionism, in a broad sense the pictorial art of the century, is, in its essential aim, limited to an immediate noting of light, movement, expression; to the exquisite record of an instant. Is it, in Browning's phrase, "the instant made eternity"? [. . .]

"The painting of nature," says Mr. MacColl, very justly, "is not always compatible with the nature of paint, and the 'sense of nature' depends as much upon humouring the nature of the paint as upon pressing the nature of the thing, upon freshness, limpid ease, untired response." "Manet and Mr. Whistler," he says elsewhere, in a sentence which might follow this one, "are the two artists of their time who are natives of paint, who make a sticky rebellious substance a magical liquid matter." In other words, it is in Manet and in Mr. Whistler, among the painters of our own age, that we can see best what the nineteenth century has been aiming at in painting. Of each it could be said, as Mr. MacColl says of Manet: "He resaw the world, remade its pictorial aspect."[23] [. . .]

To Manet, in his vision of the world, everything existed in hard outline. Late in life he tried to see more in Monet's way, but when he was using only his own eyes it was natural to him to be very heedful of the silhouette. In seeing, and in rendering what he saw, Manet, has, above all, audacity; he cannot conceal his delight in the paint which comes out of his brush like life itself. I have seen painters, standing before a canvas of Manet, lost in delight over the surprising way in which the paint comes alive, with a beauty inherent in itself, yet always on its way to express something. [. . .] Cézanne has reduced painting to a kind of science, the science of disempassioned technique. [. . .] The landscape and the still-life study are seen with exactly the same childlike intentness, seen in the child's convention of hard outline, and with all the emphasis of an eye which chases sentiment out of natural things, that it may take them naked and alone. But, it may be questioned, are things ever either naked or alone in nature? Look from Cézanne to Carrière and you will see that everything in the picture, this "Maternité," this "Mère et Fille," is made up of "correspondences," of the harmonies which envelop and unite life with life, life with nature; that here is a vision of reality so intense that the mere statement of facts no longer needs emphasis. Cézanne's "nature morte" is a lump of the world cut out with a knife; in Carrière the rhythm of his mother and child almost evades the limits of the frame, seems a wave of the sea arrested in its motion and as if still in movement.[24] [. . .]

In Whistler it is the reality that astonishes me the most, and the variety with which he represents that reality, going clean through outward things to their essence, that is, to their essential reality; never, like Fantin, setting up an invention in the place of nature.[25] It is remarkable that an artist who may seem, in his words, to have denied nature, or to have put himself arrogantly in the place of nature, should, in his pictures, have given us no image, no outline, no shade or colour, which is not evoked out of a thing really seen and delicately remembered. [. . .] Whatever "The White Girl" or "At the Mirror" owed to Rossetti was a debt already paid before the picture was finished. Japan and Velasquez, whenever they are seen, are seen through creative eyes. And just as in the landscapes and seascapes we see the paint thinning, clarifying, becoming more exquisitely and exactly expressive, so in the portraits and figure-pieces we can trace the elimination of effort, the spiritualising of paint itself; [. . .]

Whistler begins by building his world after nature's, with supports as solid and as visible. Gradually he knocks away support after support, expecting the structure to support itself by its own consciousness, so to speak. At the perfect moment he gives to the eye just enough to catch in the outlines of things that it may be able to complete them by that imaginative sympathy which is part of the seeing of works of art. [. . .]

III.

In the nineteenth century, as in every century, there have been painters who have deliberately turned backwards or aside; haters of their own time, haters of reality, dreamers who have wanted to gather in some corner of unlimited space. Poets rather than painters, the visible world has seemed too narrow for them; and one, like Monticelli, has tried to paint in terms of music, and another, like Rossetti, has tried to put the spiritual mysteries of passion, or like Watts, the bodily form of great emotion and high duties, literally upon the canvas.[26] [. . .]

One, the unluckiest, of these dreamers who have made a world "*à rebours*," and have lived persistently in it [. . .] is Simeon Solomon, a painter who, I suppose, is still living, forgotten somewhere or other. Mr. MacColl does not mention him, though two of his pictures were in the Glasgow Exhibition; but it seems to me that he has his place, not far from Burne-Jones, in any record of the painting of the nineteenth century. [. . .] perhaps what was most significant in this strange temperament is seen in such pictures as "The Sleepers and the One that Waketh." Three faces, faint with languor, two with closed eyes and the other with eyes wearily open, lean together, cheek on cheek, between white, sharp-edged stars in a background of dim sky. These faces, with their spectral pallor, the robes of faint purple tinged with violet, are full of morbid delicacy, like the painting of a perfume. Here, as always, there is weakness, insecurity, but also a very personal sense of beauty, which this only half-mastered technique is undoubtedly able to bring out upon the canvas, in at least a suggestion of everything that the painter meant.

In later years Solomon restricted himself to single heads drawn in coloured chalks, [. . .] The drawing becomes more and more nerveless, the expression loses delicacy and hardens into the caricature of an emotion, the faint suggestions of colour become more pronounced, more crudely assorted. In the latest drawings of all we see no more than the splintering wreck of a painter's technique [. . .] They have legends under them out of the Bible, in Latin, or out of Dante, in Italian; or they have the names of the Seven Virtues, or of the Seven Deadly Sins; or are images of Sleep and Death and Twilight. "A void and wonderfully vague desire" fills all these hollow faces, as water fills the hollow pools of the sand; they have the sorrow of those who have no cause for sorrow except that they are as they are in a world not made after their pattern. The lips are sucked back and the chins thrust forward in a languor which becomes a mannerism, like the long thin throats and heavy half-closed eyes and cheeks haggard with fever or exhaustion. [. . .] These faces are without sex; they have brooded among ghosts of passions till they have become the ghosts of themselves; the energy of virtue or of sin has gone out of them, and they hang in space, dry, rattling, the husks of desire.

IV.

Clearly marked off from these painters to whom paint has been no more than a difficult, never really loved or accepted, medium for the translation of dreams or ideas into visible form, yet not without some of their desire of the impossible in paint, Monticelli, to whom Mr. MacColl devotes a few, not unsympathetic lines, seems to unite several of the tendencies of modern painting, in a contradiction all his own. I confess that he interests me more than many better painters. He tries to do a thing wholly his own, and is led into one of those confusing and interesting attempts to make one form of art do the work of another form of art as well as its own, which are so characteristic of our century, and which appeal, with so much illegitimate charm, to most speculative minds.[27]

To Monticelli colour is a mood; or is it that he is so much a painter that mood to him is colour? Faust and Margaret, or a woman feeding chickens, or a vase of flowers on a table, or a conversation in a park, or a cottage interior, it is as much the same to him as one title or another is the same to a musician. The mood of his own soul, or the fiery idea at the heart of these mere reds and greens and yellows; that is his aim, and the form which offers itself to embody that desire is a somewhat unimportant accident to him. [. . .]

But he himself, doubtless, is content with the arabesque of the intention, with a voluptuous delight in daring harmonies of colour, as a musician might be content to weave dissonances into fantastic progressions, in a kind of very conscious madness, a Sadism of sound. Monticelli's delights are all violent, and, in their really abstract intoxication of the eyes, can be indicated only in terms of lust and cruelty. Beauty, with him, is a kind of torture, as if sensuality were carried to the point of a rejoicing agony. His colour cries out with the pain of an ecstasy greater than it can bear. [. . .] The painting itself is like the way of seeing, hurried, fierce, prodigal, the paint laid on by the palette-knife in great lumps which stand out of the canvas. [. . .] At the proper distance the colours clash together in that irreconcilable way which Monticelli meant, crude tone against crude tone: their conflict is the picture.[28]

In writing of Monticelli it is impossible not to use terms of hearing at least as often as terms of sight. All his painting tends towards the effect of music, with almost the same endeavour to escape from the bondage of matter; [. . .] Monticelli is scarcely at all dependent on what he sees, or rather he sees what he likes, and he always likes the same thing. He tries to purify vision to the point of getting disembodied colour. Other painters have tried to give us the spiritual aspect of colour. He seems to paint listening. [. . .] His painting often conveys the effect of tapestry, as in the large 'Meeting in the Park,' with its colour as if stitched into the canvas. His world is a kind of queer, bright, sombre fairy-land of his own, where fantastic people sing and dance on the grass, and wander beside fountains, and lie under trees, always in happy landscapes which some fierce thought has turned tragic; the painter being indeed indifferent to more than the gesture of his puppets in solid paint, who make so little pretence to any individual life of their own. Their faces are for the most part indistinguishable; all the emotion being in the colour of their dresses, in their gesture, and in the moment's pattern which they make upon the green grass or against ancient walls.

And Monticelli has at least this great quality, among others less great: every touch of his brush expresses a personal vision, way of feeling colour, and is a protest against that vague sort of seeing everything in general and feeling nothing at all, which is supposed to be seeing things as they really are. Things as they really are! that paradox for fools. For every one, probably, for the artist certainly, things are as one sees them; and if most people seem to see things in very much the same way, that is only another proof of the small amount of individuality in the average man, his deplorable faculty of imitation, his inability not only to think but to see for himself. Monticelli creates with his eyes, putting his own symbols frankly in the place of nature's: for that, perhaps, is what it means to see nature in a personal way.[29]

II.

An Introduction to the Study of Browning[1]

The dramatic poet, in the ordinary sense, in the sense in which we apply it to Shakespeare and the Elizabethans, aims at showing, by means of action, the development of character as it manifests itself to the world in deeds. His study is character, but it is character in action, considered only in connection with a particular grouping of events, and only so far as it produces or operates upon these. The processes are concealed from us, we see the result. [. . .]

But is there no other sense in which a poet may be dramatic, besides this sense of the acting drama? no new form possible, which

> "peradventure may outgrow,
> The simulation of the painted scene,
> Boards, actors, prompters, gaslight, and costume,
> And take for a nobler stage the soul itself,
> Its shifting fancies and celestial lights,
> With all its grand orchestral silences,
> To keep the pauses of the rhythmic sounds."[2]

This new form of drama is the drama as we see it in Mr. Browning, a drama of the interior, a tragedy or comedy of the soul. Instead of a grouping of characters which shall act on one another to produce a certain result in action, we have a grouping of events useful or important only as they influence the character or the mind. [. . .] We watch the workings of the mental machinery as it is slowly disclosed before us; we note its specialties of construction, its individual character, the interaction of parts, every secret of it. [. . .]

Mr. Browning's aim, then, being to see how each soul conceives of itself, and to exhibit its essential qualities, yet without a complication of incident, it is his frequent practice to reveal the soul to itself by the application of a sudden test, which shall condense the long trial years into a single moment, and so "flash the truth out by one blow." To this practice we owe his most vivid and notable work. "The poetry of Robert Browning," says Mr. Pater, "is pre-eminently the poetry of situations."[3] He selects a character, no matter how uninteresting in itself, and places it in some situation where its vital essence may become apparent – in some crisis of conflict or opportunity. The choice of good or evil is open to it, and in perhaps a single moment its fate will be decided. [. . .] These moments of intense significance, these tremendous spiritual crises, are struck out in Mr. Browning's poetry with a clearness and sharpness of outline that no other poet has achieved. [. . .]

It is only natural that a poet with the instincts of a painter should be capable of superb landscape-painting in verse; and we find in Mr. Browning this power. It is further evident that such a poet – a man who has chosen poetry instead of painting – must consider the latter art subordinate to the former, and it is only natural that we should find Mr. Browning subordinating the pictorial to the poetic capacity, and this more carefully than most other poets. His best landscapes are as brief as they are brilliant. They are as sabre-strokes, swift, sudden, flashing the light from their sweep, and striking straight to the heart. And they are never pushed into prominence for an effect of idle beauty, nor strewn about in the way of thoughtful or passionate utterance, like roses in a runner's path. They are subordinated always to the human interest; blended, *fused* with it, so that a landscape in a poem of Mr. Browning's is literally a part of the emotion. The poetry of mere description is of all verse the dreariest and the most inept; all poetry which describes in detail, however magnificent, palls on us when persisted in. [. . .]

In the exercise of his power of placing a character or incident in a sympathetic setting, Mr. Browning shows himself [. . .] singularly skilful. He never avails himself of the dramatic poet's licence of vagueness as to surroundings: he sees them himself with instant and intense clearness, and stamps them as clearly on our brain. The picture calls up the mood.[4]

Modernity in Verse[5]

There is something revolutionary about all Mr. Henley's work; the very titles, the very existence, of his poems may be taken as a sort of manifesto on behalf of what is surely a somewhat new art, the art of modernity in verse. In the *London Voluntaries*, for instance, what a sense of poetry of cities, that rarer than pastoral poetry, the romance of what lies beneath our eyes, in the humanity of streets, if we have but the vision and the point of view! Here, at last, is a poet who can so enlarge the limits of his verse as to take in London. And I think that might be the test of poetry which professes to be modern: its capacity for dealing with London, with what one sees or might see there, indoors and out.

To be modern in poetry, to represent really oneself and one's surroundings, the world as it is to-day, to be modern and yet poetical, is, perhaps, the most difficult, as it is certainly the most interesting, of all artistic achievements. In music the modern soul seems to have found expression in Wagner; in painting it may be said to have taken form and colour in Manet, Degas, and Whistler; in sculpture, has it not revealed itself in Rodin? on the stage it is certainly typified in Sarah Bernhardt. Essentially modern poetry may be said to have begun in France, with Baudelaire. The art which he invented, a perverse, self-scrutinizing, troubled art of sensation and nerves, has been yet further developed, subtilized, volatilized, rather, by Verlaine, who still remains the typical modern poet. [. . .] What Mr. Henley has brought into the language of poetry is a certain freshness, a daring straightforwardness and pungency of epithet, very refreshing in its contrast with the traditional limpness and timidity of the respectable verse of the day. One feels indeed at times that the touch is a little rough, the voice a trifle loud, the new word just a little unnecessary. But with these unaccustomed words and tones Mr. Henley does certainly succeed in flashing the picture, the impression upon us, in realizing the intangible, in saying new things in a new and fascinating manner.

Paul Verlaine[6]

The art of Paul Verlaine is something new, absolutely new, to poetry. *Romances sans Paroles* – songs without words – is the name of one of his volumes, and his poetry at its best might almost be called disembodied song. It is an art of impressionism – sometimes as delicate, as pastoral, as Watteau, sometimes as sensitively modern as Whistler, sometimes as brutally modern as Degas. It is all suggestion, evocation [. . .] – the suggestion and evocation of sensation, a restless, insistent search for the last fine shade of expression. 'Car nous voulons,' he says in that famous poem dedicated to Charles Morice, "L'Art Poetique," –

"Car nous voulons la Nuance encor,
Pas la Couleur, rien que la nuance!
Oh! la nuance seule fiance
La rêve au rêve et la flûte au cor!"[7]

La nuance – the something evanescent which haunts and teases the artist's brain, the something which cannot, which must, be expressed! "And all the rest," says Verlaine, with supreme contempt, "is literature!" Literature means the prose of things: and is that worth expressing? Is anything, when we come to consider, worth expressing except this quintessence of things – perhaps an impossible task? Verlaine has gone farther than any other poet in the direction of an art which suggests, with close-lipped, pausing reticence, "things too *subtle* and too sweet for words." [. . .]

With what Verlaine has made of his life we are concerned only so far as the life has made or modified the artistic work; and in him the two are one, as surely as the two are one in Villon. From the date of *Romances sans Paroles* to the date of *Liturgies Intimes*, every stage of the "fever called living" has been chronicled and characterized in verse.[8] The verse has changed as the life has changed, remaining true to certain fundamental characteristics, as the man, through all, has remained true to his strange and self-contradictory temperament. [. . .] Himself a creature of passions and sensations, tossed to and fro by every wind, he has given voice to all the vague desires, the tumultuous impressions, of that feeble and ravenous creature, the modern man of cities. He has set them to music that is now exquisite, as the mood is exquisite, now dissonant, as the mood is dissonant, always an acute, a floating music, that had never been heard before.

Review of George Moore's *Impressions and Opinions*[9]

Mr. Moore's new book, a collection of essays, has the appropriate name, *Impressions and Opinions*. The essays are concerned with literature, with the drama, and with pictures. [. . .] So interesting, so suggestive, so valuable a volume of critical essays has not appeared since Mr. Pater's *Appreciations*. In saying this I had no intention of comparing Mr. Pater and Mr. Moore, who certainly are, in all obvious qualities, extremely unlike. But they have, after all, [. . .] something in common. Alone among English men of letters who write criticism, they have a complete emancipation from English prejudices in art; they alone can be trusted for an unbiased opinion as to the works of, let us say, Goncourt, Flaubert, Mérimée. [. . .] Mr. Moore, like Mr. Pater, and like no one else whom I can think of, has an absolute devotion to art as art; he is rightly incapable of taking anything into consideration but the one question – is this good or is it bad art? With all those questions that haunt the ordinary English brain he is totally unacquainted – those dragging considerations of tendency, of advisability, of convention. He receives impressions, he forms opinions, and he states his opinions, he indicates his impressions, frankly, simply, without conceiving the need of reservations, without feeling impelled to insist on limitations. [. . .]

In the section devoted to art, Mr. Moore gives impressions and opinions which are specially valuable on account of his intimate technical knowledge of the subject. He at least answers to Mr. Whistler's requirement: he is a critic of pictures who has actually painted pictures himself. And nothing in the book is more admirable, both as criticism and as literature, than the brief, expressive study of Degas, the painter who has created a new art, ultra-modern, *fin de siècle*, the art of the ballet, the bathroom, the washing-tub, the racecourse, the shop-window.

The Decadent Movement in Literature[10]

The latest movement in European literature has been called by many names, none of them quite exact or comprehensive – Decadence, Symbolism, Impressionism, for instance. [. . .] These terms, as it happens, have been adopted as the badge of little separate cliques, noisy, brainsick young people who haunt the brasseries of the Boulevard Saint-Michel, and exhaust their ingenuities in theorizing over the works they cannot write. But, taken frankly as epithets which express their own meaning, both Impressionism and Symbolism convey some notion of that new kind of literature which is perhaps more broadly characterized by the word Decadence. The most representative literature of the day – the writing which appeals to, which has done so much to form, the younger generation – is certainly not classic, nor has it any relation with that old antithesis of the Classic, the Romantic. After a fashion it is no doubt a decadence; it has all the qualities that mark the end of great periods, the qualities that we find in the Greek, the Latin, decadence: an intense self-consciousness, a restless curiosity in research, an oversubtilizing refinement upon refinement, a spiritual and moral perversity. If what we call the classic is indeed the supreme art – those qualities of perfect simplicity, perfect sanity, perfect proportion, the supreme qualities - then this representative literature of to-day, interesting, beautiful, novel as it is, is really a new and beautiful and interesting disease. [. . .] And this unreason of the soul – [. . .] – this unstable equilibrium, which has overbalanced so many brilliant intelligences into one form or another of spiritual confusion, is but another form of the *maladie fin de siècle*. For its very disease of form, this literature is certainly typical of a civilization grown over-luxurious, over-inquiring, too languid for the relief of action, too uncertain for any emphasis in opinion or in conduct. It reflects all the moods, all the manners, of a sophisticated society; its very artificiality is a way of being true to nature: simplicity, sanity, proportion – the classic qualities – how much do we possess them in our life, our surroundings, that we should look to find them in our literature – so evidently the literature of a decadence?

Taking the word Decadence, then, as most precisely expressing the general sense of the newest movement in literature, we find that the terms Impressionism and Symbolism define correctly enough the two main branches of that movement. Now Impressionist and Symbolist have more in common than either supposes; both are really working on the same hypothesis, applied in different directions. What both seek is not general truth merely, but *la vérité vraie*, the very essence of truth – the truth of appearances to the senses, of the visible world to the eyes that see it: and the truth of spiritual things to the spiritual vision. The Impressionist, in literature as in painting, would flash upon you in a new, sudden way so exact an image of what you have just seen, just as you have seen it, that you may say, as a young American sculptor, a pupil of Rodin, said to me on seeing for the first time a picture of Whistler's, "Whistler seems to think his picture upon canvas – and there it is!" [. . .] The Symbolist, in this new, sudden way, would flash upon you the "soul" of that which can be apprehended only by the soul – the finer sense of things unseen, the deeper meaning of things evident. And naturally, necessarily, this endeavor after a perfect truth to one's impression, to one's intuition – perhaps an impossible endeavor – has brought with it, in its revolt from ready-made impressions and conclusions, a revolt from the ready-made of language, from the bondage of traditional form, of a form become rigid.[11] [. . .]

What the Goncourts have done is to specialize vision, so to speak, and to subtilize language to the point of rendering every detail in just the form and color of the actual impression. M. Edmond de Goncourt once said to me – [. . .] "My brother and I invented an opera-glass: the young people nowadays are taking it out of our hands."[12]

An opera-glass – a special, unique way of seeing things – that is what the Goncourts have brought to bear upon the common things about us; and it is here that they have done the "something new" here more than anywhere. They have never sought "to see life steadily, and see it whole": their vision has always been somewhat feverish, with the diseased sharpness of over-excited nerves. [. . .] But it is this morbid intensity in seeing and seizing things that has helped to form that marvellous style – "a style perhaps too ambitious of impossibilities," as they admit – a style which inherits some of its color from Gautier, some of its fine outline from Flaubert, but which has brought light and shadow into the color, which has softened outline in the magic of atmosphere. With them words are not merely color and sound, they live. That search after "l'image peinte," "l'épithète rare," is not (as with Flaubert) a search after harmony of phrase for its own sake; it is a desperate endeavour to give sensation, to flash the impression of the moment, to preserve the very heat and motion of life. And so, in analysis as in description they have found out a way of noting the fine shades; they have broken the outline of the conventional novel in chapters, with its continuous story, in order to indicate – sometimes in a chapter of half a page – this and that revealing moment, this or that significant attitude or accident or sensation. [. . .]

Joris Karl Huysmans demands a prominent place in any record of the Decadent movement.[13] His work like that of the Goncourts, is largely determined by the *maladie fin de siècle* – the diseased nerves that, in his case, have given a curious personal quality of pessimism to his outlook on the world, his view of life. Part of his work – *Marthe, Les Soeurs Vatard, En Ménage, À Vau l'Eau* – is a minute and searching study of the minor discomforts, the commonplace miseries of life, as seen by a peevishly disordered vision, delighting, for its own self-torture, in the insistent contemplation of human stupidity, of the sordid in existence. Yet these books do but lead up to the unique masterpiece, the astonishing caprice of *À Rebours*, in which he has concentrated all that is delicately depraved, all that is beautifully, curiously poisonous in modern art. *À Rebours* is the history of a typical Decadent – a study, indeed, after a real man, but a study which seizes the type rather than the personality. In the sensations and ideas of Des Esseintes we see the sensations and ideas of the effeminate, over-civilized, deliberately abnormal creature who is the last product of our society: partly the father, partly the offspring, of the perverse art that he adores. Des Esseintes creates for his solace, in the wilderness of a barren and profoundly uncomfortable world, an artificial paradise. [. . .] He delights in the beauty of strange, unnatural flowers, in the melodic combination of scents, in the imagined harmonies of the sense of taste. And at last, exhausted by these spiritual and sensory debauches in the delights of the artificial, he is left (as we close the book) with a brief, doubtful choice before him – madness or death, or else a return to nature, to the normal life.

III.

Preface to the second edition of *London Nights*[1]

[. . .] I have been attacked, then, on the ground of morality, and by people who, in condemning my book, not because it is bad art, but because they think it bad morality, forget that they are confusing moral and artistic judgments, and limiting art without aiding morality. I contend on behalf of the liberty of art, and I deny that morals have any right of jurisdiction over it. Art may be served by morality; it can never be its servant. For the principles of art are eternal, while the principles of morality fluctuate with the spiritual ebb and flow of the ages. [. . .] Is it for such a shifting guide that I am to forsake the sure and constant leading of art, which tells me that whatever I find in humanity (passion, desire, the spirit or the senses, the hell or heaven of man's heart) is part of the eternal substance which nature weaves in the rough for art to combine cunningly into beautiful patterns? The whole visible world itself, we are told, is but a symbol, made visible in order that we may apprehend ourselves, and not be blown hither and thither like a flame in the night.[2] How laughable is it, then, that we should busy ourselves, with such serious faces, in the commending or condemning, the permission or the exemption, of this accident or that, this or the other passing caprice of our wisdom or our folly, as a due or improper subject for the 'moment's monument' of a poem![3] It is as if you were to say to me, here on these weedy rocks of Rosses Point, where the grey sea passes me continually, flinging a little foam at my feet, that I may write of one rather than another of these waves, which are not more infinite than the moods of men.

The moods of men! There I find my subject, there the region over which art rules; and whatever has once been a mood of mine, though it has been no more than a ripple on the sea, and had no longer than that ripple's duration, I claim the right to render, if I can, in verse; and I claim, from my critics and my readers, the primary understanding, that a mood is after all but a mood, a ripple on the sea, and perhaps with no longer than that ripple's duration. [. . .]

Rosses Point, Sligo, *September* 2, 1896.

Mr W. B. Yeats[4]

I.

Mr Yeats is the only one among the younger English poets who has the whole poetical temperament, and nothing but the poetical temperament. He lives on one plane, and you will find in the whole of his work, with its varying degrees of artistic achievement, no unworthy or trivial mood, no occasional concession to the fatigue of high thinking. It is this continuously poetical quality of mind that seems to me to distinguish Mr Yeats from the many men of talent, and to place him among the few men of genius. A man may indeed be a poet because he has written a single perfect lyric. He will not be a poet of high order, he will not be a poet in the full sense, unless his work, however unequal it may be in actual literary skill, presents this undeviating aspect, as of one to whom the act of writing is no more than the occasional flowering of a mood into speech. And that, certainly, is the impression which remains with one after a careful reading of the revised edition of Mr Yeats' collected poems and of his later volume of lyrics, "The Wind among the Reeds." [. . .]

In [. . .] "The Wind among the Reeds," in which symbolism

extends to the cover, where reeds are woven into a net to catch the wandering sounds, Mr Yeats becomes completely master of himself and of his own resources. Technically the verse is far in advance of anything he has ever done, and if a certain youthful freshness, as of one to whom the woods were still the only talkers upon earth, has gone inevitably, its place has been taken by a deeper, more passionate, and wiser sense of the "everlasting voices" which he has come to apprehend, no longer quite joyously, in the crying of birds, the tongues of flame, and the silence of the heart. It is only gradually that Mr Yeats has learnt to become quite human. Life is the last thing he has learnt, and it is life, an extraordinarily intense inner life, that I find in this book of lyrics, which may seem also to be one long "hymn to intellectual beauty."[5]

The poems which make up a volume apparently disconnected are subdivided dramatically among certain symbolical persons, familiar to the readers of "The Secret Rose," Aedh, Hanrahan, Robartes, each of whom, as indeed Mr Yeats is at the trouble to explain in his notes, is but the pseudonym of a particular outlook of the consciousness, in its passionate, or dreaming, or intellectual moments. It is by means of these dramatic symbols, refining still further upon the large mythological symbolism which he has built up into almost a system, that Mr Yeats weaves about the simplicity of moods that elaborate web of atmosphere in which the illusion of love, and the cruelty of pain, and the gross ecstasy of hope, became changed into beauty. [. . .]

To a poet who is also a mystic there is a great simplicity in things, beauty being really one of the foundations of the world, woman a symbol of beauty, and the visible moment, in which to love or to write love songs is an identical act, really as long and short as eternity. Never, in these love songs, concrete as they become through the precision of their imagery, does an earthly circumstance divorce ecstasy from the impersonality of vision. This poet cannot see love under the form of time, cannot see beauty except as the absolute beauty, cannot distinguish between the mortal person and the eternal idea. Every rapture hurries him beyond the edge of the world and beyond the end of time.[6]

The conception of lyric poetry which Mr Yeats has perfected in this volume, in which every poem is so nearly achieved to the full extent of its intention, may be clearly defined; for Mr Yeats is not a poet who writes by caprice. A lyric, then, is an embodied ecstasy, and an ecstasy so profoundly personal that it loses the accidental qualities of personality, and becomes a part of the universal consciousness.

The Symbolist Movement in Literature[7]

INTRODUCTION

"It is in and through Symbols that man, consciously or unconsciously, lives, works, and has his being: those ages, moreover, are accounted the noblest which can the best recognise symbolical worth, and prize it highest."

CARLYLE[8]

Without symbolism there can be no literature; indeed, not even language. What are words themselves but symbols, almost as arbitrary as the letters which compose them, mere sounds of the voice to which we have agreed to give certain significations, as we have agreed to translate these sounds by those combinations of letters? Symbolism began with the first words uttered by the first man, as he named every living thing; or before them, in heaven, when God named the world into being. And we see, in these beginnings, precisely what Symbolism in literature really is: a form of expression, at the best but approximate, [. . .] for an unseen reality apprehended by the consciousness. [. . .] "In a Symbol," says Carlyle, "there is concealment and yet revelation: hence therefore, by Silence and by Speech acting together, comes a double significance." And, in that fine chapter of *Sartor Resartus*, he goes further, vindicating for the word its full value: "In the Symbol proper, what we can call a Symbol there is ever, more or less distinctly and directly, some embodiment and revelation of the Infinite; the Infinite is made to blend itself with the Finite, to stand visible, and as it were, attainable there."

It is in such a sense as this that the word Symbolism has been used to describe a movement which, during the last generation, has profoundly influenced the course of French literature. All such words, used of anything so living, variable, and irresponsible as literature, are, as symbols themselves must so often be, mere compromises, mere indications. Symbolism, as seen in the writers of our day, would have no value if it were not seen also, under one disguise or another, in every great imaginative writer. What distinguishes the Symbolism of our day from the Symbolism of the past is that it has now become conscious of itself, in a sense in which it was unconscious even in Gérard de Nerval, to whom I trace the particular origin of the literature which I call Symbolist. The forces which mould the thought of men change, or men's resistance to them slackens; with the change of men's thought comes a change of literature, alike in its inmost essence and in its outward form: after the world has starved its soul long enough in the contemplation and the re-arrangement of material things, comes the turn of the soul; and with it comes the literature of which I write in this volume, a literature in which the visible world is no longer a reality, and the unseen world no longer a dream. [. . .]

In most of the writers whom I have dealt with as summing up in themselves all that is best in Symbolism, it will be noticed that the form is very carefully elaborated, [. . .] There is such a thing as perfecting form that form may be annihilated. All the art of Verlaine is in bringing verse to a bird's song, the art of Mallarmé in bringing verse to the song of an orchestra. In Villiers de l'Isle-Adam drama becomes an embodiment of spiritual forces, in Maeterlinck not even their embodiment, but the remote sound of their voices. It is all an attempt to spiritualise literature, to evade the old bondage of rhetoric, the old bondage of exteriority. Description is banished that beautiful things may be evoked, magically; the regular beat of verse is broken in order that words may fly, upon subtler wings. Mystery is no longer feared, as the great mystery in whose midst we are islanded was feared by those to whom that unknown sea was only a great void. [. . .]

Here, then, in this revolt against exteriority, against rhetoric, against a materialistic tradition; in this endeavour to disengage the ultimate essence, the soul, of whatever exists and can be realised by the consciousness; in this dutiful waiting upon every symbol by which the soul of things can be made visible; literature, bowed down by so many burdens, may at last attain liberty, and its authentic speech. In attaining this liberty, it accepts a heavier burden; for in speaking to us so intimately, so solemnly, as only religion had hitherto spoken to us, it becomes itself a kind of religion, with all the duties and responsibilities of the sacred ritual.

GÉRARD DE NERVAL[9]

Gérard de Nerval lived the transfigured inner life of the dreamer. "I was very tired of life!" he says. And like so many dreamers, who have all the luminous darkness of the universe in their brains, he found his most precious and uninterrupted solitude in the crowded and more sordid streets of great cities. He who had loved the Queen of Sheba, and seen the seven Elohims dividing the world, could find nothing more tolerable in mortal conditions, when he was truly aware of them, than the company of the meanest of mankind, [. . .] The real world seeming to be always so far from him, and a sort of terror of the gulfs holding him, in spite of himself, to its flying skirts, he found something at all events realisable, concrete, in these drinkers of Les Halles, these vagabonds of the Place du Carrousel, among whom he so often sought refuge. [. . .]

Who has not often meditated, above all what artist, on the slightness, after all, of the link which holds our faculties together in that sober health of the brain which we call reason? Are there not moments when that link seems to be worn down to so fine a tenuity that the wing of a passing dream might suffice to snap it? The consciousness seems, as it were, to expand and contract at once, into something too wide for the universe, and too narrow for the thought of self to find room within it. Is it that the sense of identity is about to evaporate, annihilating all, or is it that a more profound identity, the identity of the whole sentient universe, has been at last realised? Leaving the concrete world on these brief voyages, the fear is that we may not have strength to return, or that we may lose the way back. Every artist lives a double life, in which he is for the most part conscious of the illusions of the imagination. He is conscious also of the illusions of the nerves, which he shares with every man of imaginative mind. Nights of insomnia, days of anxious waiting, the sudden shock of an event, any one of these common disturbances may be enough to jangle the tuneless bells of one's nerves. The artist can distinguish these causes of certain of his moods from those other causes which come to him because he is an artist, and are properly concerned with that invention which is his own function. Yet is there not some danger that he may come to confuse one with the other, that he may "lose the thread" which conducts him through the intricacies of the inner world?[10]

The supreme artist, certainly, is the furthest of all men from this danger; for he is the supreme intelligence. Like Dante, he can pass through hell unsinged. With him, imagination is vision; when he looks into the darkness, he sees. The vague dreamer, the insecure artist and the uncertain mystic at once, sees only shadows, not recognising their outlines. He is mastered by the images which have come at his call; [. . .]

The madness of Gérard de Nerval, whatever physiological reasons may be rightly given for its outbreak, subsidence, and return, I take to have been essentially due to the weakness and not the excess of his visionary quality, to the insufficiency of his imaginative energy, and to his lack of spiritual discipline. He was an unsystematic mystic; his "Tower of Babel in two hundred volumes," that medley of books of religion, science, astrology, history, travel, which he thought would have rejoiced the heart of Pico della Mirandola, of Meursius, or of Nicholas of Cusa, was truly, as he says, "enough to drive a wise man mad." [. . .] Wavering among intuitions, ignorances, half-truths, shadows of falsehood, now audacious, now hesitating, he was blown hither and thither by conflicting winds, a prey to the indefinite.[11] [. . .]

To have thus realised that central secret of the mystics, from Pythagoras onwards, the secret which the Smaragdine Tablet of Hermes betrays in its "As things are below, so they are above"; which Boehme has classed in his teaching of "signatures," and Swedenborg has systematised in his doctrine of "correspondences"; does it matter very much that he arrived at it by way of the obscure and fatal initiation of madness?[12] Truth, and especially that soul of truth which is poetry, may be reached by many roads; and a road is not necessarily misleading because it is dangerous or forbidden. Here is one who has gazed at light till it has blinded him; and for us all that is important is that he has seen something, not that his eyesight has been too weak to endure the pressure of light overflowing from beyond the world. [. . .]

Gérard de Nerval, then, had divined, before all the world, that poetry should be a miracle; not a hymn to beauty, nor the description of beauty, nor beauty's mirror; but beauty itself, the colour, fragrance, and form of the imagined flower, as it blossoms again out of the page. Vision, the over-powering vision, had come to him beyond, if not against, his will; and he knew that vision is the root out of which the flower must grow. Vision had taught him symbol, and he knew that it is by symbol alone that the flower can take visible form. He knew that the whole mystery of beauty can never be comprehended by the crowd, and that while clearness is a virtue of style, perfect explicitness is not a necessary virtue. So it was with disdain, as well as with confidence, that he allowed these sonnets to be overheard. It was enough for him to say:

J'ai rêvé dans la grotte où nage la syrène;[13]

and to speak, it might be, the siren's language, remembering her. "It will be my last madness," he wrote, "to believe myself a poet: let criticism cure me of it." Criticism, in his own day, even Gautier's criticism, could but be disconcerted by a novelty so unexampled. It is only now that the best critics in France are beginning to realise how great in themselves, and how great in their influence, are these sonnets, which, forgotten by the world for nearly fifty years, have all the while been secretly bringing new aesthetics into French poetry.

VILLIERS DE L'ISLE-ADAM[14]

À chacun son infini

I.

Count Philippe Auguste Mathias de Villiers de L'Isle-Adam was born at St. Brieuc, in Brittany, November 28, 1838; he died at Paris, under the care of the Frères Saint-Jean-de-Dieu, August

19, 1889. Even before his death, his life had become a legend, and the legend is even now not to be disentangled from the actual occurrences of an existence so heroically visionary. The Don Quixote of idealism, it was not only in philosophical terms that life, to him, was the dream, and the spiritual world the reality; he lived his faith, enduring what others called reality with contempt, whenever, for a moment, he became conscious of it. The basis of the character of Villiers was pride, and it was a pride which covered more than the universe. And this pride, first of all, was the pride of race. [. . .]

Fundamentally, the belief of Villiers is the belief common to all Eastern mystics.[15] "Know, once for all, that there is for thee no other universe than that conception thereof which is reflected at the bottom of thy thoughts." "What is knowledge but a recognition?" Therefore, "forgetting for ever that which was the illusion of thyself," hasten to become "an intelligence freed from the bonds and the desires of the present moment." "Become the flower of thyself! Thou art but what thou thinkest: therefore think thyself eternal." [. . .] "For thou possessest the real being of all things, in thy pure will, and thou art the God that thou art able to become."

To have accepted the doctrine which thus finds expression in *Axël*, is to have accepted this among others of its consequences: "Science states, but does not explain: she is the oldest offspring of the chimeras; all the chimeras, then, on the same terms as the world (the oldest of them!), are *something more* than nothing!" [. . .]

Such avowals of ignorance are possible only from the height of a great intellectual pride. Villiers' revolt against Science, so far as Science is materialistic, and his passionate curiosity in that chimera's flight towards the invisible, are one and the same impulse of a mind to which only mind is interesting. *Toute cette vieille Extériorité, maligne, compliquée, inflexible*, that illusion which Science accepts for the one reality: it must be the whole effort of one's consciousness to escape from its entanglements, to dominate it, or to ignore it, and one's art must be the building of an ideal world beyond its access, from which one may indeed sally out, now and again, in a desperate enough attack upon the illusions in the midst of which men live. [. . .]

Axël is the Symbolist drama, in all its uncompromising conflict with the "modesty" of Nature and the limitations of the stage. It is the drama of the soul, and at the same time it is the most pictorial of dramas; I should define its manner as a kind of spiritual romanticism. [. . .] The religious ideal, the occult ideal, the wordly ideal, the passionate ideal, are all presented, one after the other, in these dazzling and profound pages; Axël is the disdainful choice from among them, the disdainful rejection of life itself, or the whole illusion of life, "since infinity alone is not a deception." [. . .]

And it is a world thought or dreamt in some more fortunate atmosphere than that in which we live, that Villiers has created for the final achievement of his abstract ideas. I do not doubt that he himself always lived in it, through all the poverty of the precipitous Rue des Martyrs. But it is in *Axël*, and in *Axël*, only, that he has made us also inhabitants of that world. [. . .]

In the sense in which that word is ordinarily used, Villiers has no pathos. This is enough to explain why he can never, in the phrase he would have disliked so greatly, "touch the popular heart." His mind is too abstract to contain pity, and it is in his lack of pity that he seems to put himself outside humanity. *A chacun son infini*, he has said, and in the avidity of his search for the infinite he has no mercy for the blind weakness which goes stumbling over the earth, without so much as knowing that the sun and stars are overhead. He sees only the gross multitude, the multitude which has the contentment of the slave. He cannot pardon stupidity, for it is incomprehensible to him. He sees, rightly, that stupidity is more criminal than vice; if only because vice is curable, stupidity incurable. But he does not realise, as the great novelists have realised, that stupidity can be pathetic, and that there is not a peasant, nor even a self-satisfied bourgeois, in whom the soul has not its part, in whose existence it is not possible to be interested.

Contempt, noble as it may be, anger, righteous though it may be, cannot be indulged in without a certain lack of sympathy; and lack of sympathy comes from a lack of patient understanding. It is certain that the destiny of the greater part of the human race is either infinitely pathetic or infinitely ridiculous.

Under which aspect, then, shall that destiny, and those obscure fractions of humanity, be considered ? Villiers was too sincere an idealist, too absolute in his idealism, to hesitate. "As for living," he cries, in that splendid phrase of *Axël*, "our servants will do that for us!" And, in the *Contes Cruels*, there is this not less characteristic expression of what was always his mental attitude: "As at the play, in a central stall, one sits out, so as not to disturb one's neighbours – out of courtesy, in a word – some play written in a wearisome style and of which one does not like the subject, so I lived, out of politeness": *je vivais par politesse*. In this haughtiness towards life, in this disdain of ordinary human motives and ordinary human beings, there is at once the distinction and the weakness of Villiers.[16] [. . .]

Meanwhile, he had been preparing the spiritual atmosphere of the new generation. Living among believers in the material world, he had been declaring, not in vain, his belief in the world of the spirit; living among Realists and Parnassians, he had been creating a new form of art, the art of the Symbolist drama, and of Symbolism in fiction. He had been lonely all his life, for he had been living in his own lifetime, the life of the next generation. [. . .]

And after all, the last word of Villiers is faith; faith against the evidence of the senses, against the negations of materialistic science, against the monstrous paradox of progress, against his own pessimism in the face of these formidable enemies. He affirms; he "believes in soul, is very sure of God"; requires no witness to the spiritual world of which he is always the inhabitant; and is content to lose his way in the material world, brushing off its mud from time to time with a disdainful gesture as he goes on his way (to apply a significant word of Pater) "like one on a secret errand."[17]

JULES LAFORGUE[18]

The prose and verse of Laforgue, scrupulously correct, but with a new maner of correctness, owe more than any one has realised to the half-unconscious prose and verse of Rimbaud. Verse and prose are alike a kind of travesty, making subtle use of colloquialism, slang, neologism, technical terms, for their allusive, their factitious, their reflected meanings, with which one can play, very seriously. The verse is alert, troubled, swaying, deliberately uncertain, hating rhetoric so piously that it prefers, and finds its piquancy in, the ridiculously obvious. It is really *vers libre*, but at the same time correct verse, before *vers libre* had been invented. And it carries, as far as that theory has ever been carried, the theory which demands an instantaneous notation (Whistler, let us say) of the figure or landscape which one has been accustomed to define with such rigorous exactitude. Verse, always elegant, is broken up into a kind of mockery of prose.

> Encore un de mes pierrots mort;
> Mort d'un chronique orphelinisme;
> C'était un coeur plein de dandysme
> Lunaire, en un drôle de corps;

he will say to us, with a familiarity of manner, as of one talking languidly, in a low voice, the lips always teased into a slightly bitter smile; and he will pass suddenly into the ironical lilt of

> Hôtel garni
> De l'infini,
> Sphinx et Joconde
> Des défunts mondes;[19]

[. . .] The old cadences, the old eloquence, the ingenuous seriousness of poetry, are all banished, on a theory as self-denying as that which permitted Degas to dispense with recognisable beauty in his figures. Here, if ever, is modern verse, verse which dispenses with so many of the privileges of poetry, for an ideal quite of its own. [. . .]

In these always "lunar" parodies, *Salomé*, *Lohengrin*, *Fils de Parsifal*, *Persée et Andromède*, each a kind of metaphysical myth, he realises that *la créature va hardiment à être cérébrale, anti-naturelle*, and he has invented these fantastic puppets with an almost Japanese art of spiritual dislocation. They are, in part, a way of taking one's revenge upon science, by an ironical borrowing of its very terms, which dance in his prose and verse, derisively, at the end of a string.[20]

In his acceptance of the fragility of things as actually a principle of art, Laforgue is a sort of transformed Watteau, showing his disdain for the world which fascinates him, in quite a different way. He has constructed his own world, lunar and actual, speaking slang and astronomy, with a constant disengaging of the visionary aspect, under which frivolity becomes an escape from the arrogance of a still more temporary mode of being, the world as it appears to the sober majority. He is terribly conscious of daily life, cannot omit, mentally, a single hour of the day; and his flight to the moon is in sheer desperation. He sees what he calls *l'Inconscient* in every gesture, but he cannot see it without these gestures. [. . .]

It is an art of the nerves, this art of Laforgue, and it is what all art would tend towards if we followed our nerves on all their journeys. There is in it all the restlessness of modern life, the haste to escape from whatever weighs too heavily on the liberty of the moment, that capricious liberty which demands only room enough to hurry itself weary. It is distressingly conscious of the unhappiness of mortality, but it plays, somewhat uneasily, at a disdainful indifference. And it is out of these elements of caprice, fear, contempt, linked together by an embracing laughter, that it makes its existence. [. . .] There is a great pity at the root of this art of Laforgue: self-pity, which extends, with the artistic sympathy, through mere clearness of vision, across the world. His laughter, which Maeterlinck has defined so admirably as "the laughter of the soul," is the laughter of Pierrot, more than half a sob, and shaken out of him with a deplorable gesture of the thin arms, thrown wide. He is a metaphysical Pierrot, *Pierrot lunaire*, and it is of abstract notions, the whole science of the unconscious, that he makes his showman's patter. [. . .] He has invented a new manner of being René or Werther.[21] An inflexible politeness towards man, woman, and destiny. He composes love-poems hat in hand, and smiles with an exasperating tolerance before all the transformations of the eternal feminine. He is very conscious of death, but his *blague* of death is, above all things, gentlemanly. He will not permit himself, at any moment, the luxury of dropping the mask: not at any moment. [. . .]

And yet one realises, if one but reads him attentively enough, how much suffering and despair, and resignation to what is, after all, the inevitable, are hidden away under this disguise, and also why this disguise is possible. Laforgue died at twenty-seven: he had been a dying man all his life, and his work has the fatal evasiveness of those who shrink from remembering the one thing which they are unable to forget. [. . .] He thinks intensely about life, seeing what is automatic, pathetically ludicrous in it, almost as one might who has had no part in the comedy. He has the double advantage, for his art, of being condemned to death, and of being, in the admirable phrase of Villiers, "one of those who come into the world with a ray of moonlight in their brains."

STÉPHANE MALLARMÉ[22]

I.

Stéphane Mallarmé was one of those who love literature too much to write it except by fragments; in whom the desire of perfection brings its own defeat. With either more or less ambition he would have done more to achieve himself; he was always divided between an absolute aim at the absolute, that is, the unattainable, and a too logical disdain for the compromise by which, after all, literature is literature. [. . .] It was "the work" that he dreamed of, the new art, more than a new religion, whose precise form in the world he was never quite able to settle.

Un auteur difficile, in the phrase of M. Catulle Mendès, it has always been to what he himself calls 'a labyrinth illuminated by flowers' that Mallarmé has felt it due to their own dignity to invite his readers. To their own dignity, and also to his. Mallarmé was obscure, not so much because he wrote differently, as because he thought differently, from other people. His mind was elliptical, and, relying with undue confidence on the intelligence of his readers, he emphasised the effect of what was unlike other people in his mind by resolutely ignoring even the links of connection that existed between them. Never having aimed at popularity, he never needed, as most writers need, to make the first advances. He made neither intrusion upon nor concession to those who, after all, were not obliged to read him. [. . .]

"Poetry," said Mallarmé, "is the language of a state of crisis"; and all his poems are the evocation of a passing ecstasy, arrested in mid-flight. This ecstasy is never the mere instinctive cry of the heart, the simple human joy or sorrow, which, like the Parnassians, but for not quite the same reason, he did not admit in poetry. It is a mental transposition of emotion or sensation, veiled with atmosphere, and becoming, as it becomes a poem, pure beauty. [. . .]

It is the distinction of Mallarmé to have aspired after an impossible liberation of the soul of literature from what is fretting and constraining in "the body of that death," which is the mere literature of words. Words, he has realised, are of value only as a notation of the free breath of the spirit; words, therefore, must be employed with an extreme care, in their choice and adjustment, in setting them to reflect and chime upon one another; yet least of all for their own sake, for what they can never, except by suggestion, express. "Every soul is a melody," he has said, "which needs to be readjusted; and for that are the flute or viol of each." The word, treated indeed with a kind of "adoration," as he says, is so regarded in a magnificent sense, in which it is apprehended as a living thing, itself the vision rather than the reality; at least the philtre of the evocation. The word, chosen as he chooses it, is for him a liberating principle, by which the spirit is extracted from matter; takes form, perhaps assumes immortality. Thus an artificiality, even, in the use of words, that seeming artificiality which comes from using words as if they had never been used before, that chimerical search after the virginity of language, is but the paradoxical outward sign of an extreme discontent with even the best of their service. [. . .]

These seem to me the main lines of Mallarmé's doctrine. It is the doctrine which, as I have already said, had been divined by Gérard de Nerval; but what in Gérard, was pure vision, becomes in Mallarmé a logical sequence of meditation. Mallarmé was not a mystic, to whom any thing came unconsciously; he was a thinker, in whom an extraordinary subtlety of mind was exercised on always explicit, though by no means the common, problems. "A seeker after something in the world, that is there in no satisfying measure, or not at all,"[23] he pursued his search with unwearying persistence, with a sharp mental division of dream and idea, certainly very lucid to himself, however he may have failed to render his expression clear to others. And I, for one, cannot doubt that he was, for the most part, entirely right in his statement and analysis of the new conditions under which we are now privileged or condemned to write. His obscurity was partly his failure to carry out the spirit of his own directions; but, apart from obscurity, which we may all be fortunate enough to escape, is it possible for a writer, at the present day, to be quite simple, with the old, objective simplicity, in either thought or expression? To be *naïf*, to be archaic, is not to be either natural or simple; I affirm that it is not natural to be what is called "natural" any longer. We have no longer the mental attitude of those to whom a story was but a story, and all stories good; we have realised, since it was proved to us by Poe, not merely that the age of epics is past, but that no long poem was ever written; the finest long poem in the world being but a series of short poems linked together by prose. And, naturally, we can no longer write what we can no longer accept. Symbolism, implicit in all literature from the beginning, as it is implicit in the very words we use, comes to us now, at last quite conscious of itself, offering us the only escape from our many imprisonments. We find a new, an older, sense in the so worn out forms of things; the world, which we can no longer believe in as the satisfying material object it was to our grandparents, becomes transfigured with a new light; words, which long usage had darkened almost out of recognition, take fresh lustre. And it is on the lines of that spritualising of the word, that perfecting of form in its capacity for allusion and suggestion, that confidence in the eternal correspondences between the visible and the invisible universe, which Mallarmé taught, and too intermittently practised, that literature must now move, if it is in any sense to move forward.

MAETERLINCK AS A MYSTIC[24]

The secret of things which is just beyond the most subtle words, the secret of the expressive silences, has always been clearer to Maeterlinck than to most people; and, in his plays, he has elaborated an art of sensitive, taciturn, and at the same time highly ornamental simplicity, which has come nearer than any other art to being the voice of silence. To Maeterlinck the theatre has been, for the most part, no more than one of the disguises by which he can express himself, and with his book of meditations on the inner life, *Le Trésor des Humbles*, he may seem to have dropped his disguise.

All art hates the vague; not the mysterious, but the vague; two opposites very commonly confused, as the secret with the obscure, the infinite with the indefinite. And the artist who is also a mystic hates the vague with a more profound hatred than any other artist. Thus Maeterlinck, endeavouring to clothe mystical conceptions in concrete form, has invented a drama so precise, so curt, so arbitrary in its limits, that it can safely be confided to the masks and feigned voices of marionettes. His theatre of artificial beings, who are at once more ghostly and more mechanical than the living actors whom we are accustomed to see, in so curious a parody of life, moving with a certain freedom of action across the stage, may be taken as itself a symbol of the aspect under which what we fantastically term "real life" presents itself to the mystic. [. . .]

"I have come to believe," he writes, in *Le Tragique Quotidien*, "that an old man seated in his armchair, waiting quietly under the lamplight, listening without knowing it to all the eternal laws which reign about his house, interpreting without understanding it all that there is in the silence of doors and windows, and in the little voice of light, enduring the presence of his soul and of his destiny, bowing his head a little, without suspecting that all the powers of the earth intervene and stand on guard in the room like attentive servants, not knowing that the sun itself suspends above the abyss the little table on which he rests his elbow, and that there is not a star in the sky nor a force in the soul which is indifferent to the motion of a falling eyelid or a rising thought – I have come to believe that this motionless old man lived really a more profound, human, and universal life than the lover who strangles his mistress, the captain who gains a victory, or the husband who 'avenges his honour.'"

That, it seems to me, says all there is to be said of the intention of this drama which Maeterlinck has evoked; [. . .], [it] is a drama founded on philosophical ideas, apprehended emotionally; on the sense of the mystery of the universe, of the weakness of humanity, [. . .] It is a drama in which the interest is concentrated on vague people, who are little parts of the universal consciousness, their strange names being but the pseudonyms of obscure passions, intimate emotions. [. . .]

Maeterlinck has realised, better than any one else, the significance, in life and art, of mystery. He has realised how unsearchable is the darkness out of which we have but just stepped, and the darkness into which we are about to pass. And he has realised how the thought and sense of that twofold darkness invade the little space of light in which, for a moment, we moved; the depth to which they shadow our steps, even in that moment's partial escape. But in some of his plays he would seem to have apprehended this mystery as a thing merely or mainly terrifying; the actual physical darkness surrounding blind men, the actual physical approach of death as the intruder; he has shown us people huddled at a window, out of which they are almost afraid to look, or beating at a door, the opening of which they dread. Fear shivers through these plays, creeping across our nerves like a damp mist coiling up out of a valley. And there is beauty, certainly, in this "vague spiritual fear"; [. . .]

But, after all, the claim upon us of this book is not the claim of a work of art, but of a doctrine, and more than that, of a system. Belonging, as he does, to the eternal hierarchy, the unbroken succession, of the mystics, Maeterlinck has apprehended what is essential in the mystical doctrine with a more profound comprehension, and thus more systematically, than any mystic of recent times. He has many points of resemblance with Emerson, on whom he has written on essay which is properly an exposition of his own personal ideas; but Emerson, who proclaimed the supreme guidance of the inner light, the supreme necessity of trusting instinct, of honouring emotion, did but proclaim all this, not without a certain antimystical vagueness: Maeterlinck has systematised it. A more profound mystic than Emerson, he has greater command of that which comes to him unawares, is less at the mercy of visiting angels.[25] [. . .]

This old gospel, of which Maeterlinck is the new voice, has been quietly waiting until certain bankruptcies, the bankruptcy of Science, of the Positive Philosophies, should allow it full credit. Considering the length even of time, it has not had an unreasonable space of waiting; and remember that it takes time but little into account. [. . .]

Jacob Boehme has said, very subtly, "that man does not perceive the truth but God perceives the truth in man"; that is, that whatever we perceive or do is not perceived or done consciously by us, but unconsciously through us. Our business, then, is to tend that "inner light" by which most mystics have symbolised that which at once guides us in time and attaches us to eternity. This inner light is no miraculous descent of the Holy Spirit, but the perfectly natural, though it may finally be overcoming, ascent of the spirit within us. The spirit, in all men, being but a ray of the universal light, it can, by careful tending, by the removal of all obstruction, the cleansing of the vessel, the trimming of the wick, as it were, be increased, made to burn with a steadier, a brighter flame. In the last rapture it may become dazzling, may blind the watcher with excess of light, shutting him in within the circle of transfiguration, whose extreme radiance will leave all the rest of the world henceforth one darkness.[26] [. . .]

And it is towards this point that all the words of this book tend. Maeterlinck, unlike most men ("What is man but a God who is afraid?") is not "miserly of immortal things." He utters the most divine secrets without fear, betraying certain hiding-places of the soul in those most nearly inaccessible retreats which lie nearest to us. All that he says we know already; we may deny it, but we know it. It is what we are not often at leisure enough with ourselves, sincere enough with ourselves, to realise; what we often dare not realise; but, when he says it, we know that it is true, and our knowledge of it is his warrant for saying it. He is what he is precisely because he tells us nothing which we do not already know, or it may be, what we have known and forgotten.

The Choice[27]

That a man like Huysmans should have accepted the Church, should have found the most closely formulated theory of religion still possible, and more than a mere refuge, is certainly significant. It is significant, among other things, as a confession on the part of a great artist, that art alone, as he has conceived it, is not finally satisfying without some further defence against the world. In "A Rebours" he showed us the sterilising influence of a narrow and selfish conception of art, as he represented a particular paradise of art for art's sake turning inevitably into its corresponding hell. Des Esseintes is the symbol of all those who have tried to shut themselves in from the natural world, upon an artificial beauty which has no root there. Worshipping colour, sound, perfume, for their own sakes, and not for their ministrations to a more divine beauty, he stupefies himself on the threshold of ecstasy. And Huysmans, we can scarcely doubt, has passed through the particular kind of haschish dream which this experience really is. He has realised that the great choice, the choice between the world and something which is not visible in the world, but out of which the visible world has been made, does not lie in the mere contrast of the subtler and grosser senses. He has come to realise what the choice really is, and he has chosen. Yet perhaps the choice is not quite so narrow [. . .]; perhaps it is a choice between actualising this dream or actualising that dream. In his escape from the world, one man chooses religion, and seems to find himself; another, choosing love, may seem also to find himself; and may not another, coming to art as to a religion and as to a woman, seem to find himself not less effectually? The one certainty is, that society is the enemy of man, and that formal art is the enemy of the artist. We shall not find ourselves in drawing-rooms or in museums. A man who goes through a day without some fine emotion has wasted his day, whatever he has gained in it. And it is so easy to go through day after day, busily and agreeably, without ever really living for a single instant. Art begins when a man wishes to immortalise the most vivid moment he has ever lived. Life has already, to one not an artist, become art in that moment. And the making of one's life into art is after all the first duty and privilege of every man. It is to escape from material reality into whatever form of ecstasy is our own form of spiritual existence. There is the choice; and our happiness, our "success in life," will depend on our choosing rightly, each for himself, among the forms in which that choice will come to us.[28]

1900.

IV.

Preface to *Plays, Acting and Music*[2]

This book is intended to form part of a series, on which I have been engaged for many years. I am gradually working my way towards the concrete expression of a theory, or system of aesthetics, of all the arts. In my book on "The Symbolist Movement in Literature" I made a first attempt to deal in this way with literature; other volumes, now in preparation, are to follow. The present volume deals mainly with the stage, and, secondarily, with music; it is to be followed by a volume called "Studies in Seven Arts," in which music will be dealt with in greater detail, side by side with painting, sculpture, architecture, handicraft, dancing, and the various arts of the stage. And, as life too is a form of art, and the visible world the chief storehouse of beauty, I try to indulge my curiosity by the study of places and of people. A book on "Cities" is now in the Press, and a book of "imaginary portraits" is to follow, under the title of "Spiritual Adventures." Side by side with these studies in the arts I have my own art, that of verse, which is, after all, my chief concern.

In all my critical and theoretical writing I wish to be as little abstract as possible, and to study first principles, not so much as they exist in the brain of the theorist, but as they may be discovered, alive and in effective action, in every achieved form of art. I do not understand the limitation by which so many writers on aesthetics choose to confine themselves to the study of artistic principles as they are seen in this or that separate form of art. Each art has its own laws, its own capacities, its own limits; these it is the business of the critic jealously to distinguish. Yet, in the study of art as art, it should be his endeavour to master the universal science of beauty.

Ballet, Pantomime, and Poetic Drama[2]

I. THE WORLD AS BALLET

The abstract thinker, to whom the question of practical morality is indifferent, has always loved dancing, as naturally as the moralist has hated it. The Puritan, from his own point of view, is always right, though it suits us, often enough, for wider reasons, to deny his logic. The dance is life, animal life, having its own way passionately. Part of that natural madness which men were once wise enough to include in religion, it began with the worship of the disturbing deities, the Gods of ecstasy, for whom wantonness and wine, and all things in which energy passes into an ideal excess, were sacred.[3] It was cast out of religion when religion cast out nature; for, like nature itself, it is a thing of evil to those who renounce instincts. From the first it has mimed the instincts. It can render birth and death, and it is always going over and over the eternal pantomime of love; it can be all the passions, and all the languors; but it idealises these mere acts, gracious or brutal, into more than a picture; for it is more than a beautified reflection, it has in it life itself, as it shadows life; and it is farther from life than a picture. Humanity, youth, beauty, playing the part of itself, and consciously, in a travesty, more natural than nature, more artificial than art: but we lose ourselves in the boundless bewilderments of its contradictions.

The dance, then, is art because it is doubly nature; and if nature, as we are told, is sinful, it is doubly sinful. A waltz, in a drawing-room, takes us suddenly out of all that convention, away from those guardians of our order who sit around the walls, approvingly, unconsciously; in its winding motion it raises an invisible wall about us, shutting us off from the whole world, in with ourselves; in its fatal rhythm, never either beginning or ending, slow, insinuating, gathering impetus which must be held back, which must rise into the blood, it tells us that life flows even as that, so passionately and so easily and so inevitably; and it is possession and abandonment, the very pattern and symbol of earthly love. Here is nature (to be renounced, to be at least restrained) hurried violently, deliberately, to boiling point. And now look at the dance, on the stage, a mere spectator. Here are all these young bodies, made more alluring by an artificial heightening of whites and reds on the face, displaying, employing all their natural beauty, themselves full of the sense of joy in motion, or affecting that enjoyment, offered to our eyes like a bouquet of flowers, a bouquet of living flowers which have all the glitter of artificial ones. As they dance, under the changing lights, so human, so remote, so desirable, so evasive, coming and going to the sound of a thin, heady music which marks the rhythm of their movements like a kind of clinging drapery, they seem to sum up in themselves the appeal of everything in the world that is passing, and coloured, and to be enjoyed: everything that bids us take no thought for the morrow, and dissolve the will into slumber, and give way luxuriously to the delightful present.[4]

How fitly, then, in its very essence, does the act of dancing symbolise life; with so faithful a rendering of its actual instincts! And to the abstract thinker, as to the artist, all this really primitive feeling, all this acceptance of the instincts which it idealises, and out of which it makes its own beauty, is precisely what gives dancing its pre-eminence among the more than imitative arts. The artist, it is indeed true, is never quite satisfied with his statue, which remains cold, does not come to life. In every art men are pressing forward, more and more eagerly, farther and farther beyond the limits of their art, in the desire to do the impossible – to create life. Realising all humanity to be but a masque of shadows, and this solid world an impromptu stage as temporary as they, it is with a pathetic desire of some last illusion, which shall deceive even ourselves, that we are consumed with this hunger to create, to make something for ourselves, of at least the same shadowy reality as that about us. The art of the ballet awaits us, with its shadowy and real life, its power of letting humanity drift into a rhythm so much of its own, and with ornament so much more generous than its wont.

And something in the particular elegance of the dance, the scenery; the avoidance of emphasis, the evasive, winding turn of things; and, above all, the intellectual as well as sensuous appeal of a living symbol, which can but reach the brain through the eyes, in the visual, concrete, imaginative way; has seemed to make the ballet concentrate in itself a good deal of the modern ideal in matters of artistic expression. Nothing is stated, there is no intrusion of words used for the irrelevant purpose of describing; a world rises before one, the picture lasts only long enough to have been there; and the dancer, with her gesture, all pure symbol, evokes, from her mere beautiful motion, idea, sensation, all that one need ever know of event. There, before you, she exists, in harmonious life; and her rhythm reveals to you the soul of her imagined being.[5]

II. PANTOMIME AND THE POETIC DRAMA

It might be contended that in the art of the theatre an absolute criticism can admit nothing between pantomime and the poetic drama. In these two extremes, drama in outline, and drama elaborated to the final point, the appeal is to the primary emotions, and with an economy and luxuriance of means, each of which is in its own way inimitable. It is an error to believe that pantomime is merely a way of doing without words, that it is merely the equivalent of words. Pantomime is thinking overheard. It begins and ends before words have formed themselves, in a deeper consciousness than that of speech. And it addresses itself, by the artful limitations of its craft, to universal human experience, knowing that the moment it departs from those broad lines it will become unintelligible. It risks existence on its own perfection, as the rope-dancer does, to whom a false step means downfall. And it appeals, perhaps a little too democratically, to people of all nations. Becoming aristocratic, getting sheer through the accidents of life without staying by the way in the manner of the realistic drama, it adds the beauty of words to the beauty of primary emotions, and is the poetic drama. Between lie the non-essentials, a kind of waste.

All drama, until one comes to the poetic drama, is an imitation of life, as a photograph is an imitation of life; and for this reason it can have, at the best, but a secondary kind of imaginative existence, the appeal of the mere copy. To the poetic drama nature no longer exists; or rather, nature becomes, as it has been truly said nature should become to the painter, a dictionary.[6] Here is choice, selection, combination: the supreme interference of beauty. Pantomime, in its limited way, is again no mere imitation of nature: it is a transposition, as an etching transposes a picture. It observes nature in order that it may create a new form for itself, a form which, in its enigmatic silence, appeals straight to the intellect for its comprehension, and, like ballet, to the intellect through the eyes.

And pantomime has that mystery which is one of the requirements of true art. To watch it is like dreaming. How silently, in dreams, one gathers the unheard sound of words from the lips that do but make pretence of saying them! And does not everyone know that terrifying impossibility of speaking, which fastens one to the ground for the eternity of a second, in what is the new, perhaps truer, computation of time in dreams? Something like that sense of suspense seems to hang over the silent actors in pantomime, giving them a nervous exaltation which has its subtle, immediate effect upon us, in tragic or comic situation. The silence becomes an atmosphere, and with a very curious power of giving distinction to form and motion.

I do not see why people should ever break silence, on the stage, except to speak poetry. Here, in pantomime, you have a gracious, expressive silence, beauty of gesture, a perfectly discreet appeal to the emotions, a transposition of the world into an elegant, accepted convention: in a word, all the outlines of the picture. Poetry comes, not only looking beautiful, not only excluding what should not be there, but saying beautiful things, the only things worth saying when once words begin to be used, not for their mere utility (the ordering of dinner, a bargain, the arrangement of one's affairs), but for their beauty, in a form of art. Here is the picture completed, awaiting only, for its ideal presentment, the interpretative accompaniment of music, which Wagner will give it, in what is so far the most complete form of art yet realised.

III. THE LESSON OF *PARSIFAL*[7]

The performance of *Parsifal*, as I saw it last year at Bayreuth, seemed to me the one really satisfying performance I had ever seen in a theatre; and I have often, since then, tried to realise for myself exactly what it was that one might learn from that incarnation of the ideas, the theoretical ideas, of Wagner. I have not read any of his theoretical writings, and I can only make my own deductions from what I actually saw, there on the stage.

Parsifal, then, presents itself as before all things a picture. The music, soaring up from hidden depths, and seeming to drop from the heights, and be reflected back from shining distances, though it is, more than anything I have ever heard, like one of the great forces of nature, the sea or the wind, itself makes pictures, abstract pictures; but even the music, as one watches the stage, seems to subordinate itself to the visible picture there. And, so perfectly do all the arts flow into one, the picture impresses one chiefly by its rhythm, the harmonies of its convention. The lesson of *Parsifal* is the lesson that, in art, rhythm is everything. Every movement in the acting of this drama makes a picture, and every movement is slow, deliberate, as if automatic. No actor makes a gesture which has not been regulated for him; there is none of that unintelligent haphazard known as being "natural"; these people move like music, or with that sense of motion which it is the business of painting to arrest. [. . .] It is difficult to express the delight with which one sees, for the first time, people really motionless on the stage. After all, action, as it has been said, is only a way of spoiling something. The aim of the modern stage, of all drama, since the drama of the Greeks, is to give a vast impression of bustle, of people who, like most actors, when they are not making irrelevant speeches, are engaged in frantically trying to make us see that they are feeling acute emotion, by I know not what restlessness, contortion, and ineffectual excitement. If it were once realised how infinitely more important are the lines in the picture, than these staccato extravagances which do but aim at tearing it out of its frame, breaking violently through it, we should have learnt a little, at least, of what the art of the stage should be, of what Wagner has shown us that it can be.

Distance from the accidents of real life, atmosphere, the space for a new, fairer world to form itself, being of the essence of Wagner's representation, it is worth noticing how adroitly he throws back this world of his, farther and farther into the background, by a thousand tricks of lighting, the actual distance of the stage to the proscenium, and by such calculated effects, as that long scene of the Graal, with its prolonged movement and ritual, through the whole of which Parsifal stands motionless, watching it all. How that solitary figure at the side, merely looking on, though, unknown to himself, he is the centre of the action, also gives one the sense of remoteness, which it was Wagner's desire to produce, throwing back the action into a reflected distance, as we watch someone on the stage who is watching it!

The beauty of this particular kind of acting and staging is of course the beauty of convention. [. . .] Here is none of that base, tricky realism, which would have us believe too prosaically in the real existence of what is going on before us: a reality neither more nor less, not more fortunate, or more unfettered, or less trivial, than our own, here in the stalls. [. . . .] And this is partly because the beauty of convention includes, though it may, when it pleases, disregard, what we call nature. Convention, here as in all plastic art, is founded on natural truth very closely studied. The rose is first learned, in every wrinkle of its petals, petal by petal, before that reality is elaborately departed from, in order that a new, abstract beauty may be formed out of those outlines, all but those outlines being left out.

And *Parsifal*, which is thus solemnly represented before us, has in it, in its very essence, that hieratic character which it is the effort of supreme art to attain. At times one is reminded of the most beautiful drama in the world, the Indian drama *Sakuntalá*: in that litter of leaves, brought in so touchingly for the swan's burial, in the old hermit watering his flowers. There is something of the same universal tenderness, the same religious linking together of all the world, in some vague enough, but very beautiful, Pantheism. I think it is beside the question to discuss how far Parsifal himself is either Christ or Buddha, and how far Kundry is a new Magdalen. Wagner's mind was the mind to which all legend is sacred, every symbol of divine things to be held in reverence; but symbol, with him, was after all a means to an end, and could never have been accepted as really an end in itself. I should say that in *Parsifal* he is profoundly religious, but not because he intended, or did not intend, to shadow the Christian mysteries. His music, his acting, are devout, because the music has a disembodied ecstasy, and the acting a noble rhythm, which can but produce in us something of the solemnity of sensation produced by the service of the Mass, and are in themselves a kind of religious ceremonial.[8]

A New Art of the Stage[9]

I.

In the remarkable experiments of Mr. Gordon Craig, I seem to see the suggestion of a new art of the stage, an art no longer realistic, but conventional, no longer imitative, but symbolical. In Mr. Craig's staging there is the incalculable element, the element that comes of itself, and cannot be coaxed into coming. [. . .] Our stage painters can imitate anything, but what they cannot give us is the emotion which the playwright, if he is an artist, wishes to indicate by means of his scene. It is the very closeness of the imitation which makes our minds unable to accept it. The eye rebounds, so to speak, from this canvas as real as wood, this wood as real as water, this water which is actual water. Mr. Craig aims at taking us beyond reality; he replaces the pattern of the thing itself by the pattern which that thing evokes in his mind, the symbol of the thing. As, in conventional art, the artist unpicks the structure of the rose to build up a mental image of the rose, in some formal pattern which his brain makes over again,[10] [. . .] so, in this new convention of the stage, a plain cloth, modulated by light, can stand for space or for limit, may be the tight walls of a tent or the sky and the clouds. The eye loses itself among these severe, precise, and yet mysterious lines and surfaces; the mind is easily at home in them; it accepts them as readily as it accepts the convention by which, in a poetical play, men speak in verse rather than in prose. [. . .]

The whole stage art of Mr. Craig is a protest against realism, and it is to realism that we owe whatever is most conspicuously bad in the mounting of plays at the present day. [. . .] No scene-painter, no scene-shifter, no limelight man, will ever delude us by his moon or meadow or moving clouds or water. His business is to aid the poet's illusion, that illusion of beauty which is the chief excuse for stage plays at all, [. . .]. The distinction, the incomparable merit, of Mr. Craig is that he conceives his setting as the poet conceives his drama. [. . .] What Mr. Craig does, or would do if he were allowed to do it, is to open all sorts of 'magic casements,' and to thrust back all kinds of real and probable limits, and to give at last a little scope for the imagination of the playwright who is also a poet.

William Blake[11]

INTRODUCTION

I.

When Blake spoke the first word of the nineteenth century there was no one to hear it, and now that his message, the message of emancipation from reality through the "shaping spirit of imagination," has penetrated the world, and is slowly remaking it, few are conscious of the first utterer, in modern times, of the message with which all are familiar. Thought to-day, wherever it is most individual, owes either force or direction to Nietzsche, and thus we see, on our topmost towers, the Philistine armed and winged, and without the love or fear of God or man in his heart, doing battle in Nietzsche's name against the ideas of Nietzsche. No one can think, and escape Nietzsche; but Nietzsche has come after Blake, and will pass before Blake passes.

The Marriage of Heaven and Hell anticipates Nietzsche in his most significant paradoxes, and, before his time, exalts energy above reason, and Evil, "the active springing from energy," above Good, "the passive that obeys reason." [. . .] He trusted the passions, because they were alive; and, like Nietzsche, hated asceticism, because

> "Abstinence sows sand all over
> The ruddy limbs and flaming hair,
> But desire gratified
> Plants fruits of life and beauty there."[12]

"Put off holiness," he said, "and put on intellect." And "the fool shall not enter into heaven, let him be ever so holy." Is not this a heaven after the heart of Nietzsche? [. . .]

Yet, to Nietzsche, with his strange, scientific distrust of the imagination, of those who so "suspiciously" say "We see what others do not see," there comes distrust, hesitation, a kind of despair, precisely at the point where Blake enters into his liberty. [. . .]

The philosophy of Nietzsche was made out of his nerves and was suffering, but to Blake it entered like sunlight into the eyes.

Nietzsche's mind is the most sleepless of minds; with him every sensation turns instantly into the stuff of thought; he is terribly alert, the more so because he never stops to systematise; he must be for ever apprehending. He darts out feelers in every direction, relentlessly touching the whole substance of the world. His apprehension is minute rather than broad; [. . .] His personality stands to him in the place of a system. Speaking of Kant and Schopenhauer, he says: "Their thoughts do not constitute a passionate history of the soul." His thoughts are the passionate history of his soul. It is for this reason that he is an artist among philosophers rather than a pure philosopher. And remember that he is also not, in the absolute sense, the poet, but the artist. He saw and dreaded the weaknesses of the artist, his side-issues in the pursuit of truth. But in so doing he dreaded one of his own weaknesses.

Blake, on the other hand, receives nothing through his sensations, suffers nothing through his nerves. "I know of no other Christianity," he says, "and of no other Gospel than the liberty both of body and mind to exercise the divine arts of Imagination: Imagination, the real and eternal world of which this vegetable universe is but a faint shadow, and in which we shall live in our eternal or imaginative bodies, when these vegetable mortal bodies are no more."[13] To Nietzsche the sense of a divine haunting became too heavy a burden for his somewhat inhuman solitude, the solitude of Alpine regions, with their steadfast glitter, their thin, high, intoxicating air. "Is this obstrusiveness of heaven," he cried, "this inevitable superhuman neighbour, not enough to drive one mad?" But Blake, when he says, "I am under the direction of messengers from heaven, daily and nightly," speaks out of natural joy, which is wholly humility, and it is only "if we fear to do the dictates of our angels, and tremble at the tasks set before us," it is only then that he dreads, as the one punishment, that "every one in eternity will leave him."[14] [. . .]

III.

[. . .] Blake was the first, and remains the only, poet who has in the complete sense made his own books with his own hands: the words, the illustrations, the engraving, the printing, the colouring, the very inks and colours, and the stitching of the sheets into boards. With Blake, who was equally a poet and an artist, words and designs came together and were inseparable; and to the power of inventing words and designs was added the skill of engraving, and thus of interpreting them, without any mechanical interference from the outside. To do this must have been, at some time or another, the ideal of every poet who is a true artist, and who has a sense of the equal importance of every form of art, and of every detail in every form. Only Blake has produced a book of poems vital alike in inner and outer form, and, had it not been for his lack of a technical knowledge of music, had he but been able to write down his inventions in that art also, he would have left us the creation of something like an universal art. [. . .]

To define the poetry of Blake one must find new definitions for poetry; but, these definitions once found, he will seem to be the only poet who is a poet in essence; [. . .]. In his verse there is, if it is to be found in any verse, the "lyrical cry"; and yet, what voice is it that cries in this disembodied ecstasy? The voice of desire is not in it, nor the voice of passion, nor the cry of the heart, nor the cry of the sinner to God, nor of the lover of nature to nature. It neither seeks nor aspires nor laments nor questions. It is like the voice of wisdom in a child, who has not yet forgotten the world out of which the soul came. It is as spontaneous as the note of a bird, it is an affirmation of life; in its song, which seems mere music, it is the mind which sings; it is lyric thought. [. . .]

IV.

[. . .] Blake is the only poet who sees all temporal things under the form of eternity. To him reality is merely a symbol, and he catches at its terms, hastily and faultily, as he catches at the lines of the drawing-master, to represent, as in a faint image, the clear and shining outlines of what he sees with the imagination; through the eye, not with it, as he says. Where other poets use reality as a spring-board into space, he uses it as a foothold on his return from flight. Even Wordsworth seemed to him a kind of atheist, who mistook the changing signs of "vegetable nature" for the unchanging realities of the imagination. "Natural objects," he wrote in a copy of Wordsworth, "always did and now do weaken, deaden, and obliterate imagination in me. Wordsworth must know that what he writes valuable is not to be found in nature."[15] And so his poetry is the most abstract of all poetry, although in a sense the most concrete. It is everywhere an affirmation, the register of vision; never observation. To him observation was one of the daughters of memory, and he had no use for her among his Muses, which were all eternal, and the children of the imagination. "Imagination," he said, "has nothing to do with memory." For the most part he is just conscious that what he sees as "an old man grey" is no more than a "frowning thistle":

> "For double the vision my eyes do see,
> And a double vision is always with me.
> With my inward eyes, 'tis an old man grey,
> With my outward, a thistle across my way."[16]

In being so far conscious, he is only recognising the symbol, not admitting the reality. [. . .]

And when I say that he reads lessons, let it not be supposed that Blake was ever consciously didactic. Conduct does not concern him; not doing, but being. He held that education was the setting of a veil between light and the soul. [. . .] "When I am endeavouring to think rightly, I must not regard my own any more than other people's weaknesses"; so, in his poetry, there is no moral tendency, nothing that might not be poison as well as antidote; nothing indeed but the absolute affirmation of that energy which is eternal delight. He worshipped energy as the well-head or parent fire of life; and to him there was no evil, only a weakness, a negation of energy, the ignominy of wings that droop and are contented in the dust.

And so, like Nietzsche, but with a deeper innocence, he finds himself "beyond good and evil," in a region where the soul is naked and its own master.[17] Most of his art is the unclothing of the soul, and when at last it is naked and alone, in that "thrilling" region where the souls of other men have at times penetrated, only to shudder back with terror from the brink of eternal loneliness, then only is the soul exultant with the supreme happiness.

X.

There are people who still ask seriously if Blake was mad. If the mind of Lord Macaulay is the one and only type of sanity, then Blake was mad.[18] If imagination, and ecstasy, and disregard of worldly things, and absorption in the inner world of the mind, and a literal belief in those things which the whole 'Christian community' professes from the tip of its tongue; if these are signs and suspicions of madness, then Blake was certainly mad. [. . .] "When opposed by the superstitious, the crafty, or the proud," says Linnell again, "he outraged all common-sense and rationality by the opinions he advanced"; and Palmer gives an instance of it: "Being irritated by the exclusively scientific talk at a friend's house, which talk had turned on the vastness of space, he cried out, 'It is false. I walked the other evening to the end of the heath, and touched the sky with my finger.'"[19]

It was of the essence of Blake's sanity that he could always touch the sky with his finger. "To justify the soul's frequent joy in what cannot be defined to the intellectual part, or to calculation": that, which is Walt Whitman's definition of his own aim, defines Blake's. Where others doubted he knew; and he saw where others looked vaguely into the darkness. He saw so much further than others into what we call reality, that others doubted his report, not being able to check it for themselves; and when he saw truth naked he did not turn aside his eyes. [. . .] "God forbid," he said, "that Truth should be confined to mathematical demonstration. He who does not know Truth at sight is unworthy of her notice." And he said: "Error is created, truth is eternal. Error or creation will be burned up, and then, not till then, truth or eternity will appear. It is burned up the moment men cease to behold it."[20]

It was this private certainty in regard to truth and all things that Blake shared with the greatest minds of the world, [. . .]

And truth has moved, or we have. After *Zarathustra*, *Jerusalem* no longer seems a wild heresy. People were frightened because they were told that Blake was mad, or a blasphemer. Nietzsche, who has cleared away so many obstructions from thought, has shamed us from hiding behind these treacherous and unavailing defences. We have come to realise, what Rossetti pointed out long ago, that, as a poet, Blake's characteristic is above all things that of "pure perfection in *writing verse.*" We no longer praise his painting for its qualities as literature, or forget that his design has greatness as design. And of that unique creation of an art out of the mingling of many arts which we see in the "illuminated printing" of the engraved books, we have come to realise what Palmer meant when he said long ago: "As a picture has been said to be something between a thing and a thought, so, in some of these type books over which Blake had long brooded with his brooding of fire, the very paper seems to come to life as you gaze upon it – not with a mortal life, but an indestructible life." And we have come to realise what Blake meant by the humble and arrogant things which he said about himself. "I doubt not yet," he writes in one of those gaieties of speech which illuminate his letters, "to make a figure in the great dance of life that shall amuse the spectators in the sky."[21] If there are indeed spectators there, amused by our motions, what dancer among us are they more likely to have approved than this joyous, untired, and undistracted dancer to the eternal rhythm?

Notes

WALTER PATER

I. Diaphaneitè

1. This is Pater's first essay, read to an Oxford literary group in 1864, and published after his death in *Miscellaneous Studies* in 1895. The title suggests the transparence of the 'clear crystal nature' Pater describes in the essay, which is the type of all his autobiographical 'Imaginary Portraits', including the most extended and important of these, *Marius the Epicurean.*
2. Pater begins on solidly romantic ground, placing the artist between the religious mystic and the philosopher. The suggestion here that 'the main current of the world's energy' is a spiritual, mental phenomenon suggests that Pater has already been exposed to German Romantic thought, particularly Hegel and his notion of the developing *Geist* or world spirit. Cf. his elaboration of this idea in the essay on 'Romanticism' (q.v.).
3. The characteristic figure of purification, concentration, intensity, which was to make such an appeal to Pater throughout his life. Compare the 'Conclusion' to *The Renaissance* (q.v.) written four years later.
4. 'To be united with himself and (made) inwardly simple'; from Thomas à Kempis's *De Imitatione Christi*, a famous fifteenth-century work of mystical theology which charts the soul's path to perfection by gradually disengaging itself from the world and uniting itself with God.
5. George Eliot's *Romola* (1863) draws an intense portrait of Fra Girolamo Savonarola (1452–98), a Dominican monk who preached at Florence against the new licence of the Renaissance and gradually became enmeshed in political machinations.
6. This blending of the restraint of classical style and the passion of romantic philosophy was to become one of Pater's most characteristic and influential ideas. He found his ideal type of cultural hero in Goethe, as his essays on Coleridge (q.v.) and Winckelmann make clear. The ensuing identification between 'the artist' and 'he who has treated life in the spirit of art' already begins to suggest the figure of Wilde and subsequent generations of aesthetes.
7. Georges Danton (1759–94), a statesman during the French Revolution, who eventually came into conflict with Robespierre and was guillotined. Carlyle drew a splendid portrait of him in *The French Revolution* (1837).
8. χλιδή (*klidé*) means 'delicacy', 'wantonness', 'luxury', usually in a derogatory sense. Pater appears to be employing artistic licence, distorting the meaning of the word for his own ends.
9. Charlotte Corday was the assassin of Marat. Carlyle's fascination with the woman's mingling of beauty and terror is highly congenial to Pater, and this strain appears with increasing frequency throughout his work.

I. From *The Renaissance*

Preface

1. Pater opens by distinguishing his critical effort from that of the German Idealist philosophers, who sought abstract and universal definitions of beauty. Following Blake, who thought that to generalize was to be an idiot, Pater announces his intention to focus on the particular and individual claims of each work of art. This allows him both to concentrate on the personal expression and genius of each artist, and to place the burden on the critic's fine powers of discrimination. At the same time, of course, it lays the foundation for his beliefs about the 'relative spirit' of modern analysis. Cf. 'Coleridge' (q.v.).
2. The quotation refers to Matthew Arnold and the opening of his famous essay 'The Function of Criticism at the Present Time'. Pater politely, but firmly, rejects the objective conception behind Arnold's view for a more subjective approach, as the rest of the paragraph makes clear. Compare the opening of Poe's 'The Poetic Principle' (q.v.).
3. The emphasis on *pleasure* here is significant, as it looks back to Wordsworth's 'Preface' to *Lyrical Ballads*, where the insistence on 'the grand elementary feeling of pleasure' in man has a moral overtone; but it also heralds the wholly self-pleasing aesthetic of Wilde which was to come.
4. 'To limit themselves to knowing beautiful things at first hand, and to develop themselves by these as sensitive amateurs, as accomplished humanists.'
5. From Blake's Annotations to Sir Joshua Reynolds's *Discourses on Art*. Blake actually wrote: 'Ages are all Equal. But Genius is Always Above The Age.'
6. Another appearance of Pater's crucial notion of *ascêsis*, or spiritual purgation; compare the development of this concept of artistic creation in Pater's essay on 'Romanticism' (q.v.).
7. In his famous selection of Wordsworth's poetry, Matthew Arnold had made substantially the same point about Wordsworth, although the two men disagreed about what the poet's 'genius' was.
8. Note this paragraph's desire to extend the Renaissance beyond its usually assumed origins in fourteenth-century Italy to twelfth-century France. In opposition to the then current theorizing, championed by Ruskin, Pater was among the first cultural historians to broaden the Renaissance to the High Middle Ages – a concept which is canonical today.
9. Here Pater touches on a romantic theory of renascence, of continual recurrence, perhaps derived from Hegel. Stressing the emotion of awakening, or re-birth, he compares the Florence of Lorenzo de Medici (1449–92), which nurtured Leonardo and Michelangelo, to the Athens of Pericles in the fifth century B.C. This idea is developed further in 'Romanticism' (q.v.).
10. A veiled reference to the French romantic formula 'art for art's sake', expressed by Gautier, with whose work Pater was already familiar. The expression recurs more boldly in the 'Conclusion' to *The Renaissance*.

Luca della Robbia

11. Here as so often in his work, Pater establishes a dialectic between the romantic, which is active, personal and expressive, and the classical, which is calm, impersonal and formal. His major disquisition on this subject is the essay 'Romanticism' (q.v.), though the polarity pervades both *The Renaissance* and *Marius the Epicurean.*
12. Pater identifies Michelangelo with the romantic temperament, as did most of the Romantic poets, and he uses this attribution to go on and link Luca della Robbia with the personal and expressive strain.

Leonardo da Vinci

13. This essay originally appeared in the *Fortnightly Review* in November 1869. The Latin motto, 'A man, servant, and interpreter of nature', is from Francis Bacon's *Novum Organum,* which stressed the dominion of human knowledge over nature by means of patient, scientific inquiry and the discovery of forms.
14. That is to say, romantic ideas of interiorized genius and personal expression in art. Jules Michelet was a French historian whose book *La Renaissance* (1855) was an important source for Pater. It is important to note that all the attendant notions of 'modern ideas', of exotic beauty, of artist as magician or priest, and of carelessness with one's genius were adopted by the subsequent 'aesthetic' generation, especially Wilde.
15. Terror had been seen as a crucial element of the sublime since Edmund Burke had written on the subject in the previous century; but Pater manages to give the concept a uniquely morbid twist that was highly influential upon later sensibility. This too has romantic roots: cf. Shelley's poem 'On the Medusa of Leonardo da Vinci'. (This painting is not now attributed to Leonardo.)
16. Compare this statement with the definition in 'Romanticism' (q.v.) that 'It is the addition of strangeness to beauty that constitutes the romantic character in art.'
17. 'How princely, how characteristic of Leonardo, the answer, *Quanto più, un' arte porta seco fatica di corpo, tanto più è vile!'* ['The more evidence of physical, strain an art reveals the lower it is!' Pater's own note.]
18. The moment of inspiration, deriving ultimately from Longinian ideas of the imagination. Here again, the essentially romantic idea is exaggerated and intensified out of proportion: Wordsworth's attendance on this moment did not stop him from beginning *The Prelude.*
19. Here Pater returns to the notion of art for art's sake and stresses its logical corollary, the concentration on *effect.* Compare Poe's 'Philosophy of Composition' and the extreme exaggeration of the idea in George Moore and Wilde (qq.v.).
20. 'Yet for Vasari there was some further magic of crimson in the lips and cheeks, lost for us.' [Pater's own note.]
21. For Pater, the Mona Lisa's smile signifies the birth of the 'modern', i.e. 'romantic' era as it brings in all the difficulties and delights of extreme self-consciousness. Cf. Wilde's development of this idea in 'The English Renaissance in Art' (q.v.).
22. This sentence was arranged in free verse form by W. B. Yeats as the first 'modern' poem, in *The Oxford Book of Modern Verse* of 1930.

The School of Giorgione

23. This essay first appeared in *The Fornightly Review* of October 1877; it was incorporated into the third edition of *The Renaissance* in 1888.
24. Here at the beginning of his most significant aesthetic speculations, Pater distinguishes himself not only from the German Idealists, concerned to find the common essence of all art, but also from Ruskin, whose insistence on the moral foundation of art led him continually to rank the arts, placing poetry above painting and music. Pater, in contrast, argues for the autonomy of each individual form of art, based in each case on a unique and untranslatable union of form and content. In particular, Pater goes on to criticize that prevalent nineteenth-century tendency to regard painting in terms of literature.
25. G. E. Lessing's *Laokoon* (1776) is an important essay of the German aesthetic philosophy, which attempts to contrast the sculpture of Laocoon and his sons battling against the sea serpents with Virgil's description, so as to distinguish between the plastic and poetic arts.
26. This sentence, freeing art from its dependence on moral or philosophical ideas, and granting the work of art autonomy entirely in its own sensuous terms, is in fact the foundation of modern art, and, as the next sentence suggests, leads directly to abstract art. It is hardly surprising that Whistler, who was to make the same defence of his art, should likewise have been interested in oriental art, with its pure, sensuous appeal.
27. Having established the autonomy of the individual arts, Pater then proceeds to argue their essential similarity in striving for an ideal fusion of form and content. 'Anders-streben' is a German philosophical term meaning 'striving to go beyond', and the term, probably derived from Hegel, is used by Pater to suggest each individual art's effort to transcend the limitations of its medium. Thus he argues that music is the truly ideal art form since in it form and content are least distinguishable.
28. Here again Pater follows romantic theory by regarding the intense expressive powers of lyric as the highest form of poetry.
29. Pater wrote an essay on *Measure for Measure* which he included in *Appreciations*. The essay makes much of the problematic nature of the play, praising its 'romantic' lust for life in the face of evil, imprisonment and death. Mariana's song 'Take, O take those lips away' (IV, i) also had a powerful impact on Tennyson, who wrote two poems inspired by it.
30. This translation of the aesthetic emphasis from art to life was to bear greater fruit in Wilde; cf. 'The Decay of Lying' (q.v.).
31. Here Pater details the romantic 'moment', the 'epiphany' wherein the world of time suddenly intersects with eternity. Compare the 'Conclusion' to *The Renaissance*, where this idea is developed in relation to Pater's own strategy for life.

Conclusion

32. 'This brief "Conclusion" was omitted in the second edition of this book, as I conceived it might possibly mislead some of those young men into whose hands it might fall. On the whole, I have thought it best to reprint it here, with some slight changes which bring it closer to my original meaning. I have dealt more fully in *Marius the Epicurean* with the thoughts

suggested by it.' [Pater's own note.] These pages first appeared as part of a review of William Morris's *Poems* in the *Westminster Review* of October 1868. Pater subsequently kept them intact as the 'Conclusion' to *The Renaissance* and published the rest of the review as 'Aesthetic Poetry', an essay included in the first edition of *Appreciations* (1889). A succinct history of the vicissitudes of this piece can be found in Appendix b.2 of Samuel Wright's *Bibliography of Walter Pater* (Garland, 1975).

33. The focus on physical man here suggests that to his foundation of Hegelian ideas, Pater has added the influence of Darwin. Compare this to the essay on Coleridge (q.v.).
34. Here Pater reduces the human position to one of absolute solipsism, from which the rest of the essay attempts to escape.
35. 'To philosophize is to cast off inertia, to bring oneself to life.' Novalis (Friedrich von Hardenberg) (1772–1801) was an important German Romantic poet.
36. Here Pater may be seen launching the cult of experience for its own sake in which much of the modern world still wanders.
37. Auguste Comte (1798–1857), the French positivist philosopher, and Georg Wilhelm Friedrich Hegel (1770–1831), the German Idealist philosopher, were both important early influences on Pater.
38. Pater's fullest statement of his own ethos at this early stage – striving for an intensity of perception which lifts the spirit free for a moment of 'epiphany' and thus evades the looming consciousness of death.

III. The Child in the House

1. The first of Pater's 'Imaginary Portraits', this piece was first published in *Macmillan's Magazine* of August 1878. It is by far and away the most autobiographical of this highly autobiographical genre, detailing Pater's childhood in the London suburb of Enfield. The period was in many respects the happiest of Pater's life, and it is not surprising that these recollections of childhood are coloured by numerous echoes of Wordsworth.

   This article provides perhaps the best concentrated introduction to Pater's temperament, subtly interweaving all of his most characteristic themes – the extreme sensitivity to sensuous phenomena which shades into morbidity, the 'aesthetic' preoccupation with the relation between beauty and pain, the enormous awareness of flux and corresponding fear of death, and the yearning to reconcile a love of the physical with a passionate idealism producing a humanized quasi-religion.

IV. From *Appreciations*

Romanticism

1. This essay originally appeared in the November 1876 issue of *Macmillan's Magazine*. It was reprinted in a slightly revised version as the 'Postscript' to *Appreciations* in 1889, from which this text is taken.
2. The image is from John Bunyan's *Pilgrim's Progress*. The House Beautiful is the palace in which Christian gains a glimpse of the Delectable

Mountains, the goal of his pilgrimage. The Study of this House contains a record of all followers and acts of God from Antiquity, which are impervious to decay. Pater's use of the term here, to suggest an imaginative structure which the creative minds of all time have been constructing, was a familiar concept of the German Romantics, and recurs in Shelley's *Defence of Poetry*. It is also just conceivable that Pater would have known Blake's aphorism: 'The ruins of time build mansions in Eternity.'

3. Here Pater distinguishes nicely between the accidents and essence of romanticism.
4. This concept of eternal recurrence of the romantic spirit forms the critical foundation for *The Renaissance*.
5. This definition, which in effect marries the French and English strains of Romanticism, is fundamental to all Pater's aesthetic criticism. While Pater is here careful to argue for a balance, other essays (such as those on Botticelli and Leonardo in *The Renaissance*) make clear that the desire for exotic strangeness in beauty was already exerting the more forceful appeal. Compare the recurrence of this strain in Moore, Wilde, and Symons (qq.v.).
6. Compare this description of the 'romantic spirit' with Pater's account of 'Aesthetic Poetry' (q.v.).
7. Jean Valjean, hero of Victor Hugo's *Les Misérables* (1862); Redgauntlet, hero of Sir Walter Scott's novel, *Redgauntlet* (1824).
8. Anne Louise Germaine, Baroness de Staël (1766–1817), daughter of a wealthy Swiss banker who became familiar with Goethe, Schiller and Schlegel, and in 1810 published *De l'Allemagne*, introducing the German Romantic movement to the rest of Europe. Heinrich Heine (1797–1856), German Romantic poet who settled in Paris in 1831. *The Romantic School*, a critical study of his contemporaries, was published in 1833. Ludwig Tieck (1773–1853), prominent Romantic novelist and playwright, deeply influenced by Shakespeare.
9. This is an example of Pater's critical acumen, since seeing the origin of romanticism in Rousseau has today become a standard view among cultural historians.
10. Pater refers to three characteristic figures of European romanticism, the heroes respectively of Goethe's *The Sorrows of Young Werther* (1774), Chateaubriand's *René* (1802), and Senancour's *Obermann* (1804) – all young men of extreme sensibility. It is instructive to compare this passage with the ending of Pater's essay on Coleridge (q.v.).
11. Cf. Pater's elaboration of this idea in his essay on Prosper Mérimée (q.v.).
12. Pater incisively connects this sense of ideal escapism with the poetry of William Morris and Rossetti in the two essays immediately preceding this piece in *Appreciations*, 'Aesthetic Poetry' and 'Dante Gabriel Rossetti' (qq.v.).
13. Stendhal (1783–1842), was the pseudonym of Henri Beyle, an important French novelist and critic, whose taste for painting as well as literature influenced Gautier and Baudelaire. This is another example of Pater's critical insight, since Stendhal was far from being a well-known figure at this date.
14. The clear, classical light, product of a harmonious soul, meant much to one such as Pater, who sought ease from anxieties and doubt. The concept

recurs in the essay on Winckelmann in *The Renaissance*, as well as in Pater's most ambitious work, *Marius the Epicurean*.

15. This is a direct allusion to the Hegelian ideas which underlie Pater's thought. *Hernani* (1830) was Hugo's tragic play at whose première the youthful forces of French Romanticism routed the Classicist opposition. Cf. the headnote for Gautier.
16. Pater's idea of *ascêsis* here emerges as a constituent part of romanticism.
17. This final paragraph, added for the publication in *Appreciations*, illustrates the care with which Pater crafted his work. These ideas about 'literary art' recapitulate the arguments developed in 'Style', which was the first essay in *Appreciations*. Thus Pater's book would have opened and closed on the same note.

Coleridge

18. Pater's first published essay, which appeared in *The Westminster Review* in January 1866, was a review of a selection of Coleridge's writings. He subsequently revised and enlarged the essay when he reprinted it in *Appreciations*, which is the text given here.
19. This sentence, with its suggestive interest in decadence, might be thought of as Pater's signature theme. As both this essay and *Marius the Epicurean* make clear, Pater conceived of himself as living in an age of overripe decline from its high romantic beginnings in the late eighteenth and early nineteenth centuries. The Coleridge he delineates in this essay is the poet and speculator who led the way to the great Victorian compromise and so initiated that decline.
20. Pater is here clearly invoking the dissolvent current of Darwinian theory, which was at that time undermining the Victorian faith in absolutes.
21. Pater's dissolvent rhetoric subtly attacks the moral and religious canons of Victorian orthodoxy. Such ethical beliefs had been defended by Ruskin (q.v.), but this attack was to prove the most attractive aspect of Pater's writings to Wilde and subsequent aesthetes (q.v.).
22. From Plato's *Phaedrus*, 247C. The passage from which these words are taken can be translated: 'For the colourless, formless, intangible really existing essence, with which all true knowledge deals, keeps this region [above the heavens] and is visible only to the mind, which is pilot to the soul.'
23. The attitude suggested here was to have a profound impact on Wilde and his spiritual descendants, though Pater has in mind the more restrained cultural urbanity of Goethe.
24. Pater decisively traces Coleridge's idealism back to the German Romantic philosophers, where many of Pater's own conceptions have their root. In particular he mentions Immanuel Kant (1724–1804) and Friedrich Schelling (1775–1854), two of the greatest figures of that movement who, as the *Biographia Literaria* makes clear, had a profound influence on Coleridge.
25. The quotations are from Coleridge's Lectures on Shakespeare; cf. *Coleridge's Shakespeare Criticism*, ed. T. M. Rayson (Constable, 1930), vol. 1, p. 224.
26. Pater criticizes Coleridge's ideal of *organic* form as not giving sufficient credit to the conscious and deliberate craft of the artist. This, which was to be one of Pater's most far-reaching ideas, echoes the ideal expressed in Poe's 'Philosophy of Composition' (q.v.), and was taken to an extreme in

Pater's essay on 'Style' (q.v.). It was subsequently developed in the praise of artifice by Wilde and Symons (qq.v.).

27. This whole passage startlingly suggests that Coleridge is the 'unacknowledged legislator' of 'aesthetic' or decadent poetry.
28. This is Coleridge's moving poem 'To William Wordsworth' of 1807.
29. The heart of Pater's essay is an incisive contrast between the poetry and temperament of Wordsworth and of Coleridge – an analysis which has been elaborated and extended, but not superseded. Significantly, it is Coleridge's fall from Wordsworth's faith in the natural ideal that Pater highlights, since for all his attachment to the sensual world and his disagreement with orthodox Christianity, this is the position toward which Pater himself is drawn. The exceptional resonance or sympathy with his subject, overtly announced in the peroration, is what makes this essay superior to the one on Wordsworth included in *Appreciations*.
30. From Wordsworth's 'Prospectus' to *The Excursion*, ll. 62–71.
31. From Coleridge's 'Dejection: An Ode' (1802), ll. 39–46.

Style

32. This essay was originally published as a review article of 'The Life and Letters of Flaubert' in *The Fortnightly Review* of December 1888. Pater then used it as the opening piece for his volume of literary criticism, *Appreciations*, in 1889; as such it forms a kind of artistic *credo* for Pater.
33. Pater opens by emphasizing his romantic foundations by invoking the authority of Wordsworth over Dryden for the sort of prose-poetry he is interested in. He is undoubtedly thinking of Wordsworth's great 'Preface' to *Lyrical Ballads*, with its assertion that 'there neither is nor can be any *essential* difference between the language of prose and metrical composition'. In this essay Pater follows the example of the romantic essayists, such as William Hazlitt and Thomas De Quincey (1785–1859), arguing for extreme attention to the craft of writing in an attempt to make prose as sonorous and artfully constructed as poetry. De Quincey's distinction between the literature of knowledge and of power occurs in his essay on 'The Poetry of Pope'.
34. Further intensifying his romantic argument, Pater figures literature as the *expression* of the writer's own mind, and goes on to suggest that art grows more perfect as it matches the internal vision. The extreme subjective basis of art here reflects the same attitude taken with respect to criticism in the 'Preface' to *The Renaissance*.
35. Pater claims imaginative prose as 'the special and opportune art of the modern world' not only because of the 'multitudinousness', the increasing external complexity of that world (which Matthew Arnold had also seen), but also because of the greatly increased self-consciousness of the individual within that world. The combination of these two factors produces the 'relative spirit' of the modern temper, which Pater described in 'Coleridge' (q.v.). It is this spirit which imaginative prose seems best able to convey.
36. Milton's elegy 'Lycidas' (1637), William Thackeray's novel *The History of Henry Esmond* (1852), and John Henry Newman's *The Idea of a University Defined* (1873) were all much admired by Pater. This expression of art as refuge from a hostile world was to gain great currency in the aesthetic generation.

37. Henry Longueville Mansel (1820–71) was dean of St. Paul's for the last three years of his life. His *Prolegomena Logica* was published in 1851, and followed the Kantian-based philosophy of Sir William Hamilton, which held that since knowledge was phenomenal and relative we cannot know fully ultimate reality or absolutes. This of course throws the emphasis on the 'apprehending mind', which would have been very agreeable to Pater.
38. This ideal of an indissoluble union of form and content in prose is an extension of the aesthetic ideal advanced in 'The School of Giorgione' (q.v.).
39. Here Pater reveals the true end of one stand of his thought: that 'the style is the man' in that style is the vehicle for the revelation of the writer's unique temperament or personality. This belief not only underlies Pater's criticism, in which he seeks the temperament of the artist through the work, but also accounts for his aesthetic practice: his 'Imaginary Portraits' are all examples of disguised autobiography in which the mask frequently slips to reveal his own personality.

Aesthetic Poetry

40. This essay first appeared as a review of three volumes of William Morris's poetry in the *Westminster Review* of October 1868. The coda of that review became the 'Conclusion' of *The Renaissance*, and the rest was modified into essay form for the first edition of *Appreciations* in 1889. The essay was deleted from all subsequent editions, however, perhaps because Pater felt the article betrayed a youthful excess of 'aesthetic' enthusiasm.
41. By linking this essay with the one on Rossetti which followed immediately upon it in the first edition of *Appreciations*, Pater makes clear that by 'aesthetic poetry' he means Pre-Raphaelite poetry. Identifying this poetry as a late romantic offshoot, Pater thus links it with the recurrent cultural phase traced in the essay on 'Romanticism' (q.v.).
42. Pater draws a distinction between the sterile and codified version of Neo-classicism at the beginning of the eighteenth century, and the more genuine passion for Greek art at its close. This distinction is at the core of his study of Winckelmann in *The Renaissance*.
43. *Goetz von Berlichingen* (1771) is Goethe's play about a medieval German Knight; *Iphigenie auf Tauris* (1787) is his adaptation of Euripides' drama. Compare this argument, with that in 'Romanticism' (q.v.).
44. Pater's interest in Provençal poetry underlies his essay on Joachim du Bellay in *The Renaissance*. This interest passed to Wilde and Symons (qq.v.) and thence to Ezra Pound.
45. In these sentences the tinge of 'decadence', in the sense of a half guilty indulgence in sensual passion, emerges more strongly than ever again in Pater's career. This essay, like that on Rossetti, suggests a naturalized supernaturalism in the transformation of the extra-worldly ideal of orthodox religion into an equally intense ideal of physical love.
46. As Michael Levey has observed in his recent book on Pater, these lines apply with particular force to Pater himself, whose writing always betrays the strain of masking both his loss of faith and his homoerotic impulses.
47. Having stressed the ideal, Pater now turns toward the real. The Pre-Raphaelites moved between the extremes of these two poles, which is why Pater was so sensitive to their work.

Dante Gabriel Rossetti

48. This essay, written in 1883, appeared for the first time in *Appreciations*.
49. This 'new school' is of course the Pre-Raphaelites. Cf. Wilde's elaboration of this matter in 'The English Renaissance' (q.v.).
50. Pater identifies Rossetti as a poet in the romantic strain by insisting on his devotion to personal *expression* in art. The essay goes on to recapitulate the argument in 'Style' (q.v.), where thought and expression fuse in a transparency which perfectly expresses the artist's personality.
51. Here again is the characteristic blending of the real and ideal, the sensuous and concrete with the visionary, which Pater developed from the Pre-Raphaelites. The rest of the essay expands on this point.
52. From Rossetti's translation of Francois Villon's 'Ballad of Dead Ladies' (1450), first published in *Poems*, 1870.
53. From Rossetti's poem, 'The Stream's Secret', ll. 163–8; 25–8.
54. Pater figures Rossetti as sustaining himself at that pitch of intensity which constitutes 'success in life', as he put it in the 'Conclusion' to *The Renaissance* (q.v.).
55. From Rossetti's sonnet sequence, 'The House of Life', Song 1.

Prosper Mérimée

1. This is one of Pater's late essays, given as a lecture in November 1890, and published in December of that year in *The Fortnightly Review*. By this time Pater was in regular attendance at the College chapel; what is surprising about this essay, therefore, is the degree to which it comprehends and sympathizes with the disillusionment of the romantic ideal. It is likely that Pater's bland mask in later life concealed its own bitter humours.
2. Pater is undoubtedly thinking of the second part of Kant's *Critique of Pure Reason*, the so-called Dialectic, in which Kant criticizes the pretensions of human knowledge to pass beyond certain limits, attacking rational attempts to prove God's existence or human immortality. In effect Kant negates the Cartesian strain of philosophy and, presumably, the hope that went with it, though not without his own bases of optimism.
3. Obermann is the hero of a romance by Senancour, a man who is at length exhausted by the demands of his own sensibility. The work was also a favourite of Matthew Arnold, and is used as a point of reference in Pater's assessment of Coleridge (q.v.).
4. Compare this account of art as opiate or narcotic with its desperately beatific function in the 'Conclusion' to *The Renaissance* (q.v.).
5. Here Pater anticipates with striking precision the 'age of irony' which has yielded the greater part of modern art.
6. Heroes and heroines of Mérimée's short stories.

JAMES WHISTLER

1. This lecture, Whistler's most coherent essay in aesthetics, was delivered in St. James's Hall, London, on 20 February 1885. It was repeated in Cambridge on 24 March, and in Oxford on 30 April of the same year, and was eventually published in *The Gentle Art of Making Enemies* in 1890.

2. This is clearly a thrust at William Morris, whose series of lectures on art and society had recently been published as *Hopes and Fears for Art* (1882). The attack on notions of the utility of art, particularly with regard to decorative art, continues throughout the first section of the lecture. Compare Gautier's Preface to *Mademoiselle de Maupin* (q.v.).
3. Rembrandt Van Rijn (1606–69), the greatest of the Dutch seventeenth-century painters, largely ignored by Ruskin. In fact Rembrandt had frequently painted biblical or historical scenes, though modelled from the faces and costume of people he saw in Amsterdam. Whistler's point is simply that for the great artist aesthetic values predominate, and Rembrandt was inspired by something very different from the extra-artistic longing that guided the work of the Pre-Raphaelites and Morris.
4. Jacopo Robusti Tintoretto (1518–94), Paulo Caliari Veronese (1528–88), masters of the Venetian school, whose emphasis on painterly values at the expense of the religious or mythological was attractive to Whistler. The reference is either to the *Infanta Margherita* (1653) or to *Las Meninas* (1658–9), both of which portray the Infanta, the daughter of the king and queen of Spain.
5. Whistler's view of the history of art follows logically from the principles already set forth – namely that as the artist has always been different from and superior to the mass of humanity, art history has been the succession of solitary geniuses with whom the public is always belatedly catching up. The same idea is expressed more incisively in Blake's adage that 'Ages are all Equal. But Genius is Always Above The Age', which Pater quotes in the Preface to *The Renaissance*. Compare this historiography with that advanced by Morris in 'The Beauty of Life' (q.v.).
6. Here it becomes apparent that Whistler shared some of Morris's and Ruskin's contempt for the levelling commercialism of the age. The difference is that the older men associated the failing with the greed of the manufacturers while Whistler locates the flaw within the public itself.
7. Whistler is perhaps adapting Baudelaire's conceit (in the 'Salon of 1846', q.v.) of the artist selecting from Nature's vast dictionary. From this point on, at any rate, the attack becomes more clearly directed against Ruskin and his extravagant worship of Nature.
8. This prose-poem suggests one of Whistler's own 'Nocturnes' in which he attempted to render an impression of the Thames at twilight.
9. This is one of the most pregnant of Whistler's remarks. The hatred of 'literature', that anecdotal or literary component which supported so much of nineteenth-century painting, has hardened into one of the canons of modern and abstract art.
10. Compare this account of the painter's 'poetry' with that which Pater describes in 'The School of Giorgione' (q.v.).
11. The most direct attack on Ruskin, who until recently had been Slade Professor of Fine Art at Oxford.
12. The final contemporary whom Whistler attacks in the lecture is Oscar Wilde, once an ebullient disciple who had begun to outrun the master. Whistler not only charges that Wilde's cult following is a middle-class rather than aristocatic following, but also that as he was not a painter Wilde could offer no real guidance in aesthetic matters. Cf. Wilde's reply in 'The Relation of Dress to Art' (q.v.).
13. This is the Prado, founded in 1818 by Ferdinand VII. It contains most of

the important works by Velasquez. Whistler always intended to go and see the museum, but for obscure reasons never did so.

14. Compare this with Rossetti's account of artistic election in 'Hand and Soul' (q.v.).
15. Mount Fujiyama is the highest and most distinctive mountain in Japan, rising to an almost symmetrical snow-capped cone which makes it a favourite subject of Japanese artists. Katsushika Hokusai (1760–1849), one of the foremost masters of the Japanese colour-block print, whose bold simplification of design and original colouring helped to transform the genre. This form of Oriental art became the rage of Paris in the mid-century, and Whistler was profoundly affected by Hokusai early in his career. Thus he did much to spread the taste for 'Japan' in England.

GEORGE MOORE

1. This pamphlet, published by Vizetelly in 1885, bore an epigraph from Carlyle attacking the 'Mudie mountain' of respectability. Herein Moore develops the line of protest on behalf of literary freedom begun by Swinburne (q.v.).
2. From Arnold's famous essay of 1864, 'The Function of Criticism at the Present Time'.
3. Moore's use of scientific and Darwinian terminology here in discussing his work is intended to suggest the Naturalist theories of Zola, by which he was influenced at this time. Cf. the section relating to Zola in the *Confessions of a Young Man* (q.v.).
4. This book was first published in 1888, though several of the chapters had appeared in magazines the previous year. Moore adjusted, expanded and revised the text many times, the most significant revision occurring for the second edition of 1889. This text is taken from the fourth English edition of 1916, though the passages printed are virtually identical with the second edition.
5. Identified by Moore's biographer as Jim Browne, a minor painter evidently in the Pre-Raphaelite style. Gustave Doré (1832–83) was the most famous French illustrator of the nineteenth century, renowned for his engravings of the *Divine Comedy*.
6. Julian, a peasant from the south of France, founded one of the most influential teaching studios of the day. Moore gives a more extended account of this extraordinary individual in an essay, 'Messonier and the Salon Julian', published in *Impressions and Opinions* (1891).
7. Compare this with the 'Conclusion' to *The Renaissance* (q.v.). Moore was influenced a good deal more by Pater than he admitted.
8. Henry Marshall (elsewhere Lewis Ponsonby Marshall) was one Lewis Weldon Hawkins, a cosmopolitan dandy and painter who introduced Moore to the extravagant pleasures of Parisian life. This room, with its garden of earthly delights and somewhat sinister aestheticism, prefigures the dwelling of Des Esseintes, the hero of Huysman's novel, *A Rebours*.
9. 1830 was the date of the famous production of Victor Hugo's *Hernani*, commonly regarded as inaugurating French romanticism. Cf. the headnote for Gautier.
10. Stéphane Mallarmé (1842–98), leader of the French Symbolist poets; his most famous poem, 'L'Après-midi d'un faune' appeared in 1876. *Rienzi* was Wagner's first opera, based on Bulwer Lytton's novel of the same

name; it was afterwards repudiated by the composer, who would not let it be performed. *The Valkyrie* is the second of the four operas which make up *The Ring of the Nibelung* (1853–70), Wagner's mature work. *Red Cotton Night-Cap Country* (1873), a prolix poem by Browning depicting the spiritual experiences of a wealthy Spaniard in France; René Ghil (1862–1925) French poet and one of the chief theorists of the Symbolists. Moore's lack of critical acumen is displayed here; compare this account of Symbolism with that of Yeats or Symons (qq.v.).

11. Paul Verlaine (1844–96), the most attractive and accessible of the French Symbolist poets in contrast to the difficult Mallarmé. *Les Fêtes Galantes* (1870) was his first book of poems.
12. 'Silence' and 'Leonore' are poems by Poe; 'The Island of the Fay' is one of Poe's short prose fantasies.
13. M. Duval was one Bernard Lopez, an elderly *littérateur* who collaborated with Moore on one of his plays. Émile Zola (1840–1902), French novelist who founded the school of Naturalism, dedicated to analysing character on pseudo-scientific lines. He became notorious for detailed descriptions of vice and poverty. Moore did much to make his work known in England, even though he gradually fell away from Zola's influence.
14. Honoré de Balzac (1799–1850), one of the greatest French novelists, whose sequence of novels depicting all strata of Parisian life became known as *La Comédie humaine*, with reference to Dante. His combination of great descriptive powers, a trenchant grasp of detail and a visionary imagination was a lasting influence on Moore.
15. *Marius the Epicurean* (1885) is Pater's extended 'imaginary portrait' of a philosophical youth in the Rome of the Antonines. Cf. Yeats's estimate of the book in 'The Tragic Generation' (q.v.).
16. 'I find the earth as beautiful as heaven, and think that correct form is virtue'; from ch. IX of *Mademoiselle de Maupin*, the credo of the 'art for art's sake' movement.
17. Originally published in *The Hawk* for 25 February 1890, and reprinted in *Impressions and Opinions*. Moore was the first to call attention to Verlaine in England, anticipating Symons's more searching enthusiasm (q.v.). This vision of a *poète maudit*, of the artist neglected and ruined by ordinary bourgeois society, is one that Verlaine helped to make famous.
18. First published in *The Magazine of Art* for November 1890, and reprinted in *Impressions and Opinions*.
19. The first anecdote refers to a party at Zola's following the publication of his novel, *L'Oeuvre* (1886). Its central character is Claude Lantier, a painter whose revolutionary technique smacks of Impressionism. The novel is full of the savour of artistic life and work in later nineteenth-century Paris. Charpentier was Zola's publisher.
20. A reference to Whistler's famous White House in Tite Street, Chelsea, whose interior walls were painted a pastel lemon yellow in order to show his own paintings and etchings to advantage. Throughout this essay, Moore contrasts Whistler's pursuit of notoriety with Degas' desire to avoid it.
21. Jean François Millet (1814–75), French painter of naturalistic rural scenes.
22. Moore sees that Degas extends artistic subject matter to the contemporary, the urban, and the trivial. Cf. Baudelaire, 'The Salon of 1846' (q.v.). (See illustrations.)

23. 'The human animal who is self-absorbed; a cat who washes herself.' Here again, Moore attributes the detached, scientific observation of human beings as prescribed by the Naturalists to Degas; in this he is not without some justice.
24. A compilation from two of Moore's articles for *The Speaker*: 'The Subject' (14 November 1891), and 'Curiosity in Art' (21 November 1891), printed as an essay in *Modern Painting*, 1893.
25. Jean-Baptiste Greuze (1725–1805), French painter of genre subjects; it is really to genre painting that Moore is objecting in this essay, albeit with a somewhat inaccurate sense of art history. His protest against the overwhelmingly 'literary' character of Victorian art is to some extent justified, however, though probably borrowed from Whistler.
26. Compiled from three *Speaker* articles: 'The Society of Portrait Painters' (11 July 1891); 'Mr. Whistler: The Man and His Art' (26 March 1892), and 'Mr. Whistler's Portraits' (2 and 9 April 1892). Published as an essay in *Modern Painting*.
27. Whistler's portrait of his mother, entitled by him 'Arrangement in Grey and Black: No. 1', is now in the Louvre.
28. Whistler's portrait of Miss Cicely Alexander, 'Harmony in Grey and Green' is in the Tate Gallery, London; Velasquez's famous painting of the Spanish Infanta and her attendants, 'Las Meninas', is in the Prado.
29. This argument is reminiscent of Baudelaire's comments about Delacroix in the 'Salon of 1846' (q.v.), where the artist selects from 'the vast dictionary' of nature. Compare the observations about the painter's relation to nature here with those in Symons's article, 'The Painting of the Nineteenth Century' (q.v.).
30. Jean Baptiste Siméon Chardin (1699–1779), French painter of exquisite still life and genre scenes. Moore is acute here in realizing how much Whistler owed to Velasquez.
31. Whistler's painting, 'The White Girl', is indisputably Pre-Raphaelite in inspiration; here again Moore displays considerable intelligence and acumen.

OSCAR WILDE

1. This lecture, composed for Wilde's tour of America, was first delivered in New York on 9 January 1882.
2. This opening is heavily indebted to Pater; compare the Preface to *The Renaissance*, and 'Romanticism' (qq.v.).
3. Wilde's historical sense is acute here since he not only links Aestheticism with the Romantic energies released by the French Revolution, but also traces the line further back, to the trust in the powers of the human mind which arose during the Enlightenment. This recognition supports his subsequent analysis of the self-conscious, psychological element in 'modern' art.
4. The first quotation comes from Blake's *Descriptive Catalogue* (No. XV); the second is from his Annotations to Sir Joshua Reynolds's *Discourses on Art* (No. II).
5. Here Wilde clearly announces the turn away from high romantic belief in a transcendent reality which had been implicit in Pater's writings. Cf. the discussion in the headnote.
6. 'Personality is what will save us' (Baudelaire?). Compare this emphasis on

the Self with Pater's essays 'Leonardo da Vinci' and 'Luca della Robbia'. (qq.v.).

7. Here and throughout the following passage, Wilde stresses the importance of conscious technique in art, anticipating the modernist doctrines of Eliot and Pound wherein the making of poetry becomes the subject of the poem, its sentiment being less important than its deliberately crafted expression.
8. Having argued that 'modern' art has no interest in the transcendent, Wilde now turns and posits an ideal aesthetic realm, divorced from the hurly-burly of contemporary life. This strain, which hearkens back to the Pre-Raphaelites, became ever more prominent in Wilde's thought. Cf. the discussion in the headnote, and his witty dialogue, 'The Decay Of Lying' (q.v.).
9. Compare the original expression of this idea in Pater's essay, 'The School of Giorgione' (q.v.).
10. From Keats's letter to J. H. Reynolds, dated 9 April 1818.
11. This reflective review of Whistler's 'Ten O'Clock Lecture' appeared in *The Pall Mall Gazette* on 28 February 1885. Throughout the piece Wilde subverts Whistler's ideas by arguing that life should be taken to the condition of art – a principle on which he organized his own life. Cf, discussion in the headnote.
12. From Baudelaire's 'Salon of 1846', Sect. XVIII, 'Of The Heroism of Modern Life' (q.v.).
13. This review of Joseph Knight's *Life of Dante Gabriel Rossetti* appeared in *The Pall Mall Gazette* on 18 April 1887.
14. Thomas Henry Hall Caine (1853–1931), a minor novelist who shared a house with Rossetti during the last months of the painter's life; William Sharp (1855–1905), who wrote mystical prose and verse under the pen name of 'Fiona Macleod', published a life of Rossetti in 1882.
15. Edmund Gosse (1849–1928) was one of the principal men of letters in the later nineteenth century, a close friend of Swinburne, R. L. Stevenson and Henry James. The *Bab Ballads* were humorous ballads by W. S. Gilbert, many of which formed the basis of Gilbert and Sullivan operettas.
16. This review was first published in *The Pall Mall Gazette* on 11 June, 1887.
17. This review of *Appreciations* appeared in *The Speaker* on 22 March 1890. It contains Wilde's highest public praise for the exceptional, self-conscious artistry of his master.
18. From Swinburne's sonnet on Gautier's *Mademoiselle de Maupin.*
19. This charming paradox is the core of Wilde's dialogue, 'The Decay Of Lying' (q.v.).
20. This dialogue first appeared in *The Nineteenth Century* in January 1889. It was collected with two other dialogues and an essay in *Intentions*, published in 1894.
21. Compare this 'anti-modern' view with the opposing aesthetic advanced by Baudelaire and Whistler (qq.v.).
22. *Laodamia* (1814) is Wordsworth's poem on the wife of Protesilaus, a Greek hero killed in the Trojan war, for whom she mourned excessively; the 'great Ode' is the 'Intimations of Immortality From Recollections of Early Childhood' (1803); 'Peter Bell' (1819), 'To the Spade of a Friend' (1806), and 'The Thorn' (1798) are all somewhat unfortunate poems by Wordsworth.

23. Titles of paintings by Edward Burne-Jones.
24. Wilde's novel, *The Picture of Dorian Gray*, first began appearing in *Lippincott's Monthly Magazine* for July 1890. This aphoristic 'Preface' was published in *The Fortnightly Review* in March 1891, and was incorporated in the first edition of the novel in July.
25. This collection of aphorisms appeared in an undergraduate magazine, *The Chameleon*, in December 1894. They were offered as evidence of Wilde's 'immorality' during the trial for libel which he brought against the Marquess of Queensbury.

WILLIAM BUTLER YEATS

1. This piece, under the title of *Four Years: 1887–1891*, first appeared in *The London Mercury* of June, July and August 1921. It was published as *The Trembling of the Veil*, the second volume of Yeats's autobiographical writings, in October 1922.
2. Charles Emile Auguste Carolus-Duran (1838–1917) and Jules Bastien-Lepage (1848–84), French painters of the Realist school, opposed to the imaginative painting that Yeats admired. Compare Baudelaire's disdain for the copy of nature in the 'Salon of 1846' (q.v.).
3. T. H. Huxley (1825–95), the philosopher of Evolution; J. Tyndall (1820–93), physicist; cited here as representatives of the scientific anti-religious outlook.
4. A BBC radio lecture given by Yeats on 11 October 1936. First published in *The Listener*, 14 October 1936.
5. Rhymers' Club: a famous but short-lived society of young poets, founded in 1891. It played a considerable part in Yeats's development. Disciples of Pater and Rossetti, and open also to influences from France, they were typical representatives of the new 'aesthetic' school of the end of the century, rejecting scientific and materialist thought for the higher claims of art. The principal members besides Yeats himself were Lionel Johnson (1867–1908), Ernest Dowson (1867–1900), and Arthur Symons (1865–1945).
6. Charles Conder (1860–1909), a decorative painter much admired by the Rhymers' circle. Aubrey Beardsley (1872–98), the outstanding artist of this school. His book-illustrations in black and white were considered to be the typical examples of 'decadent' art, and were immensely influential on the graphic design of this and the succeeding generation. The verse is from Dowson's 'Villanelle of the Poet's Road'.
7. This sentence is a deliberate echo of Pater's 'Conclusion'; Yeats attributes to his friends Pater's leading ideas, and combines several of his memorable phrases. The 'church in the style of Inigo Jones' is the Chapel of the Ascension on Bayswater Road, designed by Herbert Horne and A. H. MacMurdo. MacMurdo was a Rhymer.
8. Paul Verlaine (1844–96), the French poet whose subtle verse and disreputable life caused him to be regarded as a type and model by Yeats and his friends. Verlaine is discussed at length by Arthur Symons (q.v.). This desire for short inspired lyrics looks back to the conception which emerges fully in Edgar Allan Poe; cf. his essay on 'The Poetic Principle' (q.v.).

9. This piece first appeared as 'More Memories' in *The London Mercury*, May to August 1922. It was published as 'The Tragic Generation' in *The Trembling of the Veil* in October 1922.
10. 'Love's Nocturne' is a poem by Rossetti; Yeats's estimate of this Pre-Raphaelite erotic reverie may seem excessive, but his loyalty to Rossetti was very strong.
11. Francis Thompson (1859–1907) was a poet who, while not a member of the Rhymers, nevertheless shared some of the same characteristics. His best known poem is 'The Hound of Heaven', included in his first volume, *Poems* (1893).
12. *Lilith* and *Sibylla Palmifera* are paintings by Rossetti, consisting chiefly of women's heads in his spiritual-erotic manner.
13. Yeats here salutes Pater as the philosopher and theorist of the movement to which he belongs, and Rossetti as the imaginative forerunner. *Marius the Epicurean* (1885), Pater's great philosophic romance, is ostensibly set in the Rome of Marcus Aurelius, but it is in effect an allegory of the aesthetic and religious preoccupations of late-Victorian intellectuals. It became a sort of Bible to Yeats's generation, and, like Wilde and Symons, Yeats's prose is full of Paterian echoes and allusions.
14. An obscure passage; but Yeats finds in the contrast between the severe scholarly pretensions and the disorderly lives of his friends an unconscious search for 'antithesis' or conflict, which he in common with Blake thought of as the spring of creativity.
15. This essay first appeared in *The New Weekly* on 20 and 27 June 1914. Included in *The Cutting of an Agate*, it was reprinted in *Essays 1924*.
16. Wilson and Potter: minor artists, successors of the Pre-Raphaelites and friends of Yeats's painter father in his earlier days.
17. Hallam's essay (q.v.) had presented Tennyson in terms which made him look like an ancestor of the Pre-Raphaelites and the Rhymers – as a 'poet of Sensation . . . unconnected with any political party or peculiar system of opinions'. This is essentially the state of mind that Ruskin described as Aesthesis (Vol. I, pp. 32–4), and regarded as incomplete, requiring to be supplemented by Theoria. Yeats, without recognizing Ruskin's argument, is following a similar train of thought in the rest of this essay. Compare Whistler's rejection of 'literature' or discursive content in art in his 'Ten O'Clock Lecture' (q.v.), the position against which Yeats argues here.
18. Guillaume de Lorris (*c.* 1212–*c.* 1240), author of the first part of the *Roman de la Rose* (*c.* 1240), a long poem whose allegorical presentation of courtly love deeply influenced Chaucer.
19. This is an allusion to Heinrich Heine's essay *The Gods In Exile* (1836; 1853) about the movement of the displaced pagan gods among men – a work and concept which appealed powerfully to Pater.
20. This essay appeared in the *Cornhill Magazine* in March 1902, and was reprinted in *Ideas of Good and Evil* (1903). It represents Yeats's desire to recover the early romantic union between the poet or artist and the mass of men.
21. An enchanted garden, the generative source of the whole natural world, in *The Faerie Queene*, Bk III, canto vi.
22. From the poem by Thomas Nashe 'Farewell! adieu man's bliss' (*c.* 1592).
23. This essay first appeared in *The Dome* in April 1900, and was reprinted in *Ideas of Good and Evil*. One of Yeats's most important prose works, the

essay clearly displays his attachment to the Romantic conception of a higher, esoteric 'reality' to which imaginative art – particularly poetry – provides the key. His advance is to see the means of access concentrated into expressive and inexplicable 'symbols' which structure an imaginative work. Compare Arthur Symons's handling of this idea in *The Symbolist Movement in Literature* (q.v.).

24. Giovanni Bardi was a Florentine nobleman of the late sixteenth century; a literary and musical scholar, he devoted himself to the renewal of music in Italy. The Pléiade was a circle of poets in sixteenth-century France, of which the most important members were Pierre de Ronsard and Joachim du Bellay. The pamphlet in question is Du Bellay's 'Défense et Illustration de la Langue Française'. These poets were of great interest to Pater, who has a fine essay on Du Bellay in *The Renaissance*.
25. From Robert Burns's poem beginning 'Oh, open the door'.
26. From Blake's poem *Europe*, Plate 14, l. 3; from Shakespeare's *Timon of Athens*, Act V, sc. I, ll. 215ff.
27. Arthur William Edgar O'Shaughnessy (1844–81) was a poet and friend of Rossetti; this line is from his best-known poem, 'Ode', which begins 'We are the music makers, And we are the dreamers of dreams'.
28. From Blake's poem 'The Mental Traveller', l. 62; the verse is from Francis Thompson's 'The Heart (ii)', ll. 12–14.
29. Gerard de Nerval (1808–55), Maurice Maeterlinck (1862–1949), and Villiers de L'Isle-Adam (1838–89) were all mystical and visionary French authors. Symons, who introduced Yeats to these writers, discusses them at length in *The Symbolist Movement in Literature* (q.v.).
30. This essay, important for its outright statement of Yeats's occult beliefs, appeared in the *Monthly Review* in September 1901. It was reprinted in *Ideas of Good and Evil* (1903).
31. *Carmina Cadelica: Hymns and Incantations from the Highlands of Scotland*, collected and translated by A. Carmichael, 1900.
32. Finn MacCumhal, a legendary Irish hero.
33. This essay first appeared in *The Academy* of 19 June 1897, and was reprinted in *Ideas of Good and Evil*. It both expands Swinburne's view of Blake as the fount of the aesthetic movement (q.v.), and develops the idea of Blake as visionary, attached to the romantic absolutes of Imagination and Eternity, which passed on to Symons (q.v.).
34. From Browning's essay on Shelley (1851).
35. Jacob Boehme (1575–1624) was a German theologian and mystic who influenced the Romantic writers, among them Coleridge. He had followers in England during the eighteenth century, Behmenists as they were called, and Blake was at one time associated with them.
36. *Vala* (1797) is the first version of *The Four Zoas*, Blake's first attempt at a major epic poem.
37. This, the most substantial of Yeats's critical essays on other poets, first appeared in *The Dome* in July 1900. It was reprinted in *Ideas of Good and Evil*.
38. '*Marianne's Dream* was certainly copied from a real dream of somebody's, but like images come to the mystic in his waking state.' [Yeats's own note.]
39. Jean-Jacques Rousseau (1712–78), Swiss-born philosopher who posited that man's natural state was one of goodness and happiness, and exercised a profound influence on the European Romantic movement. In Shelley's

last, unfinished poem, *The Triumph of Life* (1822), Rousseau appears as an enigmatic ghost, guiding the poet through a dream landscape.

40. Plato's cave. in *Republic*, Bk VII, the world is allegorized as a cave in which men are confined, in such a way as to prevent them from seeing the ideal reality.
41. Porphyry on the Cave of the Nymphs. Porphyry, a Platonist of the third century A.D., wrote an interpretation of Homer's description of the cave of the nymphs in *Odyssey* Bk XII, seeing it as an allegory of the descent of the soul into earthly life. Yeats read it in Thomas Taylor's translation, and regarded it as of great symbolic importance.
42. 'Wilde told me that he had read this somewhere. He had suggested it to Burne-Jones as a subject for a picture. 1924' [Yeats's own note.] Proclus was a Neo-Platonic philosopher of the fifth century A.D.
43. Emilia Viviani was one of Shelley's ideal loves, to whom his poem *Epipsychidion* (1821) is addressed.

ARTHUR SYMONS

I.

Walter Pater

1. This reverential 'appreciation' of Symons's critical master originally appeared in *The Savoy* of December 1896, and was reprinted a year later in *Studies in Two Literatures*. The aspects of Pater's subjective, discriminating temperament emphasized in the piece are the foundations of Symons's own critical enterprise.
2. From the 'Conclusion' to *The Renaissance* (q.v.).
3. From Pater's essay on Charles Lamb in *Appreciations*.
4. Antoine Watteau (1684–1721), French painter whose graceful pictures often suggest an undertone of melancholy in the midst of delight. He was thus very appealing to the 'aesthetic' school on both sides of the Channel, and forms the subject of one of Pater's 'imaginary portraits' entitled 'A Prince of Court Painters'. Symons acutely places Pater in a tradition which is antithetic to the main stream of Victorian moralists.
5. In what was to be one of his key ideas, Symons correctly sees Pater working in the same direction as Baudelaire, preferring an imaginative and abstracted artifice to natural form. In the ensuing sentences, no doubt striving for the same effect, Symons begins to parody his master; compare Pater's 'Aesthetic Poetry' (q.v.).
6. This ideal of mathematical as opposed to organic form, placing the artist in complete control of his material, has roots in the theories of Poe and Baudelaire (qq.v.). It runs throughout Symons's criticism; cf., for example, 'The Lesson of *Parsifal*' (q.v.).
7. As the rest of this paragraph suggests, this interest in a romantic subjectivity had been developed in Symons's earlier *Introduction to the Study of Browning* (q.v.).
8. This same phrase, with its implied praise of artifice, recurs in the study of Mallarmé in *The Symbolist Movement in Literature* (q.v.).

Dante Gabriel Rossetti

9. This, one of the most penetrating early studies of Rossetti, benefits greatly from Symons's work on the French Symbolists which preceded it. The article appeared in *The Speaker* on 18 June 1904, and was subsequently published in the miscellaneous collection of essays, *Figures of Several Centuries*, 1916.
10. This is perhaps a reference to Rossetti's own harrowing tale of the Siren, 'The Orchard Pit' (q.v.).
11. Compare this suggestive figuration of the poet caught between the two worlds of imagination and reality with the argument in 'Gérard de Nerval' in *The Symbolist Movement* (q.v.). The quotation is from Pater's essay on Rossetti (q.v.).
12. These sentences recall the study of Mallarmé's pursuit of vision through the recalcitrant medium of words in *The Symbolist Movement* (q.v.).

Charles Baudelaire

13. This article, composed in 1906, appeared in *The Saturday Review* on 26 January 1907, and was later included in the revised edition of *The Symbolist Movement in Literature* of 1919. It is Symons's most coherent account of Baudelaire, clearly placing him as a forerunner to the Symbolists.
14. Charles-Augustin Sainte-Beuve (1804–69), great French critic who in his early career championed the French Romantics. He exercised a strong influence on Matthew Arnold and Pater.
15. The first quotation (Hypocrite reader, my fellow man, my brother) is the closing line of the opening poem, 'Preface', to Baudelaire's *Les Fleurs du Mal*; the second (the sorry monk) is from a poem of the same title. Symons displays great critical acumen here, as he begins to grasp the paradoxical and contradictory tensions which animated Baudelaire in a deeper way than so sympathetic an observer as Swinburne had done.

The Decay of Craftmanship in England

16. This article, prompted by the annual exhibition of the Society of Arts and Crafts, indicates the impact which Ruskin, Morris and Whistler had had on domestic arts by the turn of the century. Originally appearing in *The Weekly Critical Review* on 19 and 26 March 1903, it was later reprinted in *Studies in Seven Arts* (1906).
17. This is a Ruskinian argument; cf. 'The Nature of Gothic' (q.v.).
18. This ideal of subdued, harmonized interiors, meant for the display of paintings, comes from Whistler; it is clearly a thrust at Morris's overpatterned wallpapers.
19. This protest against commercialism and the dulling effect of mechanization recalls Morris's arguments in *Hopes and Fears for Art* (q.v.). Yet Symons's complaint against automatic piety before any handicraft, however shoddy, has an unexpectedly modern ring.

The Painting of the Nineteenth Century

20. This review of D. S. MacColl's study of *Nineteenth Century Art* (Glasgow, 1902) was first published in *The Fortnightly Review* in March 1903. It was slightly revised for *Studies in Seven Arts*, which is the version given here.
21. Probably an allusion to Robert de la Sizeranne's *Ruskin et la religion de la beauté*, published in 1897. It was this book which inspired Marcel Proust to undertake his study (and later his translations) of Ruskin.
22. This deeply romantic argument goes back through Ruskin to the Romantic poets; Symons's balancing of the natural and imaginative worlds here would have been acceptable to both Turner and Wordsworth.
23. At this point, though Symons does not note it, the argument begins to shift in favour of the artist's re-constituted 'reality'; to 'remake the pictorial aspect' of the world is not quite the same thing as entertaining a 'guardian fidelity or sense of honour towards nature'. Symons is in fact tracing the turn from romantic to late romantic feeling; compare the similar conflicts in the section on Rossetti and the Pre-Raphaelite Brotherhood (q.v.).
24. Eugène Carrière (1849–1906), French artist, known for family scenes and portraits of contemporary painters and writers. Symons's dispraise of the great pioneer of modern art, Paul Cézanne (1839–1906), brands him as a man of the nineteenth century still; yet interestingly enough, the contrast between Cézanne and Carrière which Symons draws at this point precisely outlines the distinction between abstraction and empathy which the German aesthetician, Wilhelm Worringer, saw as the foundation of modern art. Cf. Frank Kermode's cogent discussion in ch. 7 of *Romantic Image*.
25. Henri Fantin-Latour (1836–1904), French painter renowned for portrait groups of contemporary artists and writers, and a great friend of Whistler. Here too Symons undertakes some awkward manoeuvring to evade the direction in which his argument is taking him.
26. Adolphe Joseph Thomas Monticelli (1824–86), French painter whose works are characterized by blurred masses and warm, luxuriant colour; G. F. Watts (1817–1904), English painter of heavily allegorical figures; Simeon Solomon (1841–1905), late Pre-Raphaelite painter, one-time friend of Swinburne, whose sensitive appreciation of the artist (q.v.) Symons would appear to have read.
27. Following the lead of Pater's argument in 'The School of Giorgione' (q.v.), Symons suggests that Monticelli's painting 'aspires to the condition of music', with a complete fusion of form and content. This 'experiment' clearly takes the painter towards the extreme of pure abstract art which Symons has warily avoided throughout the essay. Nonetheless, here in the closing section of the piece Symons comes close to apprehending some of the principal features of modern art.
28. This description could equally apply to Van Gogh, or to such Fauvist painters as Vlaminck and Matisse. (See illustrations.)
29. Here Symons has travelled far from his original romantic premise in the essay, and his last-minute effort to harmonize the two positions is awkward in the extreme. He is on the point of realizing the thrust behind abstract art, where the painter's imaginative reality breaks completely away from natural forms.

II.

An Introduction to the Study of Browning

1. This, Symons's first major book, was published in 1886 when he was only twenty-one. It was written, he said, 'as an act of homage to a poet worshipped from boyhood', and Browning, together with George Meredith, became a strong influence on his own verse.
2. From Elizabeth Barrett Browning's *Aurora Leigh* (1856), Bk v, ll. 337–43.
3. From Pater's essay 'Winckelmann' in *The Renaissance*.
4. Here, in his early criticism, Symons's concern for a distinct and communicable impression is consistent, despite the use of the term 'mood', which will later mean something quite different. (Cf. the Preface to the second edition of *London Nights*, q.v.) This notion of an external representation of an inner emotion also anticipates T. S. Eliot's concept of the 'objective correlative'.

Modernity in Verse

5. This review of William Ernest Henley's third book of poems, *London Voluntaries and Other Verses*, was printed in *The Fortnightly Review* in August 1892, and afterwards included in *Studies in Two Literatures*. Henley remains a minor figure, but at this time he dealt with the contemporary world in a frank, sometimes harsh and ironic fashion, uncharacteristic of verse of the day.

Paul Verlaine

6. This article appeared in *The National Review* in June 1892 and formed the basis for the section on Verlaine included in 'The Decadent Movement in Literature' the following year. Symons thought of Verlaine (1844–96) as the greatest living French poet, an enthusiasm sustained through the reversals of opinion in *The Symbolist Movement* six years later.
7. For we want the Nuance over again,
   Not Colour, nothing but nuance
   Oh it alone can affiance
   Dream to dream and flute to horn.
8. The *Romances sans Paroles*, detailing a vagabond existence with the 'marvellous boy' of French poetry, Arthur Rimbaud, date from 1874; the *Liturgies Intimes*, after Verlaine's conversion to Catholicism, appeared in 1892. Symons suggests that the subjective, impressionistic character of Verlaine's art remains a constant through personal vicissitudes.

Review of George Moore's *Impressions and Opinions*

9. This review of Symons's immediate precursor in contemporary French studies appeared in *The Academy* on 21 March 1891. Cf. Moore's essays on Whistler and Degas (qq.v.).

The Decadent Movement in Literature

10. This essay was published in *Harper's New Monthly Magazine* in November 1893.
11. Here is the seed that was to grow into Symons's subsequent and more considerable work, *The Symbolist Movement in Literature*. The romantic basis of this insight is suggested in the perhaps unconscious paraphrase of Wordsworth's 'Preface' to *Lyrical Ballads*.
12. The Brothers Goncourt, Edmund (1822–96) and Jules (1830–70) were renowned men of letters and collaborative novelists in late nineteenth-century Paris. Highly nervous, overwrought and sensitive *littérateurs*, they evolved a distinct style of short, impressionistic sketches using language which borrowed many technical terms from painting. They are known today chiefly for detailed portraits of French literary life in their remarkable *Journal*.
13. Joris-Karl Huysmans (1848–1907), Dutch novelist who lived in Paris. His novel of 1884, *A Rebours* ('Against Nature') is the epitome of *fin de siècle* decadence, detailing the passage of an aristocratic aesthete through great efforts to combat his ennui to his collapse into the Church as a final refuge. It was much admired by Oscar Wilde.

III.

Preface to the second edition of *London Nights*

1. *London Nights*, Symons's third volume of poems, was published in 1895. It had been marked by short, impressionistic renderings of contemporary London scenes, including encounters with prostitutes. In this Preface Symons sought to answer the moral opprobrium which the book had drawn, but he also announced a dramatic turn in his thinking. Cf. the discussion in the headnote.
2. Compare this language with that of Yeats's essays, e.g. 'The Autumn of the Body'.
3. From the 'Introductory Sonnet' of Rossetti's *House of Life*.

Mr W. B. Yeats

4. This review of *The Wind Among the Reeds* (1899) appeared in *The Saturday Review* on 24 December 1900. It was later incorporated with a review of Yeats's 1904 version of *Collected Poems* and printed in *Studies in Prose and Verse* (1904), from which this excerpt is taken.
5. An allusion to the poem of the same title by Shelley, one of the most lasting influences on Yeats.
6. Symons rightly places Yeats in a Symbolist context; cf. the 'Introduction' to *The Symbolist Movement in Literature*. The Romantic aspect to this context is developed by Symons in his study of Blake (q.v.).

The Symbolist Movement in Literature

7. The book was published in 1899, gathering together articles and essays from the previous five years.

8. From Thomas Carlyle's *Sartor Resartus* (1831), Bk III, ch. iii, entitled 'Symbols'. Here Carlyle speaks of the Universe as a Symbol of God, all finite things pointing to the Infinite; a development of German Romantic philosophy, this idea was well known in France, and does underpin much of Symons's concern in the volume, especially the increasingly religious language with which Symons discusses literature.
9. Gérard de Nerval (1808–55), French romantic poet, companion of Gautier, whose early readings in occult literature combined with intermittent mental breakdowns produced an astonishingly visionary literature which is the forerunner of *symbolisme*.
10. It is instructive to compare this account of an artist's difficult voyage between the realms of imagination and reality both with Symons's account of Rossetti (q.v.) and the testimony of innumerable contemporary poets.
11. Giovanni Pico della Mirandola (1463–94), Florentine scholar who attempted to reconcile Neo-Platonism with Christianity, subject of one of Pater's essays in *The Rennaissance*; Joannes Meursius (1579–1639), latinized name of Jan de Meurs, Professor of History and Greek at Leyden University, noted for a vast and somewhat confused compilation of facts about the antique world; Nicholas of Cusa (1401–64), German cardinal, scholar and mystical theologian. Nerval's fate, as Symons was perhaps beginning to realize, accurately forecasts his own.
12. Pythagoras, sixth-century B.C. Greek philosopher who founded a philosophical brotherhood on ascetic and mystical principles; Hermes Trismegistus, legendary sage of ancient Egypt, identified with the god Thoth. The 'Hermetic' writings associated with his name – magical, alchemical, theosophical – actually date from the third century A.D. The Smaragdine Tablet is a brief alchemical text attributed to Hermes. Jacob Boehme (1575–1624), German shoemaker whose mystical writings grow out of the Hermetic tradition, holding that antithetical oppositions in the universe (light and dark, good and evil, etc.) are symbolic of the relation between God and nature. Emmanuel Swedenborg (1688–1772), Swedish philosopher and mystic, whose doctrines influenced Blake.
13. From Nerval's most famous poem, the sonnet 'El Desdichado', l. 11.
14. Villiers de L'Isle-Adam (1838–89), French novelist and playwright, who extended the revulsion from science and material progress initiated by Gautier and Baudelaire. His highly poetic dramas had a marked impact on Yeats and Wilde. The epigraph is 'each to his own infinity'.
15. I am far from sure', wrote Verlaine, 'that the philosophy of Villiers will not one day become the formula of our century.' [Symons's own note.] This 'belief' is an elaboration of Neoplatonic philosophy, stressing the divine potential of human beings.
16. This restrained critique of Villiers from a humanistic position indicates that at this point Symons was not in complete sympathy with the elitist aspect of late romanticism. This is probably due to Yeats's influence, since later Symons was to be less than generous about the mass of humanity.
17. From Pater's essay on Leonardo da Vinci in *The Renaissance* (q.v.).
18. Jules Laforgue (1860–87), French poet, who inaugurated the freer form of *vers libre* in a highly self-conscious, slangy and ironic poetry. Laforgue differs from the other Symbolists in not seeking an ineffable, ideal world, but rather courting the quotidian, seeking ironic deflation of the ideal by the trivial. T. S. Eliot claimed that this essay was one of the most

rewarding features of the book, and indeed the account of Laforgue's intentions and technique outlines many features of Eliot's own verse.

19. The first verses are from Laforgue's cycle of poems *Locution des Pierrots*, verse XII, stanza ii; the second is from his 'Litanies des Derniers Quartiers de la Lune'.
20. Here is the seed of Symons's subsequent interest in the impersonal, universalizing devices of the artificial, such as make-up, puppets and Japanese drama. Among his later essays are such titles as 'An Apology for Puppets' and 'Pantomime and Poetic Drama' (q.v.). Cf. also the subsequent chapter in this book, 'Maeterlinck as a Mystic' (q.v.).
21. René and Werther are heroes of extreme sensibility in novels by Chateaubriand and Goethe respectively, and this is almost certainly an echo of Pater's essay on Coleridge (q.v.). The attitude also suggests that of Eliot's Prufrock.
22. Stéphane Mallarmé (1842–98), leader of the French Symbolist poets, and regarded highly today, though Symons always preferred Verlaine. Dispraised for his obscurity in the earlier 'Decadent Movement in Literature', Mallarmé comes into his own here, though Symons qualifies the praise and shows himself keenly aware of the dangers of incommunicability courted by the Symbolist aesthetic.
23. From the conclusion of Pater's imaginary portrait of Watteau, 'A Prince of Court Painters'. Here Symons attempts to bring together several strands of the aesthetic movement.
24. Maurice Maeterlinck (1862–1949), Belgian playwright and essayist, whose intense, poetic dramas won him the Nobel Prize in 1911. His book of essays, *The Treasure of the Humble*, was published in 1896. Symons notes many features of Maeterlinck's work which point the way to such modern experiments in the theatre as Beckett and the Theatre of the Absurd.
25. Maeterlinck's book contains an appreciative essay on Emerson.
26. Here again, Symons instructively sees the Neoplatonic tradition of philosophy as the appropriate context in which to regard the Symbolist movement.

The Choice

27. This article, originally published in *The Saturday Review* on 24 March 1900, served as the 'Conclusion' to *Studies in Prose and Verse* (1904). The title comes from the declaration (applied to Huysmans) that such a man had ultimately to choose between 'the barrel of a gun and the foot of the Cross'. Like the 'Conclusion' to *The Symbolist Movement*, this piece suggests that Symons's own position was a Paterian one, vacillating between belief in and doubt of any higher 'reality'.
28. The quotation is from the 'Conclusion' to *The Renaissance* (q.v.), and it is clear that Symons is developing the position outlined there.

IV.

Preface to *Plays, Acting and Music*

1. This 'Preface' to Symons's collection of essays *Plays, Acting and Music* was dated July 1903. It announces the intention which sustained his last important period of criticism; cf. the discussion in the headnote.

Ballet, Pantomime and Poetic Drama

2. This tripartite essay, which appeared in *The Dome* for October 1898, heralds Symons's last phase of criticism, whose vitalist and impersonal emphases marry the influences of Yeats and Nietzsche to his earlier Paterian ideals.
3. Almost certainly an allusion to Nietzche's first book, *The Birth of Tragedy* (1872), which studied the clash between Apollonian calm and Dionysiac ecstasy in Greek drama. Symons's essay on this work was included in the first edition of *Plays, Acting and Music.*
4. Compare this with the closing exhortations of the 'Conclusion' to *The Renaissance* (q.v.).
5. The dancer was one of Yeats's most powerful images of the still point of combined forces; cf. the discussion in ch. 4 of Kermode's *Romantic Image*, and Ian Fletcher's article cited in the Guide to further reading, p. 303.
6. An allusion to Baudelaire's remarks on Delacroix in the 'Salon of 1846' (q.v.).
7. This piece was inspired by a performance of *Parsifal* which created a turning point in Symons's thinking. He clearly sees Wagner approaching the ideal announced in Pater's essay, 'The School of Giorgione' (q.v.), wherein the separate arts tend towards a single, unified essence. Compare this with Baudelaire's essay on Wagner (q.v.).
8. In this last paragraph Symons is close to the argument of the 'Introduction' to *The Symbolist Movement* written the following year.

A New Art of the Stage

9. E. Gordon Craig (1872–1966), English actor and stage designer, credited with revolutionizing design in the theatre. *The Art of the Theatre*, his essays on the craft, was published in 1905. Part of this essay appeared in *The Monthly Review* for June 1902, and was later expanded for publication in *Studies in Seven Arts* (1906), from which this text is taken.
10. This idea of the artist's higher, idealized arrangement of nature, pervades Symons's criticism of this period; cf. 'The Lesson of *Parsifal*' and 'The Painting of the Nineteenth Century' (qq.v.).

William Blake

11. This book, published in 1907, can lay claim to being Symons's greatest work of criticism; cf. the discussion in the headnote. The 'Introduction' sustains an illuminating comparison between Blake and Nietzsche, one of the prime influences on Symons at this time.
12. An independent quatrain from the 1793 Note-book.
13. From Blake's epic, *Jerusalem*, Plate 77, a prose address 'to the Christians'.
14. From Blake's letter to Thomas Butts, dated 10 January 1802.
15. From Blake's Annotations to 'Poems' by Wordsworth; a capsule instance of the debate in Romanticism between naturalists and super-naturalists.
16. These verses, included in a letter to Thomas Butts dated 22 November 1802, were also mentioned in Swinburne's study of Blake (q.v.).

17. A reference to Nietzsche's book, *Beyond Good and Evil* (1886), expressing the doctrine of penetration to a realm of imaginative certainty which transcends moral calculation.
18. Thomas Babington Macaulay (1800–59), Liberal M.P., essayist and historian, who made a substantial contribution to the tone of literary and political life in the Victorian era. He is used here as a type of mid-nineteenth-century propriety and wisdom.
19. John Linnell (1792–1882), English painter and later father-in-law of Samuel Palmer (1805–81), outstanding English painter specializing in visionary landscapes. Both men were friends of Blake in his old age. The anecdotes are recounted in Gilchrist's *Life of Blake*, ch. 35.
20. The first quotation is from Blake's Annotations to Sir Joshua Reynolds's *Discourses on Art*; the second is from *A Vision of the Last Judgment*.
21. From Blake's letter to William Hayley, dated 27 January 1804.

Guide to further reading

INTRODUCTION

The Romantic Agony, Mario Praz (Oxford University Press, 1933; 2nd edn 1970). A crucial study of the dark or decadent strain of the late romantic period.

The Heritage of Symbolism, C. M. Bowra (Macmillan, 1943). A useful early study of the Symbolist influence in English literature.

The Last Romantics, Graham Hough (Duckworth, 1949). Still one of the best studies of the transition period between Romanticism and Modernism.

The Mirror and the Lamp, M. H. Abrams (Oxford University Press, 1953). The classic study of the change in aesthetic theory ushered in by the Romantic Movement, which underlies many of the writers in this anthology.

The Critic's Alchemy: A Study of the Introduction of French Symbolism Into England, Ruth Z. Temple (Twayne, 1953; College & University Press, New Haven, 1967). A stimulating consideration of the impact of Symbolism on Arnold, Swinburne, Moore and Symons.

Romantic Image, Frank Kermode (Routledge and Kegan Paul, 1957). One of the most elegant and incisive essays on the period covered by this anthology.

From Gautier to Eliot, Enid Starkie (Hutchinson, 1960). A fine study which considers the matter from a French point of view.

Beyond the Tragic Vision: The Quest for Identity in the Nineteenth Century, Morse Peckham (Geo. Brazilier, 1962; Cambridge University Press, 1981). An eccentric but often illuminating consideration of the intellectual undercurrents of the nineteenth century.

Aestheticism and Decadence: A Selective Annotated Bibliography, Linda C. Dowling (Garland Press, 1977). One of the most useful descriptive guides for students of the later nineteenth century.

WALTER PATER

Primary material

The Works of Walter Pater, 10 vols., Library Edition (Macmillan, 1910). The standard edition.

Selected Writings of Walter Pater, ed. with an introduction by Harold Bloom (New American Library, 1974). The most useful anthology of Pater's writings, with a good introduction.

Secondary material

'The Place of Pater', T. S. Eliot, 1930; reprinted as 'Arnold and Pater' in *Selected Essays* (Faber, 1932). A largely dismissive account of someone who was an important influence on Eliot himself. See Hough's corrective in *The Last Romantics*.

Walter Pater: The Idea in Nature, Anthony Ward (Hilary, 1965). A consideration of Pater's relation to Hegel; eccentic but often stimulating.

Walter Pater, Ian Fletcher (Longmans, 1959; rev. edn 1971). One of the better critical studies of Pater to date, with an excellent bibliography.

Walter Pater, Gerald Monsman (Twayne, 1977). A fine critical study of Pater with a useful bibliography.

The Case of Walter Pater, Michael Levey (Thames and Hudson, 1978). Far and away the best biography of Pater.

Walter Pater: An Imaginative Sense of Fact, ed. Philip Dodd (Frank Cass, 1981). An extremely useful collection of essays and bibliographical material.

JAMES WHISTLER

Primary material

The Gentle Art of Making Enemies, J. A. M. Whistler (Heinemann, 1890; rev. edn 1892). Contains the 'Ten O'Clock Lecture', Whistler's account of the libel suit, and assorted criticism of the day with Whistler's replies.

The Whistler Journal, ed. E. R. and J. Pennell (Heinemann, 1921). A valuable collection of letters, anecdotes and reminiscences.

Secondary material

The Life of James McNeill Whistler, E. R. & J. Pennell (Heinemann, 2 vols. 1908). The first major biography of Whistler.

Whistler, James Laver (Faber, 1930; reprinted White Lion, 1976). A good study of the relation between Whistler's art and life.

Whistler, the Man, Hesketh Pearson (Methuen, 1952; reissued Macdonald and Jane's, 1978). The only biography whose sense of style and wit approaches that of its subject.

Nocturne: The Art of James McNeill Whistler, Denys Sutton (Country Life Ltd, 1963). A beautifully produced and useful study of Whistler's art.

Whistler: A Biography, Stanley Weintraub (Collins, 1974). The most thorough and acute biography.

GEORGE MOORE

Primary material

The Works of George Moore, 20 vols. (Heinemann, 1936–7). A highly selective edition prepared by Moore himself. As his revisions were not always for the better, it is usually wise to consult the original edition of any given work.

Confessions of a Young Man (Sonnechen, 1888; rev. edn 1889, 1904, and 1916).

Impressions and Opinions (David Nutt, 1891; rev. edn T. Werner Laurie, 1913).

Modern Painting (Walter Scott, 1893; rev. edn 1896).

Literature at Nurse, or Circulating Morals (Vizetally, 1885). Issued complete with preceding correspondence in *The Pall Mall Gazette* and an Introduction by Pierre Coustillas, Harvester Press, 1976.

Secondary material

The Life of George Moore, Joseph Hone (Gollancz, 1936). The definitive biography, despite its tedious length and refusal to draw conclusions.

George Moore, A. Norman Jeffares (Longman, 1965; rev. edn 1970). The most compact treatment of Moore, with a good bibliography.

George Moore's Mind and Art, ed. Graham Owens (Oliver and Boyd, 1968). A useful collection of critical essays on Moore.

A Bibliography of George Moore, Edwin Gilcher (Northern Illinois University Press, 1970). The indispensable guide to the study of Moore, charting his many revisions.

OSCAR WILDE

Primary material

The First Collected Edition of the Works of Oscar Wilde, ed. R. Ross, 15 vols. (Methuen, 1908; reissued Dawson, 1969). The standard edition, beautifully produced.

The Letters of Oscar Wilde, ed. R. Hart-Davis (Rupert Hart-Davis Ltd, 1962). Indispensable for the serious student of Wilde.

The Artist as Critic: Critical Writings of Oscar Wilde, ed. with Introduction by Richard Ellmann (W. H. Allen, 1970). The best extant selection of criticism, with a useful introduction by one of Wilde's best critics.

Secondary material

'Oscar Wilde', Andre Gide, *Prétextes* (trans. S. Mason) (Oxford, 1905). Interesting perspective on Wilde from one of his close friends.

The Art of Oscar Wilde, E. San Juan, Jr (Princeton University Press, 1967).

Oscar Wilde: A Collection of Critical Essays, ed. R. Ellmann (Prentice-Hall, 1969). The best collection of critical material on Wilde to date.

Into the Demon Universe: A Literary Exploration of Oscar Wilde, Christopher S. Nassaar (Yale University Press, 1974). Perhaps the best single critical work on Wilde, stressing his connection with Romanticism, particularly in its decadent or demonic phase.

Oscar Wilde: A Biography, H. Montgomery Hyde (Eyre Methuen, 1976). The most complete and informed biography to date, though unfortunately laying undue emphasis on the series of high court trials Wilde endured.

WILLIAM BUTLER YEATS

Primary material

Autobiographies (Macmillan, 1955). Contains Yeats's extended reminiscences of his youth, early influences, friends, etc.

Essays and Introductions (Macmillan, 1961). The standard collection of Yeats's critical prose.

Secondary material

Yeats: The Man and the Masks, Richard Ellmann (Oxford University Press, 1949; 2nd rev. edn 1979). Perhaps the best critical biography of Yeats.

The Lonely Tower, T. R. Henn (Methuen, 1950). Particularly good on Yeats's Irish background and his use of myth.

Yeats, Harold Bloom (Oxford University Press, 1970). A powerful study stressing Yeats's place in the Romantic Tradition.

Yeats, Denis Donoghue (Fontana, 1971; 3rd edn corrected, 1976). Invigorating monograph emphasizing Yeats's connection with Nietzschean vitalism.

ARTHUR SYMONS

Primary material

The Collected Works of Arthur Symons, ed. A. Symons, 9 vols. (Martin Secker, 1924). Only nine of the projected sixteen volumes were ever produced, and as Symons's tampering at this late date is often regrettable, it is best to consult the original edition whenever possible. Those used in this selection are: *Studies in Two Literatures* (1897); *The Symbolist Movement in Literature* (1899; rev. 1908); *Plays, Acting and Music* (1903; rev. 1909); *Studies in Prose and Verse* (1904); *Studies in Seven Arts* (1906); *William Blake* (1907).

The Symbolist Movement in Literature, ed. with an Introduction by Richard Ellmann (Dutton, 1958). The Introduction provides a useful account of Symons's relation with Yeats, but slights the rest of his *oeuvre*. Also contains the essays added to the 1919 edition.

Arthur Symons: Selected Writings, ed. with an Introduction by Roger V. Holdsworth (Carcanet, 1974). Fine selection of poetry with limited extracts of prose. The Introduction is a subtle and suggestive account of Symons's impact on the major figures of modernist literature.

Secondary material

The Critic's Alchemy, Ruth Z. Temple (Twayne, 1953; reprinted College and University Press, New Haven, 1967). One of the best treatments of Symons's role as intermediary between French and English culture.

Arthur Symons: A Critical Biography, Roger Lhombreaud (Unicorn Press, 1963). The best account of Symons's life to date, vitiated by an absence of critical perspective.

Romantic Image, Frank Kermode (Routledge and Kegan Paul, 1957; rev. 1961). Contains a crucial chapter on Symons.

'Symons, Yeats, and the Demonic Dance', Ian Fletcher (*London Magazine* VII (1960), no. 6, pp. 46–60). Superb treatment of Symons's relation to Yeats, with particular regard to their treatment of the dancer.

Arthur Symons, John Munro (Twayne, 1969). The most extensive critical study to date, with a good bibliography.

Rooms In the Darwin Hotel, Tom Gibbons (University of Western Australia Press, 1973). An energetic and compact treatment of Symons's place in the critical transition between Victorian and modern culture.